Reading Essentials
An Interactive Student Workbook

in6.msscience.com

P9-DMS-499

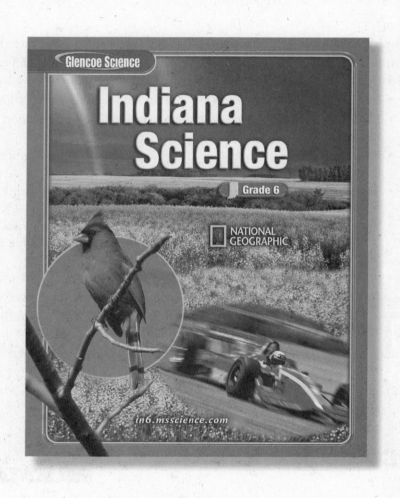

Glencoe Science

Indiana
Science
Grade 6

NATIONAL
GEOGRAPHIC

in6.msscience.com

Mc Graw Hill **Glencoe**

New York, New York   Columbus, Ohio   Chicago, Illinois   Peoria, Illinois   Woodland Hills, California

To the Student

In today's world, knowing science is important for thinking critically, solving problems, and making decisions. But understanding science sometimes can be a challenge.

Reading Essentials takes the stress out of reading, learning, and understanding science. This book covers important concepts in science, offers ideas for how to learn the information, and helps you review what you have learned.

In each chapter:

- **Before You Read** sparks your interest in what you'll learn and relates it to your world.
- **Read to Learn** describes important science concepts with words and graphics. Next to the text you can find a variety of study tips and ideas for organizing and learning information:
    - The **Study Coach** offers tips for getting the main ideas out of the text.
    - **Foldables™ Study Organizers** help you divide the information into smaller, easier-to-remember concepts.
    - **Reading Checks** ask questions about key concepts. The questions are placed so you know whether you understand the material.
    - **Think It Over** elements help you consider the material in-depth, giving you an opportunity to use your critical-thinking skills.
    - **Picture This** questions specifically relate to the art and graphics used with the text. You'll find questions to get you actively involved in illustrating the concepts you read about.
    - **Applying Math** reinforces the connection between math and science.
- Use **After You Read** to review key terms and answer questions about what you have learned. The **Mini Glossary** can assist you with science vocabulary. Review questions focus on the key concepts to help you evaluate your learning.

See for yourself. *Reading Essentials* makes science easy to understand and enjoyable.

Glencoe

The **McGraw·Hill** Companies

Send all inquiries to:
Glencoe/McGraw-Hill
8787 Orion Place
Columbus, OH 43240

ISBN 0-07-867069-1
Printed in the United States of America
4 5 6 7 8 9 10 024 09 08 07

Table of Contents

The Nature of Science

section ❶ What is science?

 Standard—6.1.2: Give examples of different ways scientists investigate natural phenomena ... to make sense of the evidence.
Also covers: 6.1.1, 6.1.3, 6.1.4, 6.1.5, 6.1.8, 6.1.9, 6.4.13, 6.7.1

● Before You Read

Have you ever wondered how something works? On the lines below, describe a time that you wondered how something worked. Did you find out how it worked? Explain how.

_____

_____

What You'll Learn
- what science is and what science cannot answer
- what theories and laws are
- identify a system and its parts
- the three main branches of science

● Read to Learn

Learning About the World

When you think of a scientist, do you think of someone in a laboratory with charts, graphs, and bubbling test tubes? Anyone who tries to learn about the natural world is a scientist—even you. <u>Science</u> is a way of learning more about the natural world. Scientists want to know why, how, or when something happened. Learning usually begins by keeping your eyes open and asking questions about what you see.

What kinds of questions can science answer?

Scientists ask many questions. How do things work? What are they made of? Why does something take place? Some questions cannot be answered by science. Science cannot help you find the meaning of a poem or decide what your favorite color is. Science cannot tell you what is right, wrong, good, or bad.

What are possible explanations?

Learning about your world begins with asking questions. Science tries to find answers to these questions. However, science can answer questions only with the information that exists at the time. Any answer found by science could be wrong or could change because people can never know everything about the world around them.

Study Coach

Outlining As you read the section, create an outline using each heading from the text. Under each heading, write the main points or ideas that you read.

FOLDABLES™

Ⓐ Build Vocabulary
Make the following Foldable to help you define and learn the vocabulary terms in this section.

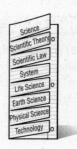

How does new information affect old explanations?

As time passes, people learn more about the world around them. As you can see in the diagram below, new information might make scientists look at old ideas and think of new explanations. Science finds only possible explanations. For example, people once thought Earth was the center of the solar system. Through the years, new information about the solar system showed this is not true.

Picture This

1. **Explain** Look at the diagram to the right. How can new information affect an old explanation for something?

_____

_____

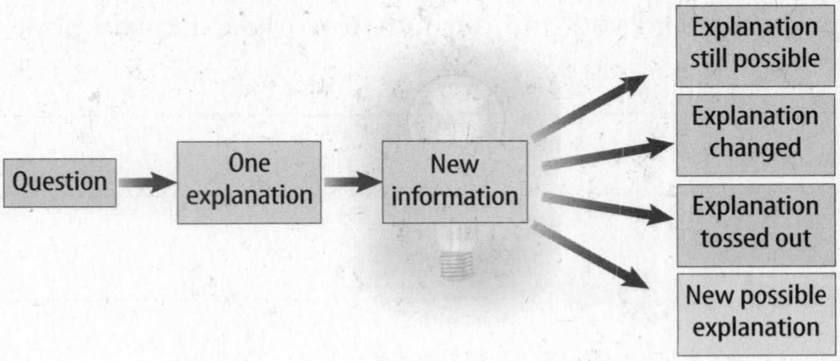

Possible outcomes

Question → One explanation → New information →
- Explanation still possible
- Explanation changed
- Explanation tossed out
- New possible explanation

What are scientific theories?

A <u>scientific theory</u> is an attempt to explain a pattern seen repeatedly in the natural world. Theories are not just guesses or opinions. Theories in science must have observations and results from many investigations to back them up. They are the best explanations that have been found so far. Theories can change. As new data are found, scientists decide how the new data fit the theory. Sometimes the new data do not support the theory. Then scientists can change the theory to fit the new data better.

What are scientific laws?

A <u>scientific law</u> is a rule that describes a pattern in nature. For an observation to become a scientific law, it must be observed happening over and over again. The law is what scientists use until someone makes observations that do not follow the law. A law helps you predict what will happen. If you hold an apple above the ground and drop it, it always will fall to Earth. The law tells you the apple will fall, but the law does not explain why the apple will fall. A law is different from a theory. It does not try to explain why something happens. It simply describes a pattern. ☑

✔ Reading Check

2. **Determine** Which describes a pattern in nature, a scientific theory or a scientific law?

_____

Systems in Science

Scientists can study many different things in nature. Some scientists study how the human body works. Others might study how planets move around the Sun. Still others might study the energy in a lightning bolt. What do all of these things have in common? All of them are systems. A **system** is a group of structures, cycles, and processes that are related to each other and work together. Your stomach is a structure, or one part of, your digestive system. ☑

Where are systems found?

You can find systems in other places besides science. Your school is a system. It has structures like school buildings, furniture, students, teachers, and many other objects. Your school day also has cycles. Your daily class schedule and the school calendar are examples of cycles. Many processes are at work during the school day. Your teacher may have a process for test taking. Before a test, the teacher might ask you to put your books away and get out a pencil. When the test is over, the teacher might ask you to put down your pencil and pass the test to the front of the room.

In a system, structures, cycles, and processes work together, or interact. What you do and what time you do it depends on your daily schedule. A clock shows your teacher that it is time for your lunch break. So, you go to lunch.

How are parts of a system related to a whole system?

All systems are made up of other systems. For example, the human body is a system. Within the human body are many other systems. You are part of your school. Your school is probably part of a larger district, state, or national system. Scientists often solve problems by studying just one part of a system. A scientist might want to know how the construction of buildings affects the ecosystem. Because an ecosystem has many parts, the scientist might study one particular animal in the ecosystem. Another might study the effect on plant life.

The Branches of Science

Science is often divided into three main parts, or branches. These branches are life science, Earth science, and physical science. Each branch asks questions about different kinds of systems.

✔ Reading Check

3. **List** What are the three parts of a system?

_____

_____

_____

💡 Think it Over

4. **Describe** Buildings usually have a heating system. Write each of the following by the part of the system it best represents. *turning on and off, thermostat, spreading heat*

Structure:

_____

Process:

_____

Cycle:

_____

What is life science?

Life science is the study of living systems and the ways in which they interact. Life scientists try to answer questions like "How do whales know where they are swimming in the ocean?" and "How do vaccines prevent disease?" Life scientists can study living things, where they live, and how they act together.

People who work in the health field, like doctors and nurses, know a lot about life science. They work with systems of the human body. Some other people that use life science are biologists, zookeepers, farmers, and beekeepers.

What is Earth science?

Earth science is the study of Earth systems and systems in space. It includes the study of nonliving things such as rocks, soil, clouds, rivers, oceans, planets, stars, meteors, and black holes. Earth science also includes the weather and climate systems on Earth. Earth scientists ask questions like "How do you know how strong an earthquake is?" and "Is water found on other planets?" They make maps and study how Earth's crust formed. Geologists study rocks and Earth's features. Meteorologists study weather and climate. There are even volcanologists who study volcanoes. ☑

What is physical science?

Physical science is the study of matter and energy. Matter is anything that takes up space and has mass. Energy is the ability to cause matter to change. All systems—living and nonliving—are made of matter.

Chemistry and physics are the two areas of physical science. Chemistry is the study of matter and the way it interacts. Chemists ask questions like "What can I do to make aspirin work better?" and "How can I make plastic stronger?" Physics is the study of energy and its ability to change matter. Physicists ask questions like "How does light travel through glass?" and "How can humans use sunlight to power objects?"

How are science and technology related?

Learning the answers to scientific questions is important. However, these answers do not help people unless they can be used in some way. **Technology** is the practical use of science in our everyday lives. Engineers use science to create technology. The study of how to use the energy of sunlight is science. Using this knowledge to create solar panels is an example of technology.

✔ **Reading Check**

5. **Apply** What might an Earth scientist study that is not on Earth?

_____

_____

💡 **Think it Over**

6. **Apply** Which of the following is an example of technology? Circle the correct answer.
   a. finding out how light travels
   b. creating solar-powered cars
   c. deciding which rock is the hardest
   d. making strong plastic

● After You Read

Mini Glossary

Earth science: the study of Earth systems and systems in space

life science: the study of living systems and the ways in which they interact

physical science: the study of matter and energy

science: a way of learning more about the natural world

scientific law: a rule that describes a pattern in nature

scientific theory: an attempt to explain a pattern seen repeatedly in the natural world

system: a group of structures, cycles, and processes that are related to each other and work together

technology: is the practical use of science in our everyday lives

1. Review the terms and their definitions in the Mini Glossary. When you see lightning strike, you probably will hear thunder soon. Is this statement a scientific theory or a scientific law? Explain.

   _____

   _____

2. Fill in the graphic organizer below with explanations of science, each branch of science, and technology.

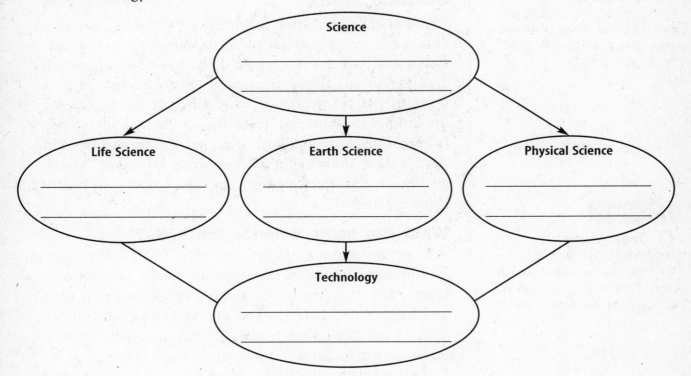

Sciencenline Visit **in6.msscience.com** to access your textbook, interactive games, and projects to help you learn more about what science is.

End of Section

Reading Essentials **5**

The Nature of Science

section ❷ Science in Action

Standard—**6.1.2:** Give examples of different ways scientists investigate natural phenomena ... to make sense of the evidence.
Also covers: 6.1.3, 6.1.5, 6.2.5, 6.2.8

What You'll Learn
- skills that scientists use
- the meaning of hypothesis
- the difference between observation and inference

 Mark the Text

Highlighting As you read the text under each heading, highlight the science skills you see. When you finish reading the section, review the skills you have highlighted.

FOLDABLES™

Ⓑ Organizing Information Make a Foldable like the one shown to describe science skills, drawing conclusions, and experiments.

● Before You Read

Think of some skills that you have. You may be good at basketball. Of all the skills you have, which do you think is your best? How did you learn that skill?

_____

_____

● Read to Learn

Science Skills

You already know that science is about asking questions. How does asking questions lead to learning? There is no single way to learn. A scientist doesn't just ask a question and then always follow the same steps to answer the question. Instead, scientists use many different skills. Some of these skills are thinking, observing, predicting, investigating, researching, modeling, measuring, analyzing, and inferring. Any of these skills might help answer a question. Some answers to scientific questions are also found with luck and using creativity.

What are some science methods?

Investigations often follow a pattern. Look at the diagram on the next page. Most investigations begin by observing, or seeing, something and then asking a question about what was seen. Scientists try to find out what is already known about a question. They talk with other scientists, and read books and magazines to learn all they can. Then, they try to find a possible explanation. To collect even more information, scientists usually make more observations. They might build a model, do experiments, or both.

A Scientific Method

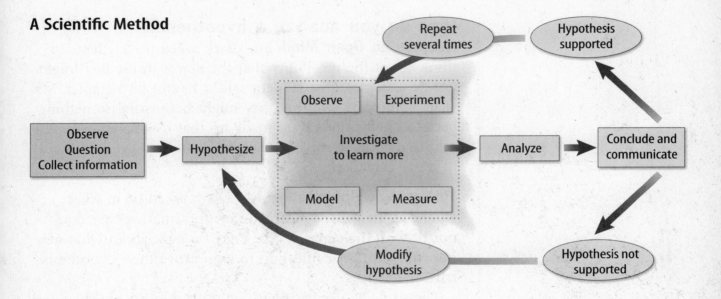

How do you question and observe?

You ask questions and make observations all the time. For example, Ms. Clark, a middle school science teacher, placed a sealed shoebox on the table at the front of the classroom. Everyone in the class began to ask questions about what was inside the box. Some students picked up the box. There was something loose inside it. Some students said it sounded like metal when it hit the sides of the box. It wasn't very heavy. Ms. Clark passed the box around. Each student made observations and wrote them in his or her journal. These students were using science skills without even knowing it.

How is guessing part of science?

Ms. Clark asked her students to guess what was in the box. One student thought it was a pair of scissors. Another student thought it was too heavy to be scissors. All agreed it was made of metal. The students then guessed that it was probably a stapler in the box. Ms. Clark told them that by guessing a stapler was in the box, they had made a hypothesis.

What is a hypothesis?

A **hypothesis** is a reasonable answer based on what you know and what you observe. The students observed that whatever was in the box was small, heavier than a pair of scissors, and made of metal. The students knew that a stapler is small, heavier than a pair of scissors, and made of metal. They used this information to make the hypothesis that there was a stapler in the box.

Picture This

1. Interpret a Diagram Why are there two arrows going in different directions at the right end of the diagram?

_____

_____

_____

Think it Over

2. Compare and Contrast How is a hypothesis different than a guess?

_____

_____

_____

How do you analyze a hypothesis?

Keeping an Open Mind Ms. Clark asked the students to think about the possibility that the object in the box might not be a stapler. One student said it had to be a stapler. Ms. Clark reminded him that they might be missing something because their minds were made up that it was a stapler. She said that good scientists keep open minds to every idea and to every explanation.

Finding New Information Ms. Clark asked them what would happen if they learned new information that does not fit with their hypothesis. They thought about what new information they could find to help prove their hypothesis true or not true.

The students decided they could get another shoebox and put a stapler in it. Then they could shake it to see whether it felt and sounded the same as the other box. By getting more information to find out if their hypothesis was correct, the students could analyze, or examine, their hypothesis.

How do you make a prediction?

Ms. Clark asked the students to predict what would happen if their hypothesis was correct. A prediction is what you think will happen. The students all agreed the second box should feel and sound like the mystery box.

How do you test a hypothesis?

Sometimes a hypothesis is tested by making observations. Sometimes building a model is the best way to test a hypothesis. To test their hypothesis, the students made a model. The new shoebox with the stapler inside of it was the model.

After making a model, you must test it to make sure it is the same as the original. So the students needed to test their model to see if it was the same as the original shoebox. When they picked up the model box, they found it was a little heavier than the first box. Also, when they shook the model box, it did not make the same sound as the first box.

The students decided to find the mass of each box. Then they would know how much more mass a stapler has compared to the object in the first box. The students used a balance to find that the box with the stapler had a mass of 410 g. The mystery box had a mass of 270 g.

Think it Over

3. Explain What will the box sound and feel like if the students' hypothesis is correct?

_____

_____

_____

How do you organize your findings?

Ms. Clark suggested that the students organize the information they had before making any new conclusions. By organizing their observations, they had a summary to look at while making conclusions. The students put their information into a table like the one below.

Observation Chart		
Questions	**Mystery Box**	**Our Box**
Does it roll or slide?	It slides and appears to be flat.	It slides and appears to be flat.
Does it make any sounds?	It makes a metallic sound when it strikes the sides of the box.	The stapler makes a thudding sound when it strikes the sides of the box.
What is the mass of the box?		

Picture This

4. Complete a Table
Using information from the previous page, complete the last row of the table.

How do you draw conclusions?

When the students looked at the observations in their table, they decided that their hypothesis was not correct. Ms. Clark asked them if that meant that there was not a stapler in the mystery box. One student said that there could be a different kind of stapler in the mystery box. The students were inferring that the object in the mystery box was not like the stapler in their test box. To **infer** means to make a conclusion based on what you observe. ☑

Another student suggested that they were right back where they started with the mystery box. Ms. Clark pointed out that even though their observations did not support their hypothesis, they knew more information than when they started.

How do you continue to learn?

A student asked if she could open the box to see what was in it. Ms. Clark explained that scientists do not get to "open the box," to find answers to their questions. Some scientists spend their entire lives looking for the answer to one question. When your investigation does not support your first hypothesis, you try again. You gather new information, make new observations, and form a new hypothesis.

Indiana Academic Standard Check

6.1.2: Give examples of different ways scientists investigate natural phenomena and identify processes all scientists use … to make sense of the evidence.

✔ **5. Determine** What did the students in Ms. Clark's class infer?

_____

_____

_____

6. Draw Conclusions
Suppose scientists did not show their methods and results to other scientists. How would this affect scientific discoveries?

_____

_____

_____

7. Explain what a dependent variable is in an experiment.

_____

_____

_____

How do you communicate your findings?

Sometimes scientists try to continue or repeat the work of other scientists. It is important for scientists to explain the results of their investigations and how they did their investigations. Scientists write about their work in journals, books, and on the Internet. They also often go to meetings and give speeches about their work. An important part of doing science is showing methods and results to others.

Experiments

Different types of questions need different types of investigations. Ms. Clark's class needed to answer the question "What is inside the mystery box?" To answer the question, they built a model to learn more about the mystery box. Some scientific questions are answered by doing a type of investigation called a controlled experiment. A **controlled experiment** involves changing only one part in an experiment and observing what that change does to another part of the experiment.

What are variables?

A **variable** is a part of an experiment that can change. Imagine an experiment that tests three fertilizers to see which one makes plants grow tallest. This experiment has two variables. One variable is the fertilizer used. Since three different fertilizers are used, each one can have a different outcome in the experiment. The second variable is the height of the plants. The different fertilizers can affect the height of the plants.

Independent Variables The **independent variable** is a variable that is changed in an experiment. The fertilizer is changed by the scientist. So, the fertilizer is an independent variable. In an experiment, there should be only one independent variable.

Dependent Variables The **dependent variable** is a variable that depends on what happens in the experiment when the independent variable is used. The dependent variable is also the variable measured at the end of the experiment. The height of the plants is the dependent variable. The height of each plant may be different, depending on which fertilizer is used. The scientist will measure the height of each plant at the end of the experiment to see what fertilizer affects the height the most. ☑

What are constants?

A __constant__ is a part of an experiment that is not changed. There can be more than one constant. In the fertilizer experiment, the constants could be the type of plant, the amount of water or sunlight the plants get, or the kind of soil the plants are planted in. The scientist keeps all of these constants the same for all the types of fertilizer that are tested.

Laboratory Safety

In your science class, you will perform many kinds of investigations. Performing investigations involves more than just following steps. You must learn how to keep yourself and those around you safe. Always obey the safety symbol warnings shown below.

Safety Symbols

 Eye Safety

 Clothing Protection

 Disposal

 Biological

 Extreme Temperature

 Sharp Object

 Fume

 Irritant

 Toxic

 Animal Safety

 Flammable

 Electrical

 Chemical

 Open Flame

 Handwashing

How do you practice safety in the lab?

When scientists work in a lab, they take many safety precautions. You must also take safety precautions in the science lab. The most important safety advice is to think before you act. You should always check with your teacher during the planning stage of your investigation. Make sure you know where the safety equipment is in your lab or classroom. You also need to make sure you know how to use the safety equipment. Safety equipment includes eyewashes, thermal mitts, and the fire extinguisher. ☑

Picture This

8. **Recognize Cause and Effect** What is one kind of experiment in which you would need to wear eye goggles?

_____

_____

☑ Reading Check

9. **Describe** What is the most important safety advice in the lab?

_____

_____

Think it Over

10. **Apply** Why should you never eat or drink in the lab?

_____

Think it Over

11. **Infer** If you are doing a science experiment in the lab or in the field, what is the one thing that you should always wear?

_____

What are some good safety habits?

Good safety habits include the following suggestions:

- Find and follow all safety symbols before you begin an investigation.

- Always wear an apron and goggles to protect yourself from chemicals, flames, and pointed objects.

- Keep goggles on until activity, cleanup, and handwashing are complete.

- Always slant test tubes away from yourself and others.

- Never eat, drink, or put on makeup in the lab.

- Report all accidents to your teacher.

- Always wash your hands after working in the lab.

How do you practice safety in the field?

Investigations are also done outside the lab. You can do investigations in streams, farm fields, and other places. Scientists call this working in the field. Scientists must follow safety regulations in the field as well as in the lab. Always wear eye goggles and other safety equipment that you need. Never reach into holes or under rocks. Always wash your hands after you have finished your work in the field or in the lab.

Why have safety rules?

Doing science in the lab or in the field can be much more interesting that just reading about it. But doing experiments can be dangerous and accidents can happen. If you follow safety rules closely, an accident is less likely to happen. Still, you cannot predict when something will go wrong.

Think of a person taking a trip in a car. Most of the time the person is not in a car accident. However, to be safe, drivers and passengers must wear their safety belts. Wearing safety gear in the lab is like wearing a safety belt in a car. It can keep you from being hurt in an accident. You should wear safety gear even if you are just watching an experiment. Always keep safety in mind when conducting an experiment.

● After You Read

Mini Glossary

constant: a part of an experiment that is not changed

controlled experiment: involves changing only one part of an experiment and observing what that change does to another part of the experiment

dependent variable: a variable that depends on what happens in the experiment when the independent variable is used

hypothesis: a reasonable answer based on what you know and what you observe

independent variable: a variable that is changed in an experiment

infer: to make a conclusion based on what you observe

variable: a part of an experiment that can change

1. Review the terms and their definitions in the Mini Glossary. In this section, what was an example of a controlled experiment?

_____

_____

2. In the flowchart below, complete the steps that a scientist might take when conducting a scientific investigation. Use these words or group of words to complete the chart:

conclude and communicate
hypothesize
experiment, investigate, or model

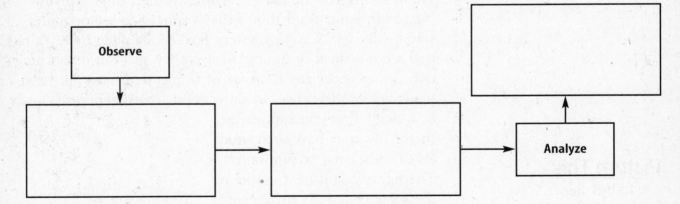

3. At the beginning of the section, you were asked to highlight science skills in the section. What is another method you could have used to learn about science skills?

_____

Science Online Visit **in6.msscience.com** to access your textbook, interactive games, and projects to help you learn more about science in action.

End of Section

The Nature of Science

section ❸ Models in Science

> **Standard—6.7.2:** Use models to illustrate processes that happen too slowly, too quickly, or on too small a scale to observe directly ....
> **Also covers:** 6.1.6, 6.1.2, 6.5.5

What You'll Learn
- to describe different types of models
- the uses of models

● Before You Read

Have you ever built a model? Why did you build the model? Tell about a model you built or want to build.

_____

_____

Study Coach

Identifying the Main Point When you read a paragraph, look for the main idea and write it down on a piece of paper or in your notebook.

● Read to Learn

Why are models necessary?

There are many ways to test a hypothesis. In the last section, Ms. Clark's class tested their hypothesis with a model of the mystery box. A **model** is something that represents an object, event, or idea in the natural world. Models can help you picture in your mind things that are hard to see or understand—like Ms. Clark's mystery box. Models can be of things that are too small or too big to see. They also can be of things that do not exist any more or of things that have not been made yet. Models also can show events that happen so slowly or quickly that you cannot see them. You may have seen models of cells, cars, or dinosaurs. The figure could be a model of the solar system. It could help you understand which planets are next to each other.

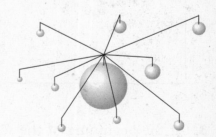

Picture This
1. **Label** the Sun in the model of the solar system.

Types of Models

There are three main types of models—physical models, computer models, and idea models. Scientists can use one or more types of models to help them answer questions. Different models are used for different reasons.

What are physical models?

Models that you can see and touch are physical models. The figure on the previous page is a physical model. A globe of Earth is also a physical model. Models show how parts relate to each other. They also can show how things look when they change position or how things react when a force is put on them.

What are computer models?

Computer models are built using computer software. You can't touch them, but you can look at them on a computer screen. Computer models can show events that happen too quickly or too slowly to see. For example, a computer can show how large plates in Earth move. They also can be used to predict when earthquakes might happen.

Computers also can model movements and positions of things that might take hours or days to do by hand, or even using a calculator. They also can predict changes caused by different systems or forces. For example, computer models help predict the weather. They use the movement of air currents in the atmosphere to make these predictions.

What are idea models?

Some models are ideas that describe what someone thinks about something in the natural world. Idea models cannot be built like physical models because they are just ideas. A famous idea model is Albert Einstein's theory of relativity. One model for this theory is the mathematical equation $E = mc^2$. This explains that mass, m, can be changed into energy, E. ☑

Making Models

Have you ever seen a sketch artist at work? The artist tries to draw a picture of someone from a description given by someone else. The more detailed the description is, the better the picture will be. Sometimes the artist uses descriptions from more than one person. If the descriptions have enough information, the sketch should look realistic. Scientific models are much the same way. The more information the scientist finds, the more accurate the model will be.

FOLDABLES

C Organize Information
Use a half sheet of paper to help you organize information about models in science.

Models in Science

Reading Check

2. **Determine** Which type of model can you see and touch: physical, computer, or idea model?

_____

_____

Think it Over

3. **Apply** Suppose you want to make a model of a plant cell for your science project. What will help you make the most accurate model?

_____

_____

Using Models

When you think of a model, you might think of a model airplane or a model of a building. Not all models are for scientific uses. You may even use models and not know it. Drawings, maps, recipes, and globes are all models.

How are models used?

Communicate Some models communicate ideas. Have you ever drawn a map to show someone how to get to your home? If so, you used a model to communicate. It is sometimes easier to show ideas than to tell them.

Test Predictions Other models test predictions. Engineers often use models of airplanes or cars in wind tunnels to test predictions about how air affects them.

Save Lives, Money, and Time Models are often used because it is safer and less expensive than using the real thing. For example, crash test dummies are used instead of people in automobile crash tests. NASA has built a special airplane that models the conditions in space. It creates freefall for 20 to 25 seconds. Astronauts can practice freefall in the airplane instead of in space. Making many trips in the airplane is easier, safer, and less expensive than a trip into space.

Limitations of Models

The solar system is too big to see all at once. So, scientists have built models. The first solar system models had the planets and the Sun revolving around Earth. Later, as scientists learned new information, they changed their models.

A new model explained the solar system in a different way, but Earth was still the center. Still later, after more observations, scientists discovered that the Sun is the center of the solar system. A new model was made to show this. Even though the first solar system models were incorrect, the models gave scientists information to build upon. Models are not always perfect, but they are a tool that scientists can see and learn from. ☑

Think it Over

4. Describe What is another model, besides a map, you could use to communicate with?

_____

_____

_____

Reading Check

5. Explain Why are models that have been proven to be wrong still helpful?

_____

_____

● After You Read

Mini Glossary

model: something that represents an object, event, or idea in the natural world

1. Review the term and its definition in the Mini Glossary. Which of the three types of models can you touch? Explain why you cannot touch the other types of models.

   _____

   _____

   _____

2. Complete the graphic organizer below to describe the three types of models and their uses.

Types of Models
Physical models are models you can see and touch.

Uses of Models
to save money, time, and lives

3. How do you think making a physical model can help you learn more about how models work?

   _____

   _____

   _____

Science Online Visit **in6.msscience.com** to access your textbook, interactive games, and projects to help you learn more about models.

End of Section

section ➍ Evaluating Scientific Explanation

Standard—6.2.8: Analyze and interpret a given set of findings, demonstrating that there may be more than one good way to do so.
Also covers: 6.1.1, 6.1.5, 6.2.5, 6.5.2

What You'll Learn

- to evaluate scientific explanations
- how to evaluate promotional claims

⬤ Before You Read

Have you ever played the game where you whisper a message into a person's ear, and then that person repeats the message to another person, and so on? What usually happens by the time the message gets to the last person?

Study Coach

Asking Questions As you read the section, write down any questions you might have about what you read.

FOLDABLES

ⓓ Finding Main Ideas
Use a half sheet of paper to help you list the main ideas about how to evaluate scientific explanations.

> Evaluating Scientific
> Explanations

⬤ Read to Learn

Believe it or not?

Think of something someone told you that you didn't believe. Why didn't you believe it? You probably decided there was not enough proof. What you did was evaluate, or judge, the reliability of what you heard. You can evaluate the reliability of a statement by asking "How do you know?" If what you are told seems reliable, you can believe it.

What is critical thinking?

When you decide to believe information you read or hear, you use critical thinking. **Critical thinking** means using what you already know and new facts to decide if you agree with something. You can decide if information is true by breaking it down into two parts. Based on what you know, are the observations correct? Do the conclusions make sense?

Evaluating the Data

Data are observations made in a scientific investigation. Data are gathered and recorded in tables, graphs, or drawings during a scientific investigation. Always look at the data when you evaluate a scientific explanation. Be careful about believing any explanation that is not supported by data.

Are the data specific?

The data given to back up a statement should be specific, or exact. Suppose a friend tells you that many people like pizza better than they like hamburgers. What do you need to know before you agree with your friend? You need some specific data. How many people were asked which food they like more? Specific data makes a statement more reliable and you are more likely to believe it.

How do you take good notes?

In this class you will keep a science journal. You will write down what you see and do in your investigations. Instead of writing "the stuff changed color," write "the clear liquid turned to a bright red when I added a drop of food coloring." It is important to record your observations when they happen. Important details can be forgotten when you wait. ☑

Evaluating Conclusions

When you think about a conclusion that someone has made, you can ask yourself two questions. First, does the conclusion make sense? Second, are there any other possible explanations? Suppose you hear that school will be starting two hours late because of bad weather. A friend decides that the bad weather is snow. You look outside. There is no snow on the roads. The conclusion does not make sense. Are there any other possible explanations? Maybe the roads are icy. The first conclusion is not reliable unless other possible explanations are proven to be wrong.

Evaluating Promotional Materials

Look at the newspaper advertisement. It seems unbelievable. You should hear some of the scientific data before you believe it. The purpose of an ad is to get you to buy something. Always keep this in mind when you read an ad. Before you believe ads like this one, evaluate the data and conclusions. Is the scientific evidence from a good, independent laboratory? An independent laboratory is not related to the company selling the product. Always evaluate data and ask questions before you spend your money.

● After You Read

Mini Glossary

critical thinking: using what you already know and new facts to decide if you should agree with something

data: observations made in a scientific investigation

1. Review the terms and their definitions in the Mini Glossary. Write one sentence using both terms.

_____

_____

2. Use the graphic organizer below to record some of the questions you should ask when you read the results of a scientific investigation.

Questions to ask when you evaluate a scientific investigation
Is the data specific?

3. How could you teach an elementary science class about how to use critical thinking?

_____

_____

 Visit **in6.msscience.com** to access your textbook, interactive games, and projects to help you learn more about evaluating scientific explanations.

 **The Solar System and Beyond**

section ❶ Earth's Place in Space

 Standard—6.1.1: Explain that some scientific knowledge, such as the length of the year, is very old and yet is still applicable today. Understand ....
Also covers: 6.2.5, 6.2.7, 6.3.3, 6.3.5, 6.3.6, 6.3.10

● Before You Read

What is different about daytime and nighttime? Write what you have noticed.

● Read to Learn

Earth Moves

Each morning the Sun seems to rise in the east. Throughout the day, it seems to move higher up in the sky. Around noon it reaches its highest point. Then it appears to fall toward the west until it disappears below the horizon. Is the Sun moving? It is Earth that is moving, with you on it.

What is Earth's rotation?

Earth spins like a top. The imaginary center line that Earth spins around is called Earth's axis. Earth spinning around its axis is Earth's **rotation** (roh TAY shun).

Earth's rotation causes day and night. As Earth rotates, the Sun appears to move across the sky. Earth rotates one time each day. That takes about 24 hours. It is the rotation of Earth that makes the Sun appear to be moving across the sky. Because the Sun only appears to move across the sky, this movement is called apparent motion.

What is Earth's revolution?

Earth's rotation causes day and night. Earth moves around the Sun in a regular, curved path called an **orbit**. The movement of Earth around the Sun is known as Earth's **revolution** (reh vuh LEW shun). Earth revolves around the Sun one time each year.

Mark the Text

Underline As you read, underline the answer to the question in each heading to help you focus on the main ideas.

FOLDABLES™

Ⓐ Compare and Contrast
Make the following two-tab Foldable to show how the movements of Earth and the movements of the Moon are similar and different.

What causes Earth's seasons?

Flowers bloom as the days get warmer. The Sun appears higher in the sky, and daylight lasts longer. Spring seems like a fresh, new beginning. What causes these changes? Earth's axis is not straight up and down—it is slightly tilted. Earth's tilted axis combined with Earth's revolution around the Sun causes seasons. ☑

In the northern hemisphere summer begins in June and ends in September. This is when the northern hemisphere is tilted toward the Sun. During summer, there are more hours of daylight. Longer days are one reason summer is warmer than winter, but not the only reason. During summer, the Sun's rays strike at a higher angle. The angle of the sunlight causes summer to be warmer than winter. More hours of daylight and more intense sunlight during summer are both caused by Earth's tilt.

Earth's Moon

The Moon's surface has many depressions called craters. It has mountainous regions, too. The mountainous areas of the Moon are called **lunar highlands.** The Moon also has dark and flat regions called **maria** (MAHR ee uh). Maria is the Latin word for seas. The maria formed when lava erupted from the Moon's interior and cooled in low areas on its surface.

What orbits Earth?

While Earth revolves around the Sun, the Moon orbits Earth. Human-made objects also orbit Earth. These include the *International Space Station*, other satellites, and debris. The debris is sometimes called space junk. Space junk can include parts from old rockets, old tools, and old equipment.

How does the Moon move?

The Moon's movements are similar to Earth's movements. Earth rotates on an axis, and so does the Moon. Earth revolves around the Sun. The Moon revolves around Earth. It takes the Moon 27.3 days to rotate once. This is the same amount of time it takes the Moon to revolve one time around Earth. Because the Moon rotates and revolves at the same rate, the same side of the Moon always faces Earth. The side of the Moon that faces Earth is called the near side. The opposite side of the Moon is called the far side.

☑ **Reading Check**

1. **Recognize Cause and Effect** What two causes can you give for Earth's seasons?

_____

_____

_____

💡 **Think it Over**

2. **Infer** Why do you think the dark, flat regions of the Moon were named maria?

_____

_____

_____

What lights the Moon?

The Moon does not have its own source of light. It reflects the light of the Sun. Just as half of Earth experiences day while the other half experiences night, half of the Moon is lighted while the other half is dark. The appearance of the Moon changes slightly each night. As the Moon revolves around Earth, you see different amounts of its lighted side. These changes are called phases of the Moon.

What is the lunar cycle?

The phase of the Moon that you see depends on the relative positions of the Moon, the Sun, and Earth. It takes one month for the Moon to go through its phases. That time is called a lunar cycle.

New Moon The lunar cycle begins with the new moon. During the new moon, the Moon is between Earth and the Sun. The lighted half of the Moon is facing the Sun and the dark side faces Earth.

Waxing After a new moon, the phases get larger. The phases are waxing because more of the lighted half of the Moon can be seen each night.

Full Moon The middle of the lunar cycle is full moon. Earth is between the Moon and the Sun. The lighted half of the Moon faces Earth.

Waning After full moon, the phases begin waning. During waning phases, less of the lighted half of the Moon can be seen each night. The Moon appears smaller and smaller until it can't be seen at all. Then the cycle begins again.

What is a solar eclipse?

When the Moon is directly between the Sun and Earth, it blocks sunlight from reaching Earth. This event is called a solar <u>eclipse</u> (ih KLIHPS). Solar eclipses happen rarely. They always take place during the new moon phase.

Only a few people can witness a total solar eclipse. The Moon is small compared to Earth. Therefore, the darkest part of the Moon's shadow falls on only a small area of Earth during a solar eclipse. Even a partial solar eclipse is unusual. **WARNING:** *Never look directly at the Sun, even during an eclipse. The light can permanently damage your eyes.*

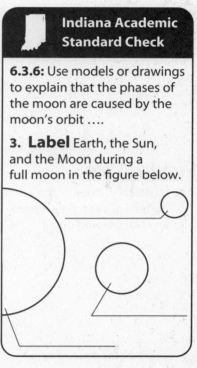

Indiana Academic Standard Check

6.3.6: Use models or drawings to explain that the phases of the moon are caused by the moon's orbit ….

3. Label Earth, the Sun, and the Moon during a full moon in the figure below.

Think it Over

4. Draw Conclusions Why do you think a solar eclipse always occurs during a new moon phase?

_____

_____

_____

Think it Over

5. Draw Conclusions Why do you think a lunar eclipse always occurs during a full moon phase?

_____

_____

Picture This

6. Identify Look at the figure. Label an area where low tides would occur.

✔ **Reading Check**

7. Recognize Cause and Effect List the two objects that cause tides on Earth.

_____

_____

What is a lunar eclipse?

When Earth is directly between the Sun and the Moon, its shadow falls on the Moon. This is called a lunar eclipse. A lunar eclipse is unusual because the Moon's orbit is not in the same plane as Earth's orbit around the Sun. When lunar eclipses do occur, it is always the full moon phase. The full moon then becomes dim and sometimes turns deep red.

What causes Earth's tides?

The Moon's gravity pulls on Earth and causes Earth's tides. **Tides** are the regular rise and fall in sea level. When the Moon is closer to a particular place on Earth, the Moon's gravity pulls harder on that place. The figure shows the effect of the Moon's gravity on Earth. Two bulges form in Earth's oceans. One bulge is on the side of Earth close to the Moon. The other bulge is on the side of Earth on the opposite side, away from the Moon. These two bulges of water are the high tides. Because Earth rotates, different places on Earth experience high or low tides.

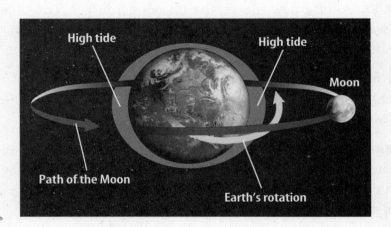

High tide · High tide · Moon · Path of the Moon · Earth's rotation

Does the Sun affect tides?

The Sun also affects tides on Earth. Because the Sun is much farther from Earth, the Sun does not affect tides as much as the Moon. When the Sun, Earth, and the Moon are lined up, high tides are higher and low tides are lower. This is called spring tide. Spring tides occur because the force of the Moon's gravity and force of the Sun's gravity combine. Together they produce a greater effect. When the Sun, Earth, and the Moon form a 90-degree angle, high tides are not as high as usual, and low tides are not as low as usual. This is called a neap tide. During neap tide, the Sun's gravity reduces the effect of the Moon's gravity. ✔

● After You Read

Mini Glossary

eclipse (ih KLIHPS): event that occurs when the Moon moves between the Sun and Earth (solar eclipse), or when Earth moves between the Sun and the Moon (lunar eclipse), and casts a shadow

lunar highlands: mountainous areas on the Moon that are about 4.5 billion years old

maria: smooth, dark regions on the Moon that formed when lava flowed onto the Moon's surface

orbit: regular, curved path around the Sun

revolution (rev uh LEW shun): movement of Earth around the Sun, which takes a year to complete

rotation (roh TAY shun): spinning of Earth on its axis, which occurs once every 24 hours, produces day and night, and causes the planets and stars to appear to rise and set

tides: the alternate rise and fall of sea level caused by the gravitational attractions of the Moon and Sun

1. Review the terms above and their definitions in the Mini Glossary. In your own words, explain the cause of tides.

   _____

   _____

2. *Circle the word or phrase that best answers the question.*

   a. What is the event called when Earth's shadow falls on the Moon or when the Moon's shadow falls on Earth?

   A. lunar highlands   **B.** eclipse   **C.** tides   **D.** maria

   b. What is caused by the tilt of Earth's axis and its revolution?

   A. eclipses   **B.** phases   **C.** tides   **D.** seasons

   c. How much time does it take for Earth to rotate one time?

   A. 24 hours   **B.** 27.3 hours   **C.** 24 days   **D.** 365 days

3. Reread the topic sentences you underlined in the text. How did this strategy help you remember the main ideas about Earth's seasons, Earth's moon, and the cause of tides?

   _____

   _____

 Science Online Visit **in6.msscience.com** to access your textbook, interactive games, and projects to help you learn more about Earth's place in space.

 End of Section

The Solar System and Beyond

section ❷ **The Solar System**

Standard—6.1.7: Explain that technology is essential for such purposes as access to outer space, sample collection ... communication of information.
Also covers: 6.2.3, 6.2.5, 6.2.7, 6.3.1, 6.3.3, 6.3.7, 6.7.2

What You'll Learn

- distances in space
- the planets and moons in the solar system
- how Earth is a unique planet

Study Coach

Create a Quiz After you have read this section, create a five-question quiz. Exchange quizzes with a partner. Review your answers together.

FOLDABLES

❸ **Build Vocabulary** Make quarter-sheet Foldables as shown below. Write the vocabulary terms and the definitions from this section.

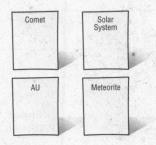

● Before You Read

On the lines below, write three facts that you know about the solar system. As you read the section, check your facts to see if you were correct.

_____

_____

● Read to Learn

Distances in Space

The **solar system** is made up of the nine planets and many other objects that orbit the Sun. Objects in the solar system are held in their orbits by the Sun's strong gravity.

The planets in the solar system revolve around the Sun in elliptical, or oval-shaped, orbits. The orbits of most of the planets are only slightly elliptical, almost circular. Pluto and Mercury have orbits that are shaped more like flattened circles.

How are distances measured?

Distances in space are hard to imagine because space is so vast. Suppose you had to measure the hallway outside your classroom or the distance from your home to school. You probably would measure the hallway using meters and the distance home using kilometers. Larger units are used to measure greater distances.

What is an astronomical unit?

Units bigger than kilometers are needed to measure the enormous distances between planets. One such measure is the astronomical (as truh NAH mih kul) unit. An **astronomical unit** equals 150 million km, the average distance from Earth to the Sun. The abbreviation for astronomical unit is *AU*.

Touring the Solar System

Now you know a little bit more about how to measure distance in the solar system. Next, you can travel outward from the Sun and take a look at the objects in the solar system. What will you see first?

Inner Planets

Traveling away from the Sun, the first group of planets is the inner planets. They are mostly solid, with minerals similar to those on Earth. Much of what is known about these planets comes from spacecraft that send data back to Earth.

Mercury Mercury is the planet closest to the Sun and the second smallest planet. Like Earth's moon, it has a lot of craters. Craters form when meteorites strike a planet's surface. Mercury has no true atmosphere. Mercury's small size and low gravity allow gases that could form an atmosphere to escape into space. Because it has no atmosphere and it is so close to the Sun, Mercury has extreme temperatures. The surface can reach temperatures as high as 425°C during the day and fall to −170°C at night. Mercury is unfit for life.

Venus Venus is the second planet from the Sun. Venus is sometimes called Earth's twin. Its size and mass are similar to Earth's. The surface of Venus is surrounded by thick clouds. The clouds trap solar energy, causing surface temperatures to average around 472°C.

Earth Earth has an atmosphere that allows life to exist on its surface. As far as scientists know, Earth is the only planet that supports life. Earth's surface temperatures allow water to exist as a solid, a liquid, and a gas. Also, ozone in Earth's atmosphere works like a screen to limit the harmful rays from the Sun that reach Earth's surface.

Mars Mars is the fourth planet from the Sun. It is sometimes called the red planet. The red color of Mars is caused by iron oxide in the soil. Several spacecraft have made missions to Mars, and some of their robots have been left behind on the surface of the planet. From these missions scientists have learned that there might once have been flowing water on Mars. There is some water there today. Polar ice caps on Mars are made of frozen water and frozen carbon dioxide. Like Earth, Mars also has seasons. Mars has two small moons, Phobos and Deimos. ☑

Think it Over

1. **Recognize Cause and Effect** What are two reasons that gases from the planet Mercury escape into space?

_____

_____

_____

Reading Check

2. **Explain** What causes the surface of Mars to appear red?

_____

_____

_____

What is the asteroid belt?

The asteroid belt is an area between Mars and Jupiter in which many asteroids travel around the Sun. Asteroids are pieces of rock made of minerals similar to those that formed the rocky planets and moons. In fact, these asteroids might have become a planet if it weren't for the giant planet, Jupiter. Jupiter's huge gravitational force might have prevented a small planet from forming in the area of the asteroid belt. The asteroid belt might be parts of larger objects that collided in space. The asteroid belt separates the solar system's planets into two groups—the inner planets and the outer planets. ☑

Outer Planets

The outer planets orbit beyond the asteroid belt. The outer planets are Jupiter, Saturn, Uranus, Neptune, and Pluto. All the outer planets, except Pluto, are huge balls of gas called gas giants. Each might have a solid core, but none of them has a solid surface. The gas giants have many moons orbiting them. They have rings made of dust and ice surrounding them. Pluto is different. It is made up of ice and rock.

Jupiter Jupiter is the fifth planet from the Sun. It is the largest planet in the solar system. Jupiter has the shortest day—less than 10 hours long. This means that Jupiter rotates faster than any other planet. A huge, red storm near the equator is called the Great Red Spot. Jupiter has 61 moons. One, called Ganymede (GA nih meed), is larger than the planet Mercury. Ganymede, along with two other moons, Europa and Callisto, might have liquid water under their icy crusts. Another of Jupiter's moons, Io, has more active volcanoes than any other object in the solar system.

Saturn Saturn is the sixth planet from the Sun. Saturn has several broad rings made up of hundreds of smaller rings. All the rings are made up of pieces of ice and rock. Some of these pieces are as small as specks of dust. Other pieces are large, even many meters across. Saturn has at least 31 moons. The largest moon is Titan. Titan has an atmosphere that is similar to the atmosphere on Earth long ago. Some scientists hypothesize that Titan's atmosphere might provide clues about how life began on Earth.

✔ Reading Check

3. Identify What separates the inner planets from the outer planets?

_____

_____

💡 Think it Over

4. Infer How might scientists learn more about Titan's atmosphere?

_____

_____

_____

Uranus Uranus is the seventh planet from the Sun. You can use the table below to find the distance between Uranus and the Sun. The axis of most planets is tilted just a little, somewhat like the handle of a broom that is leaning against a wall. The axis of Uranus is tilted almost even with the plane of its orbit, like a broomstick lying on the floor. Uranus's atmosphere is made mostly of hydrogen with smaller amounts of helium and methane. The methane gives Uranus a bluish-green color. Uranus has rings and at least 21 moons. ☑

Neptune Neptune is the eighth planet from the Sun. It's atmosphere is made up of hydrogen, helium, and methane. Like Uranus, methane gives Neptune a blue color. In 1989, *Voyager 2* sent pictures of Neptune to Earth. These pictures showed a Great Dark Spot in it's atmosphere. By 1994, the spot was gone. Neptune is the last of the big, gas planets with rings around it. It has 11 moons. Triton, the largest, has geysers that shoot gaseous nitrogen into space. Triton does not have many craters. Lava still is flowing onto its surface.

Pluto Pluto is the ninth planet from the Sun. Pluto was discovered in 1930. It is the last planet in the solar system, and it is also the smallest planet. Pluto is smaller than Earth's moon. Pluto is a rocky planet with a frozen crust. It is the only planet in the solar system that has never been visited by a spacecraft. Pluto has one moon, called Charon. Charon is about half the size of Pluto.

Solar System Data			
Planet	Distance from the Sun (AU)	Planet	Distance from the Sun (AU)
Mercury	0.39	Jupiter	5.20
Venus	0.72	Saturn	9.54
Earth	1.00	Uranus	19.19
Mars	1.52	Neptune	30.07
Asteroid belt	2–4	Pluto	39.48

How can you model the solar system?

The table above shows the distances of the planets and the asteroid belt from the Sun. Notice that the inner planets are fairly close together, and the outer planets are far apart. The distances from the Sun can be used to make a scale model of the solar system.

☑ **Reading Check**

5. **Explain** What is unique about the axis of Uranus?

_____

_____

_____

Applying Math

6. **Interpret Data** Imagine that you are making a scale model of the solar system. On your model, 1 cm equals 1 AU. How far from the Sun will Saturn be on your model?

_____

Comets

A **comet** is a large body of ice and rock that orbits the Sun. It can be as large as fifty kilometers across. Comets might come from the Oort cloud, an area far beyond the orbit of Pluto. The Oort cloud is about 50,000 AU from the Sun. Other comets come from an area called the Kuiper Belt, which lies just past the orbit of Neptune.

When a comet gets closer to the Sun, solar radiation changes some of its ice into gas. Solar winds blow gas and dust away from the comet. From Earth, the gas and dust that follow the comet appear as a bright tail. The figure below shows a comet in the night sky. ☑

✔ **Reading Check**

7. Why does a comet appear to have a tail?

_____

_____

_____

What is a meteorite?

Sometimes, chunks of rock and metal from outer space fall to Earth's surface. **Meteorites** are any fragments from space that land on Earth. Small meteorites can be the size of pebbles. A large meteorite can have a mass as large as 14.5 metric tons. Hundreds of meteorites fall to Earth each year. Only a few of the meteorites that fall are ever found.

Scientists are interested in meteorites because they help them understand more about space. For example, many meteorites seem to be about 4.5 billion years old. This gives an estimate of the age of the solar system.

There are three types of meteorites—irons, stones, and stoney-irons. Irons are made almost all of iron, with some nickel mixed in. Stones are rocky. Stoney-irons, a mixture of metal and rock, are the rarest meteorites. ☑

✔ **Reading Check**

8. Recall What are the three types of meteorites?

_____

_____

_____

● After You Read

Mini Glossary

astronomical (as truh NAH mih kul) unit: a unit of measure equal to the distance from Earth to the Sun, or about 150 million km

comet: large body of ice and rock that orbits the Sun; a comet develops a bright, glowing tail as it nears the Sun

meteorite: any rock from space that survives its plunge through the atmosphere and lands on Earth's surface

solar system: the nine planets and numerous other objects that orbit the Sun, all held in place by the Sun's gravity

1. Review the terms above and their definitions in the Mini Glossary. Use two of the vocabulary words in sentences that show you understand the words.

_____

_____

_____

2. Complete the chart below to review the main ideas and details about the solar system.

INNER PLANETS	OUTER PLANETS	OTHER OBJECTS
_____	_____	MOONS
VENUS	_____	_____
_____	_____	_____
_____	_____	_____
	PLUTO	

3. How did making a five-question quiz help you understand what you read?

_____

_____

_____

 Visit **in6.msscience.com** to access your textbook, interactive games, and projects to help you learn more about the solar system.

End of Section

chapter 2

The Solar System and Beyond

section ❸ Stars and Galaxies

 Standard—6.1.7: Explain that technology is essential for such purposes as access to outer space, sample collection … communication of information.
Also covers: 6.2.5, 6.2.6, 6.2.7, 6.3.2

What You'll Learn

- why stars appear to move across the sky
- about constellations
- how stars change over time

▶ **Study Coach**

KWL Chart Create a three-column chart to help you organize the information in this section. Before you read, write what you already know about stars and galaxies. Then write what you want to know. As you read, write what you have learned about stars and galaxies.

● Before You Read

What are some different ways that scientists have learned about stars and galaxies? Write your ideas on the lines below.

_____

_____

_____

● Read to Learn

Stars

Stars are always in the sky. You can't see them during the day because the Sun's light makes Earth's atmosphere so bright that it hides them. Earth's rotation makes it look like the stars move across the night sky, just like another star, the Sun, seems to move across the sky during the day. Earth's revolution around the Sun also causes the stars to appear as if they changed location.

What is a constellation?

<u>Constellations</u> (kahn stuh LAY shuns) are groups of stars that form patterns in the sky. Around the world, different people throughout history have given different names to the constellations. Ursa Major, Ursa Minor, Orion, and Taurus are some of the names in use today.

What makes one star different from another?

They may look about the same from Earth, but stars are actually different colors. They are different colors because they are different temperatures. Red stars are the coolest visible stars. Yellow stars have medium temperatures, and blue stars are the hottest. Stars are different sizes, too. Most stars are small. The Sun is a medium-sized, yellow star.

Can a star's brightness be classified?

Some stars are brighter than others. You can see this on a clear night. Scientists classify a star's brightness by a system called apparent magnitude. From Earth, stars that appear the dimmest have an apparent magnitude of 6. Brighter stars have smaller numbers, even numbers below zero. The Sun is the brightest with an apparent magnitude of −26.7. It looks bright because it is so close to Earth, not because it is so much brighter than other stars. The Sun is really a medium-bright star compared to other stars.

The Lives of Stars

Scientists hypothesize that stars begin as huge clouds of gas and dust. Gravity pulls together the dust and gases. Then temperatures begin to rise. When the dust and gas draw very close and the temperature gets very hot, atoms begin to merge, or join, together. This merging process is called fusion. Fusion changes matter into the energy that powers the star.

After a medium-sized star has formed and used up some of the gas at its center, it expands. The star becomes a giant. Giants are large, cool, reddish stars. The Sun will become a giant in about five billion years. It will remain a giant for about a billion years. Then the Sun will lose its outer shell, the core will shrink, and the Sun will become a white dwarf—a hot, small star. Finally, the Sun will cool and stop shining. It will become a black dwarf.

How long a star lives depends on how massive it is. Larger stars have shorter lives. Smaller stars have longer lives.

What is the life cycle of a supergiant?

When a large star begins to use up the fuel in its core, it expands to become a supergiant. Eventually, the core of the supergiant collapses. This sends an explosion through the star and the star becomes bright. The exploding star is called a **supernova**. Gas and dust are released and might become part of a new star.

The core of the supergiant may become a neutron star if it isn't too large. If the core is more than three times as massive as the Sun, it collapses to form a black hole. No light can escape from a black hole. ☑

FOLDABLES™

Ⓒ Find Main Ideas Make the following half-sheet Foldables to help you identify the main ideas about stars and galaxies.

Lives of Stars:

Types of Galaxies:

✔ Reading Check

1. **Identify** What is the end of the life of a massive supergiant?

_____

Galaxies

A **galaxy** is a group of stars, gas, and dust held together by gravity. Galaxies look like dim clumps of stars in the sky.

Are all galaxies the same?

There are different shapes and sizes of galaxies. The three major types of galaxies are elliptical, spiral, and irregular. Elliptical galaxies are shaped like huge basketballs or footballs. Spiral galaxies can be shaped like huge pinwheels. Some spiral galaxies have bars at the center. Irregular galaxies come in all sorts of shapes. They are smaller than other galaxies. ☑

What is the Milky Way galaxy?

We live in a giant spiral galaxy called the Milky Way. Hundreds of billions of stars are in the Milky Way, including the Sun. Just as Earth revolves around the Sun, stars revolve around the centers of galaxies. The Sun revolves around the center of the Milky Way about once every 225 million years.

You can see part of the Milky Way from Earth as a band of light across the night sky. The band of light is made up of the light of stars in the galaxy's disk. The Milky Way is bigger and brighter than most other galaxies in the universe. Every star you see in the night sky is part of the Milky Way Galaxy.

✔ **Reading Check**

2. **Classify** What are the three major types of galaxies?

_____

_____

_____

The Sun is located toward the edge of the Milky Way.

Cygnus arm

Perseus arm

Centaurus arm

Orion arm

Sagittarius arm

Location of the Sun

Picture This

3. **Interpret Scientific Illustrations** How many arms does the Milky Way Galaxy have.

_____

Why is the speed of light unique?

The speed of light is about 300,000 km/s. Light could go around Earth seven times in one second. Nothing travels faster. Light always travels at the same speed, no matter what. The speed of light is a constant that scientists use to talk about the large distances in the universe. The figure shows how scientists can calculate distances in space.

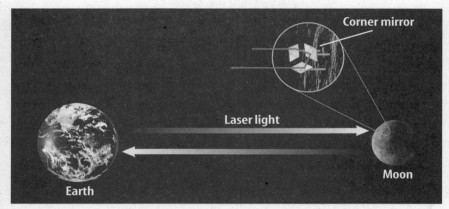

The distance from Earth to the Moon has been determined by bouncing a laser beam off mirrors left by *Apollo 11* astronauts.

What is a light-year?

One light-year is a unit of measurement that is even larger than one astronomical unit. A **light-year** is the distance light travels in one year. A light-year is about 9.5 trillion km.

Galaxies are so big that they are measured in light-years. Small galaxies are a few thousand light-years across. Large galaxies may be 100,000 light-years across. The distance between galaxies is also measured in light-years. When light from some stars reaches Earth, that light has been traveling for millions of years. ☑

The Universe

Each galaxy contains billions of stars. As many as 100 billion galaxies might exist. All these galaxies with all their billions of stars make up the universe. The universe is the great vastness of space dotted with exploding stars, black holes, and star-filled galaxies. In all this space is one small planet called Earth. In relation to the vastness of the universe, Earth is smaller than one speck of dust. Earth looks even smaller when you consider that the universe seems to be expanding. Could it be the only place where life exists?

Picture This

4. Draw Conclusions
When scientists measured the distance between Earth and the Moon, they used a laser beam and mirrors. What did they measure?

_____

_____

_____

✓ **Reading Check**

5. Explain What is measured in light-years?

_____

_____

● After You Read

Mini Glossary

constellation (kahn stuh LAY shun): group of stars that forms a pattern in the sky

galaxy: group of stars, gas, and dust held together by gravity

light-year: about 9.5 trillion km—the distance that light travels in one year—which is used to measure large distances between stars or galaxies

supernova: very bright explosion of a supergiant that takes place after its core collapses

1. Review the terms and their definitions in the Mini Glossary. Use two or more terms in a short poem about the universe. Your poem doesn't have to rhyme.

_____

_____

_____

2. Fill in the summary chart with information you have learned in this section.

Stars	_____ are made up of stars that form patterns in the sky.
	Stars begin as _____.
Galaxies	Earth is in the _____ arm of the _____ Galaxy.
The Universe	The universe has billions of _____ made up of billions of _____.

3. Reread the Know column of your K-W-L chart. Did you find out what you wanted to know by reading the section? Make sure you filled in the column labeled *Learned*. What other resources could help you find out what you want to know about stars and galaxies?

_____

_____

_____

End of Section

Science Online Visit **in6.msscience.com** to access your textbook, interactive games, and projects to help you learn more about stars and galaxies.

chapter 3 Atmosphere

section ❶ Earth's Atmosphere

> **Standard—6.3.7:** Understand and describe the scales involved in characterizing Earth and its atmosphere. Describe that Earth is ….
> Also covers: 6.2.5, 6.2.6, 6.3.13

● Before You Read

Imagine you are on a spaceship looking down at Earth. Would the view be perfectly clear? What do you think you might see surrounding Earth? Write your thoughts on the lines below.

_____

_____

_____

● Read to Learn

Importance of the Atmosphere

Earth's **atmosphere** is a thin layer of gases, solids, and liquids that surround the planet forming a protective covering. The covering keeps Earth from getting too hot or too cold. The atmosphere keeps Earth from absorbing too much heat from the Sun. It also keeps too much heat from escaping into space. Without protection from the atmosphere, life on Earth could not exist.

Makeup of the Atmosphere

Viewed from space Earth's atmosphere today has a thin layer of gases. White clouds usually cover at least half the planet. Between gaps in the clouds, the blue color of the ocean waters shows through.

Earth's early atmosphere was very different from the atmosphere we know today. The early atmosphere was produced by erupting volcanoes. They released nitrogen and carbon dioxide, but little oxygen. Then, about 2 billion years ago, the amount of oxygen in the atmosphere began to increase.

What You'll Learn
- the gases in Earth's atmosphere
- the structure of Earth's atmosphere
- what causes air pressure

Study Coach

Flash Cards Make flash cards to help you learn more about this section. Write the question on one side of the flash card and the answer on the other. Keep quizzing yourself until you know all the answers.

FOLDABLES

Ⓐ Organize Make a three-tab Foldable to help you learn about gases, solids, and liquids in Earth's atmosphere.

What caused the atmosphere to change?

Early organisms that lived in the ocean used sunlight to make food. While making food, the organisms released oxygen into the atmosphere.

The oxygen formed a layer of ozone molecules around Earth. The ozone layer protects Earth from the Sun's harmful rays. Over time, this protective ozone layer enabled green plants to grow on land. The green plants released even more oxygen. Today, many living things on Earth, including humans, depend on oxygen to survive.

Applying Math

1. **Fractions** Which is the most accurate fraction for the amount of oxygen contained in Earth's atmosphere—about 1/5, about 2/3, about 3/4?

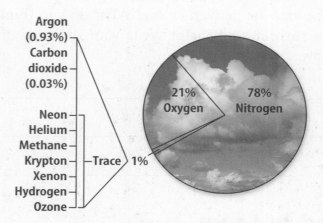

What gases make up Earth's atmosphere?

As shown in the figure above, 78 percent of Earth's atmosphere is made up of nitrogen. Oxygen makes up 21 percent of the atmosphere. Small amounts of other gases make up the remaining 1 percent.

The composition of the atmosphere is changing in small but important ways. For example, humans burn fuel for energy. As fuel is burned, carbon dioxide is released as a by-product into Earth's atmosphere. Increasing energy use may increase the amount of carbon dioxide in the atmosphere.

What solids and liquids are in Earth's atmosphere?

In addition to gases, Earth's atmosphere contains small, solid particles such as dust, salt, and pollen. Dust particles get into the atmosphere when wind picks them up off the ground. Salt is picked up from ocean spray. Plants give off pollen that becomes mixed throughout part of the atmosphere. ☑

The atmosphere also contains small liquid droplets, other than water droplets in clouds. The atmosphere moves these liquid droplets and solids from one area to another.

Reading Check

2. **List** three solids found in Earth's atmosphere.

Layers of the Atmosphere

What would happen if a glass of chocolate milk was left untouched on a kitchen counter? Eventually, a lower layer, heavy with chocolate, would separate and fall to the bottom of the glass.

Like a glass of chocolate milk, Earth's atmosphere has layers. There are five layers in the atmosphere, as shown in the figure below. There are two lower layers: the troposphere (TRO puh sfihr) and the stratosphere (STRA tuh sfihr). The three upper layers of the atmosphere are: the mesosphere (MEZ uh sfihr), the thermosphere (THUR muh sfihr), and the exosphere (EK soh sfihr). Most of the air is contained in the troposphere and the stratosphere. ☑

What are the lower layers of the atmosphere?

The <u>troposphere</u> is the layer of Earth's atmosphere that is closest to the ground. It contains 99 percent of the water vapor and 75 percent of the atmospheric gases. The troposphere is where clouds and weather occur. It extends up to about 10 km from Earth's surface.

The <u>stratosphere</u> is the layer of Earth's atmosphere directly above the troposphere. As the figure shows, the ozone layer is found within the stratosphere.

Layers of the Atmosphere

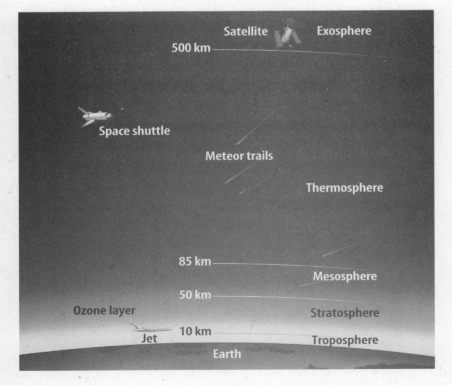

☑ Reading Check

3. **Identify** What are the two lower layers of the atmosphere?

_____

_____

Picture This

4. **Interpret** In what layer of the atmosphere do satellites orbit?

_____

6.3.7: Understand and describe the scales ... Earth and its atmosphere. Describe that ....

✔ **5. Identify** Which of these is the hottest and thickest layer of the atmosphere: the mesosphere, the thermosphere, or the ionosphere?

What are the upper layers of the atmosphere?

The **mesosphere** is the third layer of the atmosphere. It extends from the top of the stratosphere to about 85 km above Earth.

The thermosphere is named for its high temperatures. The **thermosphere** is the fourth layer of the atmosphere and is its hottest and thickest layer. It is found between 85 km and 500 km above Earth's surface. ☑

The ionosphere (I AH nuh sfihr) is within the mesosphere and thermosphere. The **ionosphere** is a layer of electrically charged particles that absorbs AM radio waves during the day and reflects them back at night. Because of this, daytime listeners cannot hear AM radio broadcasts from distant stations. When the ionosphere reflects radio waves at night, listeners can hear the distant stations they could not pick up during the day.

What causes this night and day difference between how far radio waves travel? During the day, energy from the Sun interacts with particles in the ionosphere. The interaction causes them to absorb AM radio frequencies. At night, the Sun's energy is not available and it does not interact with the particles in the ionosphere. This is why radio waves can travel greater distances at night as shown in the figure below.

The **exosphere** is the top layer of the atmosphere. The exosphere is very thin because it contains so few molecules. Beyond the exosphere is outer space.

Picture This

6. Determine What is reflected by the ionosphere at night but not during the day?

Radio Waves in the Ionosphere

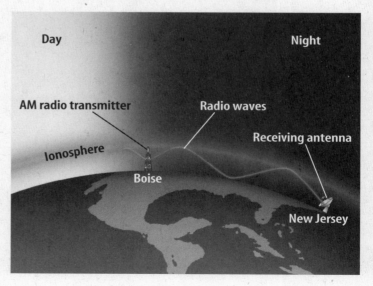

Atmospheric Pressure

Imagine a football player running with the ball. Suddenly, six other players tackle him. They pile one on top of the other. Who feels the weight more—the player on the bottom holding the ball, or the one on top? The player on the bottom, of course. Why? A great mass of bodies is pressing down on him.

What is pressure?

The molecules that make up human beings have mass. Atmospheric gases have mass, too. Atmospheric gases extend hundreds of kilometers above Earth's surface. Earth's gravity pulls these gases toward its surface. The weight of these gases presses down on the air below. As a result, the gas molecules nearer Earth's surface are closer together as shown in the figure to the right. This dense air close to the ground exerts more force than the less dense air near the top of the atmosphere. **Pressure** is the force exerted on an area.

Air Molecules

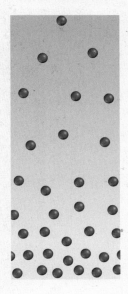

What affects air pressure?

Air pressure is greater near Earth's surface, where molecules are closer together. Air pressure decreases in air that is further from Earth's surface. In other words, air pressure decreases with altitude as shown in the graph below.

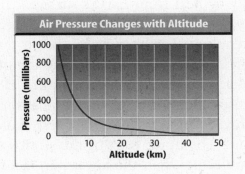

Air Pressure Changes with Altitude

Because air pressure decreases with altitude, it is harder to breathe in the mountains than it is at the seashore. Jet airplanes maintain an inside air pressure that matches the air pressure on the ground. If the inside of the plane was not pressurized, people flying high above Earth's surface could not breathe.

Picture This

7. Interpret Why do the air molecules at the bottom of the figure exert more pressure than those at the top?

_____

_____

_____

Picture This

8. Estimate What is the air pressure at an altitude of 5 km?

_____

Think it Over

9. Explain Why do different layers of Earth's atmosphere have different temperatures?

_____

_____

Temperature in Atmospheric Layers

Most of the energy on Earth comes from the Sun. This energy must pass through the atmosphere before it reaches Earth's surface. Some layers of the atmosphere contain gases that easily absorb the Sun's energy. Other layers do not contain these gases. As a result, different atmospheric layers have different temperatures as shown in the graph below.

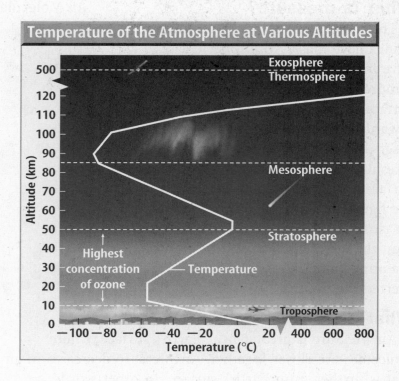

Temperature of the Atmosphere at Various Altitudes

Picture This

10. Interpret Look at the graph of atmospheric temperatures. Does the temperature in the thermosphere increase or decrease with altitude?

_____

_____

Molecules that make up the air in the troposphere are warmed mostly by heat from Earth's surface. The Sun warms Earth's surface, which then warms the air right above it. For every kilometer above Earth's surface, the air temperature falls about 6.5°C. As a result, the air at the top of a mountain usually is cooler than the air at the bottom. ☑

In the stratosphere, molecules of ozone absorb some of the Sun's energy. Energy absorbed by these molecules raises the temperature. The upper part of the stratosphere has more ozone molecules than the lower part does. Therefore, the temperature in this layer rises with increasing altitude.

Like the troposphere, the temperature in the mesosphere decreases with altitude. The thermosphere and the exosphere are closest to the Sun. These layers have fewer molecules, but each molecule has a lot of energy. Temperatures here are high.

✔ Reading Check

11. Compare Are the air molecules in the troposphere warmed mainly by the Sun's heat or by the heat from Earth's surface?

_____

_____

The Ozone Layer

The **ozone layer** lies within the stratosphere about 19 km to 48 km above the ground. Ozone is made of oxygen. All life depends on the ozone layer.

The oxygen you breathe has two atoms per molecule. An ozone molecule is made up of three oxygen atoms. The ozone layer contains a high concentration of ozone and shields you from the Sun's harmful energy. How? Ozone absorbs most of the ultraviolet radiation that enters the atmosphere. **Ultraviolet radiation** is a type of energy that comes to Earth from the Sun. Too much exposure to ultraviolet radiation can damage your skin and cause cancer. ✔

What are CFCs?

Chlorofluorocarbons (CFCs) are chemical compounds used in some refrigerators, air conditioners, aerosol sprays, and production of foam packaging. Evidence exists that CFCs are one type of air pollutant destroying Earth's protective ozone layer.

CFCs can enter the atmosphere in different ways. CFCs can leak from appliances. Sometimes CFCs escape when products containing them are not disposed of properly. ✔

Molecules from CFCs can break apart ozone molecules. Each ozone molecule is made up of three oxygen atoms bonded together. Each CFC molecule has three chlorine atoms. When a chlorine atom from a CFC molecule comes near a molecule of ozone, the ozone molecule breaks apart. One atom of chlorine can destroy about 100,000 ozone molecules. As a result, more harmful ultraviolet rays reach Earth's surface.

What is the ozone hole?

The destruction of ozone molecules by CFCs seems to cause a seasonal reduction in ozone over Antarctica called the ozone hole. Every year beginning in late August or early September the amount of ozone in the atmosphere over Antarctica begins to decrease. By October, the ozone concentration is at its lowest point. Then it begins to increase again. By December, the ozone hole disappears. ✔

In the mid-1990s, many governments banned the production and use of CFCs. As a result, there are fewer CFC molecules in the atmosphere today.

✔ Reading Check

12. Identify What does ozone absorb?

_____

_____

✔ Reading Check

13. Explain Name one way CFCs can enter the atmosphere.

_____

_____

✔ Reading Check

14. Recall Where is the ozone hole located?

_____

_____

● After You Read

Mini Glossary

atmosphere: Earth's air, which is made up of a thin layer of gases, solids, and liquids; forms a protective layer around the planet and is divided into five distinct layers

chlorofluorocarbons (CFCs): group of chemical compounds used in refrigerators, air conditioners, production of foam packaging, and aerosol sprays that may enter the atmosphere and destroy ozone

exosphere (EK soh sfihr): top layer of the atmosphere

ionosphere(I AH nuh sfihr): layer of electrically charged particles in the thermosphere that absorbs AM radio waves during the day and reflects them back at night

mesosphere (MEZ uh sfihr): third layer of the atmosphere that extends from the top of the stratosphere to about 85 km above Earth

ozone layer: layer of the stratosphere with a high concentration of ozone; absorbs most of the Sun's harmful ultraviolet radiation

pressure: the force exerted on a surface

stratosphere (STRA tuh sfihr): layer of Earth's atmosphere directly above the troposphere

thermosphere (THUR muh sfihr): fourth layer of Earth's atmosphere, and its thickest layer; has high temperatures

troposphere (TRO puh sfihr): layer of Earth's atmosphere that is closest to the ground

ultraviolet radiation: type of energy that comes to Earth from the Sun

1. Review the terms and definitions in the Mini Glossary. Write a sentence that explains why the ozone layer is important.

_____

_____

2. List the layers of the atmosphere in order. Begin with the top layer and end with the layer closest to Earth's surface.

   1. _____

   2. _____

   3. _____

   4. _____

   5. _____

End of Section

Science Online Visit **in6.msscience.com** to access your textbook, interactive games, and projects to help you learn more about Earth's atmosphere.

Atmosphere

section ❷ Energy Transfer in the Atmosphere

> **Standard—6.3.9:** Illustrate that the cycling of water in and out of the atmosphere plays an important role in determining climatic patterns.
> **Also covers: 6.3.17**

● Before You Read

Imagine you are outside on a warm, sunny day. On the lines below, describe how the Sun feels on your skin.

_____

_____

_____

What You'll Learn
- what happens to the Sun's energy on Earth
- about radiation, conduction, and convection
- what the water cycle is

● Read to Learn

Energy from the Sun

The Sun provides most of Earth's energy. The energy from the Sun drives winds and ocean currents. It allows plants to grow and produce food. Plants, in turn, serve as food for the animals that eat them. Three different things can happen to the energy Earth gets from the Sun. Some of the energy is reflected back into space by clouds, particles, and Earth's surface. Some of it is absorbed by the atmosphere. Some of the energy is absorbed by land and water on Earth's surface. The figure shows how much solar radiation is reflected and absorbed at Earth's surface.

6% reflected by the atmosphere

25% reflected from clouds

4% reflected from Earth's surface

15% absorbed by the atmosphere

50% directly or indirectly absorbed by Earth's surface

> **Mark the Text**
>
> **Identify the Main Point**
> Highlight the main point in each paragraph. Highlight in a different color a detail or example that helps explain the main point.

> **Picture This**
> 1. **Interpret** What happens to most of the Sun's energy?
>
> _____
>
> _____
>
> _____

B Illustrate and Label
Make a three-tab Foldable to illustrate and describe radiation, conduction, and convection.

Radiation | Conduction | Convection

Heat

Heat is energy that flows from an object with a higher temperature to an object with a lower temperature. Energy from the Sun reaches Earth's surface and heats it. This heat is sent, or transferred, through the atmosphere. Heat is transferred by radiation, conduction, and convection.

What is radiation?

When the sun is out, you can feel it warming your face. It warms you even though you are not in direct contact with it. How is this possible?

Energy from the Sun reaches Earth in the form of radiant energy, or radiation. **Radiation** is energy that is transferred in the form of rays or waves. Earth radiates, or sends, some of the energy it absorbs from the Sun back toward space. Radiant energy from the Sun warms your face.

What is conduction?

Walking barefoot on a hot beach will heat up your feet. Heat is transferred to your feet because of conduction. **Conduction** is the transfer of energy that occurs when molecules bump into each other. Molecules are always in motion. But molecules in warmer objects move faster than molecules in cooler objects. When objects are in contact, energy is transferred from warmer objects, like hot sand, to cooler objects, like your feet.

Radiation from the Sun heated the sand. But direct contact with the sand warmed your feet. In the same way, Earth's surface conducts, or transfers, energy directly to the atmosphere. When air moves over warm land or water, molecules in air are heated by direct contact.

What is convection?

Convection is another way heat is transferred. It occurs after the atmosphere is warmed by radiation or conduction. **Convection** is the transfer of heat by the flow of material. Convection circulates, or moves, heat throughout the atmosphere. How does this happen?

When air is warmed, the molecules in it move apart. The air becomes less dense. Air pressure decreases because fewer molecules are in the same space. In cold air, molecules move closer together. The air becomes more dense and air pressure increases. Cooler, denser air sinks while warmer, less dense air rises. This forms a convection current.

💡 **Think it Over**

2. **Explain** How do different air temperatures form a convection current?

_____

_____

_____

The Water Cycle

<u>Hydrosphere</u> is a term that describes all the water on Earth's surface. As shown in the figure below, there is a constant cycling of water between the hydrosphere and the atmosphere. This constant exchange of water helps to determine Earth's weather patterns and climate types.

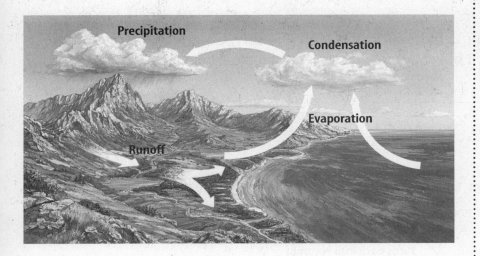

Picture This

3. **Determine** Circle the process which occurs when water falls as rain, snow, or sleet. What is the process?

_____

Here's how the water cycle works. Energy from the Sun causes water from lakes, streams, and oceans to change from a liquid to a gas by a process called evaporation. The gas, or water vapor, enters Earth's atmosphere. If the water vapor cools enough, it turns back into water. <u>Condensation</u> is the process that occurs when water vapor cools and changes back into a liquid.

Clouds form when condensation occurs high in the atmosphere. Clouds are made up of tiny droplets of water. As these tiny droplets run into each other, they form larger drops. As the water drops grow, they become too large to be held in the air. The drops fall to earth as precipitation, or rain, snow, or sleet. This completes the cycle of returning water to the hydrosphere. ☑

Earth's Atmosphere is Unique

Why doesn't life exist on Mars or Venus? The atmosphere on Mars is too thin to hold much of the Sun's heat. As a result, it is too cold on Mars for living things to survive. On the other hand, Venus is too hot to support life. Gases in Venus's dense atmosphere trap far too much heat from the Sun. Earth is neither too hot nor too cold. Its atmosphere holds just the right amount of the Sun's energy to support life.

Reading Check

4. **Identify** What process forms clouds?

_____

● After You Read

Mini Glossary

condensation: process in which water vapor changes to a liquid

conduction: transfer of energy that occurs when molecules bump into each other

convection: transfer of heat by the flow of material

hydrosphere: all the water on Earth's surface

radiation: energy transferred by waves or rays

1. Review the terms and their definitions in the Mini Glossary. Choose one term and use it in a sentence telling how it affects energy transfer in the atmosphere.

_____

_____

2. Fill in the cycle map below to show the water cycle. Use these words to help you.

Water vapor   precipitation   condensation   clouds   energy

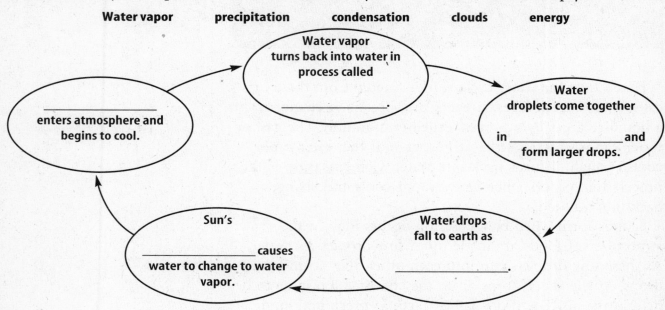

Water vapor turns back into water in process called _____.

_____ enters atmosphere and begins to cool.

Water droplets come together in _____ and form larger drops.

Sun's _____ causes water to change to water vapor.

Water drops fall to earth as _____.

3. Think about what you have learned. How would highlighting the main points and details help you to study for a test?

_____

_____

End of Section

Science Online Visit **in6.msscience.com** to access your textbook, interactive games, and projects to help you learn more about energy transfer in the atmosphere.

chapter
3 Atmosphere

section 3 Air Movement

> **Standard—6.7.2:** Use models to illustrate processes that happen too slowly, too quickly, or on too small a scale to observe directly.
> **Also covers:** 6.2.5, 6.3.11

● Before You Read

When you think of the word *wind* what comes to mind? Brainstorm some words and write them on the lines below.

_____

_____

What You'll Learn
- why different altitudes receive different amounts of solar energy
- about Coriolis effect
- how air is affected by land and water surfaces below it

● Read to Learn

Forming Wind

Earth is mostly rock or land. Three-fourths of Earth's surface is covered by the oceans. These two areas strongly affect wind systems all over Earth.

Because the Sun heats Earth unevenly, some areas are warmer than others. Remember that warmer air expands and becomes less dense than cold air. As a result, air pressure is lower in areas where air is heated. **Wind** is the movement of air from an area of higher pressure to an area of lower pressure.

What is heated air?

Different areas of Earth receive different amounts of radiation from the Sun. Why? Because Earth's surface is curved. The equator receives more radiation than areas north or south of it. The Sun's rays hit the equator more directly. Because air at the equator is warm, it is less dense. So it is displaced, or moved, by denser, colder air. Remember that when cooler, denser air sinks while warmer, less dense air rises, a convection current forms. The cold, dense air comes from the poles. They receive less radiation from the Sun, because its rays strike the poles at an angle, spreading out the energy. The resulting dense, high-pressure air sinks and moves along Earth's surface. However, there is more to wind than dense air sinking and less dense air rising.

Study Coach

State the Main Ideas As you read this section, stop after each paragraph and put what you have just read into your own words.

FOLDABLES

C Classify Make a three-column Foldable to help you understand the main causes of air movement.

Convection currents	Polar jet stream	Land breeze
Coriolis effect		
Global winds		Sea breeze

What is the Coriolis effect?

What would happen if you threw a ball to a person sitting across from you on a moving merry-go-round? By the time the ball got to the opposite side, the other person would have moved and the ball would appear to have curved.

Like the merry-go-round, the rotation of Earth causes the Coriolis (kohr ee OH lus) effect. The **Coriolis effect** causes moving air and water to appear to turn to their left in the southern hemisphere (south of the equator) and to turn to the right in the northern hemisphere (north of the equator) due to Earth's rotation. This effect is illustrated in the figure below. The flow of air caused by the Coriolis effect and by differences in the amount of solar radiation received on Earth's surface creates wind patterns on Earth's surface. These wind patterns influence the weather. ☑

✔ Reading Check

1. **Determine** What causes moving air and water to appear to turn one way in the southern hemisphere and the opposite way in the northern hemisphere?

_____

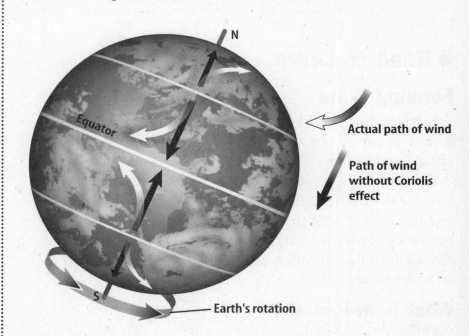

Actual path of wind

Path of wind without Coriolis effect

Earth's rotation

Picture This

2. **Explain** Do winds turn to their left or their right north of the equator?

_____

Global Winds

How did Christopher Columbus get from Spain to the Americas? The *Nina*, the *Pinta*, and the *Santa Maria* had no source of power other than the wind in their sails.

Early sailors used wind patterns to help them navigate the oceans. Near the equator, there sometimes was little or no wind to fill the sails of their ships. It also rained nearly every afternoon. Why? Because air near the equator has been heated by the Sun. Warm air rises, creating low pressure and little wind. The rising air then cools and causes rain. This windless, rainy zone near the equator is called the doldrums. ☑

✔ Reading Check

3. **Identify** What is the name of the windless, rainy zone near the equator?

_____

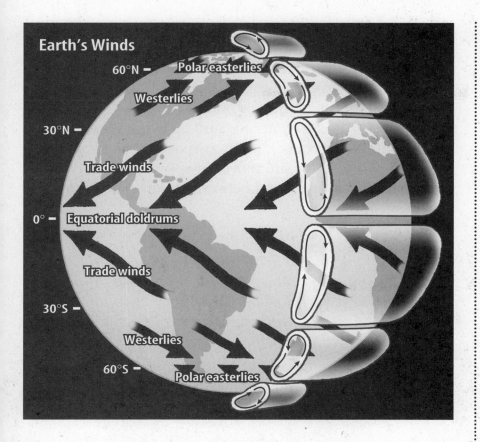

Earth's Winds

60°N — Polar easterlies

Westerlies

30°N —

Trade winds

0° — Equatorial doldrums

Trade winds

30°S —

Westerlies

60°S — Polar easterlies

Picture This

4. Identify Which winds are located on either side of the Equatorial doldrums?

_____

What winds blow near Earth's surface?

The figure above shows some of the winds that blow near Earth's surface. These prevailing winds move heat and moisture around Earth.

Trade Winds Air descending to Earth's surface near 30° north latitude and 30° south latitude creates steady winds. These winds blow in tropical regions. Early sailors liked them because they moved their ships along quickly. Sailors named them trade winds because they relied on these winds to help them sail to many places to trade goods. ☑

Prevailing westerlies Between 30° latitude and 60° latitude in the northern and southern hemispheres, winds called the prevailing westerlies blow. These winds blow in the opposite direction from the trade winds. Prevailing westerlies cause much of the movement of weather across North America.

Polar easterlies Another surface wind, polar easterlies, are found near the poles. Near the north pole, easterlies blow from northeast to southwest. Near the south pole, polar easterlies blow from the southeast to the northwest.

✔ Reading Check

5. Explain Why would sailors like trade winds?

_____

_____

_____

What winds are in the upper troposphere?

Jet streams are narrow bands of strong winds that blow near the top of the troposphere. The polar jet stream affecting North America forms along a boundary where colder air lies to the north and warmer air lies to the south. It moves faster in the winter because there is a greater difference between cold air and warm air. As the figure below shows, the polar jet stream moves in a wavy west-to-east direction. It is usually found between 10 km and 15 km above Earth's surface. ☑

6. Define What are the narrow bands of strong winds that blow near the top of the troposphere?

_____

_____

Picture This

7. Determine Trace with your pencil the direction of the polar jet stream. Is it moving east to west or west to east?

_____

_____

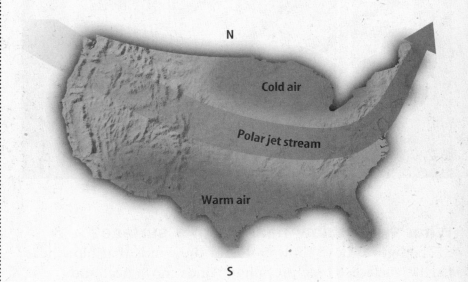

What are the effects of the jet stream?

The jet stream helps move storms across the country from the west to the east. Jet pilots use information about jet streams to help them fly. When flying to the east, planes save time and fuel. Going west, planes avoid the jet stream by flying at a different altitude. Flying from Boston to Seattle may take 30 minutes longer than flying from Seattle to Boston.

Local Wind Systems

Major weather patterns for the entire planet are determined by global wind systems. Local weather is affected by smaller wind systems. Those who live near large bodies of water experience two such wind systems. They are sea breezes and land breezes.

💡 Think it Over

8. Infer Why would it take longer to fly from east to west than from west to east?

_____

_____

Sea Breeze

Warm air

Cool air

Sea breeze

Land Breeze

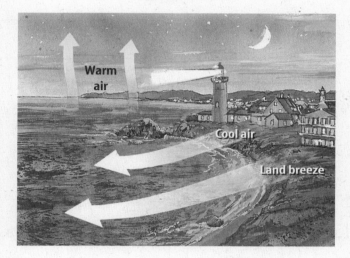

Warm air

Cool air

Land breeze

What causes sea breezes and land breezes?

Convection currents over areas where the land meets the sea can cause wind. During the day, the Sun's heat warms the land more than it warms the water. A <u>sea breeze</u> is the movement of air from sea to land during the day. Air over the land is heated by conduction. This heated air is less dense and has lower pressure. Cooler, denser air over the water has higher pressure and flows towards the warmer, less dense air above the land. A convection current results, and wind blows from the sea toward the land. ☑

At night, the land and the air above it cools much faster than ocean water. Cooler, denser air above the land moves over the water, as the warm air over the water rises. The movement of air from land to sea is a <u>land breeze</u>.

Picture This

9. Interpret What is happening to the warm air in both figures?

_____

_____

☑ **Reading Check**

10. Identify What causes wind over areas where the land and sea meet?

_____

_____

● After You Read

Mini Glossary

Coriolis (kohr ee OH lus) effect: causes moving air and water to appear to turn left in the southern hemisphere and turn right in the northern hemisphere due to Earth's rotation

jet streams: narrow bands of strong winds that blow near the top of the troposphere

land breeze: movement of air from land to sea at night, created when cooler, denser air from the land forces warmer air over the sea

sea breeze: movement of air from sea to land during the day when cooler air above the water moves over the land forcing the heated, less dense air above the land to rise

wind: the movement of air from an area of higher pressure to an area of lower pressure

1. Review the terms and definitions in the Mini Glossary. Then choose one of the definitions and write it in a sentence in your own words.

_____

_____

2. Fill in the boxes with the correct word, *cooler* or *warmer*, to show what occurs in a sea breeze and a land breeze.

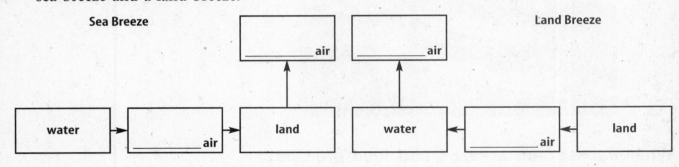

3. Think of Earth's shape. How does the shape of Earth affect the amount of heat different areas receive?

_____

_____

_____

End of Section

 **Science Online** Visit **in6.msscience.com** to access your textbook, interactive games, and projects to help you learn more about air movement.

54 Atmosphere

 Weather

section ❶ What is weather?

Standard—6.3.9: Illustrate that the cycling of water in and out of the atmosphere plays an important role in determining climatic patterns.

● Before You Read

Have you ever flown a kite or watched someone else fly one? On the lines below, describe how the kite moves in the air.

_____

_____

● Read to Learn

Weather Factors

Everybody talks about the weather. It may seem like small talk, but weather is very important to some people. Pilots, truck drivers, farmers, and other professionals study the weather because it can affect their jobs.

What is weather?

You can look out the window and see that it's raining, or snowing, or windy. But do you really know what weather is? <u>Weather</u> is the state of the atmosphere at a specific time and place. Weather describes conditions such as air pressure, wind, temperature, and moisture content in the air.

How does the Sun affect weather on Earth?

The Sun provides almost all of Earth's energy. Energy from the Sun evaporates water on Earth. Evaporated water enters the atmosphere and forms clouds. Later, the water falls back to Earth as rain or snow.

The Sun also heats Earth. Heat from the Sun is absorbed by Earth's surface, which then heats the air above it. Because of differences in Earth's surface, some places in Earth's atmosphere are warmer and other places are cooler. Air currents and water currents move the heat to different places around Earth. Weather is the result of heat and Earth's air and water.

What You'll Learn

- how pressure, wind, temperature, and moisture content of air affect weather
- how clouds form and how they are classified
- how rain, hail, sleet and snow develop

Study Coach

Think-Pair-Share Work with a partner. As you read this section, discuss what you already know about the topic and what you learn.

FOLDABLES

A Organize Use four quarter sheet note cards to record information about the factors that determine weather.

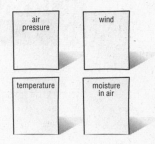

What affects temperature?

Air is made up of molecules that are always moving randomly, or without any set pattern, even when there is no wind. Temperature is a measure of the average amount of motion of molecules. When the temperature is high, air molecules move rapidly and it feels warm. When the temperature is low, air molecules move more slowly and it feels cold. ☑

What causes wind?

Have you ever flown a kite? What do you need in order to get the kite off the ground and into the air? Kites fly because air is moving. Air that moves in one direction is called wind. The Sun heats Earth unevenly, but wind helps spread the heat around.

As the Sun warms the air, the air expands and becomes less dense. Warm, expanding air has low atmospheric pressure. Cooler air is denser and sinks, which brings high atmospheric pressure. Wind is the result of air moving from areas of high pressure to areas of low pressure.

The temperature of air can affect air pressure. When air is cooler, molecules are closer together, creating high pressure. When air is heated, it expands and becomes less dense. This creates lower pressure. Beaches are often windy as a result of air moving from areas of high pressure to areas of lower pressure, as shown in the figure below.

✔ **Reading Check**

1. **Determine** When the temperature is high, how do air molecules move?

_____

_____

Picture This

2. **Label** one side of the figure *high pressure* and one side *low pressure*.

_____ pressure   _____ pressure

What tools are used to measure wind?

Some instruments measure wind direction and others measure wind speed. A wind vane, sometimes seen on houses or barns, has an arrow that points in the direction from which the wind is blowing. A wind sock, another tool that shows wind direction, has an open end to catch the wind. The wind sock fills and points in the direction toward which the wind is blowing. ☑

An anemometer (a nuh MAH muh tur) is an instrument that measures wind speed. Anemometers have four open cups that catch the wind and cause the anemometer to spin. The faster the wind blows, the faster the anemometer spins.

What is humidity?

Heat evaporates water into the atmosphere. Where does the water go? Water vapor molecules fit into spaces among the molecules that make up air. The amount of water vapor held in the air is called **humidity**.

Air does not always hold the same amount of water vapor. More water vapor can be present when the air is warm than when it its cool. At warm temperatures, the molecules of water vapor in the air move quickly. As a result, the molecules do not come together easily, as shown on the left in the figure below.

☑ **Reading Check**

3. **Explain** Name one tool for measuring wind direction and tell how it works.

_____

_____

_____

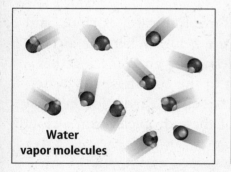

Water vapor molecules

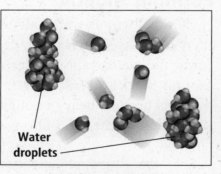

Water droplets

Picture This

4. **Determine** Circle the figure that shows droplets of water forming.

At cooler temperatures, the molecules in air move more slowly. This slower movement allows the water vapor molecules to stick together. Droplets of liquid water form, as shown on the right in the figure above. This process of liquid water forming from water vapor is called condensation. If enough water is present in the air for condensation to take place, the air is saturated.

What is relative humidity?

Weather forecasters report the amount of moisture in the air as relative humidity. **Relative humidity** is a measure of the amount of moisture held in the air compared with the amount of moisture the air can hold at a given temperature. If the weather forecaster says that the relative humidity is 50 percent, this means that the air contains 50 percent of the water needed for the air to be saturated at that temperature.

Dew Point

When the temperature drops, less water vapor can be present in the air. If temperatures are low enough, water vapor will condense to a liquid or form ice crystals. The temperature at which the air is saturated and condensation forms is the **dew point**. Dew point changes as the amount of water vapor in the air changes. ☑

You've probably seen water droplets form on the outside of a can of cold soda. The cold can cooled the air around it to its dew point. The water vapor in the air condensed, forming water droplets on the soda can. Something similar occurs when you see dew. Air near the ground cools to its dew point, and then water vapor condenses and forms dew. If temperatures are near 0° C, frost may form.

Forming Clouds

Clouds form as warm air is forced upward, expands, and then cools, as shown in the figure below. When the air cools, the water vapor molecules in the air come together around particles of dust or salt in the air. These tiny water droplets are not heavy enough to fall to Earth. So, they stay suspended in the air. Billions of these droplets form a cloud.

✔ **Reading Check**

5. Identify What is the temperature at which condensation forms called?

Picture This

6. Interpret Trace the arrows that show moist warm air rising.

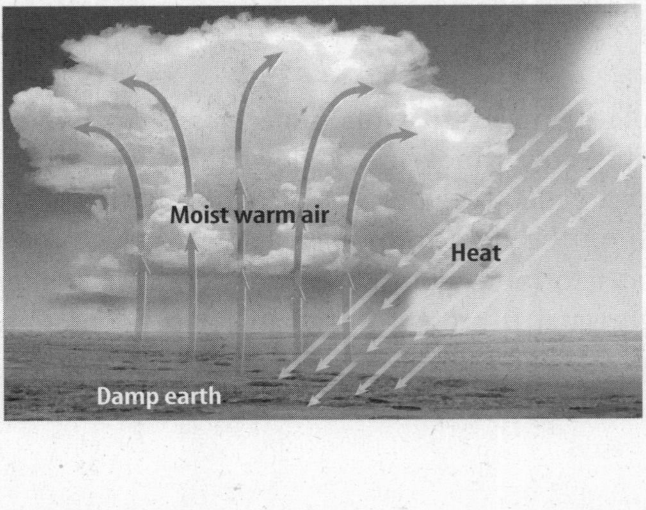

Moist warm air

Heat

Damp earth

Classifying Clouds

Clouds are grouped, or classified, by shape and height. Some clouds are tall and rise high into the sky. Some clouds are low and flat. Dense clouds can bring snow or rain. Thin clouds usually appear on sunny days. Three main factors determine the shape and height of clouds—temperature, pressure, and the amount of water vapor in the air.

What are the different types of clouds?

Stratus clouds are layered in smooth, even sheets across the sky and may be seen on fair, rainy, or snowy days. Usually stratus clouds form low in the sky. **Fog** is a stratus cloud that forms when air is cooled to its dew point near the ground.

Cumulus (KYEW myuh lus) clouds are large, white, puffy clouds that are often flat on the bottom and sometimes tower high into the sky. Cumulous clouds can be seen either in fair weather or in thunderstorms.

Cirrus (SIHR us) clouds are thin, white, feathery clouds. They form high in the atmosphere and are made of ice crystals. Although cirrus clouds are linked with fair weather, they sometimes appear before a storm.

How is height used to name clouds?

Cloud names are sometimes given prefixes to describe the height of the cloud base. Three common cloud prefixes are *cirro-*, *alto-* and *strato-*. *Cirro-* describes high clouds. *Alto-* is used for clouds that form at middle levels. *Strato-* is used for clouds that form closer to the ground.

Cirrostratus clouds are made of ice crystals and form high in the air. Usually cirrostratus clouds are a sign of fair weather. Sometimes they signal a storm is on the way. Altostratus clouds form at middle levels. If these clouds are not too thick, sunlight can filter through them.

What types of clouds produce rain and snow?

Dark clouds that contain rain or snow are called nimbus clouds. *Nimbus* is a Latin word meaning "dark rain cloud." The water content of nimbus clouds is so high that only a little sunlight can pass through them.

When a cumulus cloud grows into a thunderstorm, it is called a cumulonimbus (kyew myuh loh NIHM bus) cloud. These high clouds can tower almost 18 km. Nimbostratus clouds are layered clouds that usually bring long, steady rain or snowfall. ✔

Think it Over

7. Classify What are the three main cloud types?

_____

_____

_____

Reading Check

8. Determine When a cumulus cloud becomes a thunderstorm, what is it called?

_____

B Compare and contrast
Make a four-tab Foldable as
shown. As you read, take notes
on how the four forms of
precipitation are similar and
different.

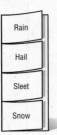

Rain

Hail

Sleet

Snow

Picture This

9. Identify In the figures,
circle the name of each type
of precipitation.

Precipitation

<u>Precipitation</u> is water falling from clouds. Precipitation occurs when cloud droplets combine and grow large enough to fall to Earth. The cloud droplets form around tiny particles like salt and dust in the air.

Why are some raindrops bigger than others?

You have probably noticed that some raindrops are bigger than others. One reason for this size difference is the strength of updrafts in a cloud. If strong updrafts of wind keep drops in the air longer, they can combine with other drops. As a result, they grow larger.

Another factor which affects raindrop size is the rate of evaporation as the drop falls to Earth. If the air is dry, the raindrop will get smaller as it falls. Sometimes the raindrop will evaporate completely before it even hits the ground.

How does temperature affect precipitation?

Air temperature determines what kind of precipitation will fall—rain, snow, sleet, or hail. How air temperature affects precipitation is shown in the figures below. When the air temperature is above freezing, water falls as rain. If the air temperature is so cold that water vapor changes to a solid, it snows. Sleet forms if raindrops fall through a layer of freezing air near Earth's surface, forming ice pellets.

During thunderstorms, hail forms in cumulonimbus clouds. Hailstones form when water freezes around tiny centers of ice. Hailstones get larger as they're tossed up and down by rising and falling air. Most hailstones are small, but sometimes they can get larger than softballs. Of all forms of precipitation, hail causes the most damage.

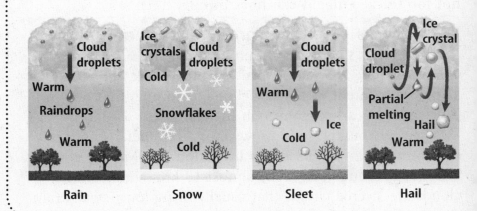

Rain   Snow   Sleet   Hail

● After You Read

Mini Glossary

dew point: temperature at which air is saturated and condensation forms

fog: stratus cloud that forms when air near the ground is cooled to its dew point

humidity: amount of water vapor held in the air

precipitation: water falling from clouds—including rain, snow, sleet, and hail—whose form is determined by air temperature

relative humidity: measure of the amount of moisture held in the air compared with the amount it can hold at a given temperature

weather: state of the atmosphere at a specific time and place; determined by air pressure, wind, temperature, and how much moisture is in the air

1. Review the terms and their definitions in the Mini Glossary. Then write one sentence describing today's weather. Use at least two of the terms.

   _____

   _____

2. Use these words to fill in the blanks and tell about clouds forming and precipitation: snow, hail, warm moist air, stratus, cumulus, rain, cirrus, sleet, water vapor, clouds

   _____ rises, expands, and cools.

   _____ condenses into tiny droplets.

   Droplets suspend in the air, forming _____.

   Three types of clouds are _____, _____, and _____.

   Four kinds of precipitation come from clouds: _____, _____, _____,

   and _____.

3. You were asked to discuss and study this section with a partner. Was this a helpful strategy for learning the information? Why or why not?

   _____

   _____

Science Online Visit **in6.msscience.com** to access your textbook, interactive games, and projects to help you learn more about weather.

End of Section

Weather

section ② Weather Patterns

 Standard—6.3.11: Identify and explain the effects of oceans on climate.
Also covers: 6.3.12

What You'll Learn
- how weather is related to fronts and high and low pressure areas
- about different types of severe weather

Mark the Text

Key Terms Highlight the key terms and their meanings as you read this section.

FOLDABLES™

© Classify Make a four-tab Foldable as shown. As you read, take notes on the four different fronts.

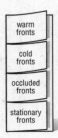

warm fronts
cold fronts
occluded fronts
stationary fronts

● Before You Read

Have you ever gone into a basement or an attic? Describe how the temperature felt compared to the rest of the building.

_____

_____

_____

● Read to Learn

Weather Changes

Sometimes when you leave school in the afternoon, the weather is different from what it was earlier in the morning. Weather constantly changes.

What are air masses?

An __air mass__ is a large body of air that has the same temperature and moisture content as the area over which it formed. For example, an air mass that develops over land is drier than one that develops over water. An air mass that develops in the tropics is warmer than one that develops over northern regions. When weather changes from one day to the next, it is because of the movement of air masses.

How does air pressure affect the weather?

Pressure in the atmosphere varies over Earth's surface. You may have heard a weather forecaster talk about high- and low-pressure systems. Low-pressure systems are masses of rising air. When air rises and cools, clouds form. That's why areas of low pressure usually have cloudy weather. But high-pressure air masses have a sinking motion. As a result, it's hard for air to rise and for clouds to form. So, high pressure usually means nice weather.

What are cyclones and anticyclones?

Winds blow from areas of high pressure to areas of low pressure. In the northern hemisphere, when wind blows into a low-pressure area, Earth's rotation causes the wind to swirl in a counterclockwise direction. These large, swirling areas of low pressure are called cyclones. Cyclones are associated with stormy weather.

Winds blow away from an area of high pressure. In the northern hemisphere, Earth's rotation causes these winds to swirl in a clockwise direction. High-pressure areas are associated with fair weather and are called anticyclones.

Fronts

A boundary between two air masses that have different temperature, density, or moisture is called a **front**. There are four main types of fronts, including cold, warm, occluded, and stationary.

What is a cold front?

A cold front occurs when cold air moves toward warm air, as shown on the left in the figure below. The cold air goes under the warm air and lifts it. As the warm air is lifted, it cools and water vapor condenses, forming clouds. If there is a large difference in temperature between the cold air and the warm air, thunderstorms and tornadoes may form.

What is a warm front?

Warm fronts form when lighter, warmer air moves over heavier, colder air, as shown on the right in the figure below. In a warm front, wet weather may last for days.

✔ Reading Check

1. Describe What type of weather are cyclones associated with?

_____

Picture This

2. Identify Color the arrow showing cold air movement in the cold front blue. Color the arrow showing warm air movement in the warm front red.

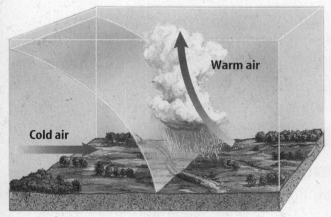

Cold Front

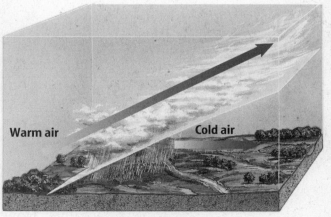

Warm Front

What is an occluded front?

Most fronts involve two air masses. But occluded fronts involve three air masses—cold air, cool air, and warm air. An occluded front, as shown in the figure below, may form when a cold air mass moves toward cool air with warm air in between. The cold air forces the warm air up. The warm air is then closed off from the surface. The term *occlusion* means "closure."

Picture This

3. Interpret Color the arrows red that show where the warm air is closed off from the surface in the occluded front.

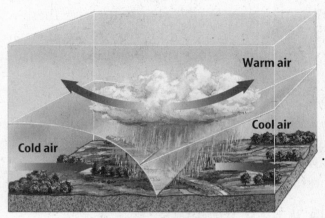

Occluded Front

What is a stationary front?

A stationary front occurs when a boundary between air masses stops moving, as shown in the figure below. Stationary fronts can stay in the same place for several days. Often there is light wind and precipitation at the stationary front.

Picture This

4. Identify Circle the area in the stationary front where neither the cold air nor warm air is moving.

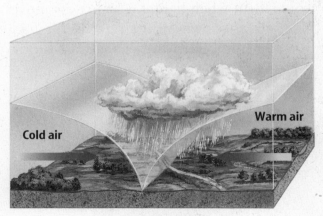

Stationary Front

Severe Weather

You usually can do your daily activities regardless of the weather. However, some weather conditions, like blizzards, tornadoes, and hurricanes, can force you to change your plans.

What causes thunderstorms?

During thunderstorms, heavy rain falls, lightning flashes, and thunder rumbles. Hail might fall. What causes these weather conditions?

Thunderstorms occur in warm, moist air masses and along fronts. Warm, moist air is forced up. It cools and condensation begins, forming cumulonimbus clouds. When rising air cools, water vapor condenses into water droplets or ice crystals. Smaller droplets collide and form larger ones. The larger, heavier droplets fall through the cloud toward Earth's surface. The falling droplets collide with more droplets and get bigger. Raindrops cool the air around them. The cool, dense air sinks. Sinking, rain-cooled air and strong updrafts of warmer air cause the strong winds that often come during thunderstorms. Hail may form as ice crystals fall. ☑

What damage do thunderstorms cause?

Sometimes thunderstorms stall in one area, causing heavy rains. When streams can no longer hold all the water running into them, flash floods occur. Because they occur with little warning, flash floods are dangerous.

Thunderstorms often bring strong winds that can cause damage. If a thunderstorm has winds over 89 km/h, it is called a severe thunderstorm. Hail from thunderstorms can dent cars, break windows, and flatten crops.

What causes lightning?

Inside a storm cloud, warm air is lifted rapidly as cooler air sinks. This movement of air can cause different parts of a cloud to have opposite charges. When an electrical current runs between areas with opposite charges, lightning flashes. Lightning can occur between two clouds, inside one cloud, or between a cloud and the ground. ☑

What causes thunder?

Thunder comes from the rapid heating of air around a bolt of lightning. Lightning can reach temperatures of about 30,000° C. That's five times hotter than the surface of the Sun. This heat causes air around the lightning to expand rapidly. Then the air cools quickly and shrinks. Because of the sudden expanding and shrinking, molecules in the air move more rapidly. The rapid movement of molecules creates sound waves. Thunder is the sound waves you hear.

✔ Reading Check

5. **Explain** How do water droplets falling out of a thundercloud get bigger as they fall toward Earth's surface?

_____

_____

_____

✔ Reading Check

6. **Determine** What causes different parts of a cloud to have opposite charges?

_____

_____

What are tornadoes?

Some severe thunderstorms produce tornadoes. A **tornado** is a violently rotating column of air that touches the ground. Severe thunderstorms produce wind at different heights which blow at different speeds and in different directions. This difference in wind speed and direction is called wind shear. Wind shear creates a rotating column parallel to the ground. Updrafts in a thunderstorm can tilt the rotating column upward, creating a funnel cloud. If the funnel cloud touches the ground, it is called a tornado. ☑

The figure below shows a diagram of a tornado. Notice the different levels of winds and the rotating updraft. The strong updraft usually forms at the base of a type of cumulonimbus cloud called a wall cloud.

☑ **Reading Check**

7. Identify What is a violently rotating column of air that touches the ground called?

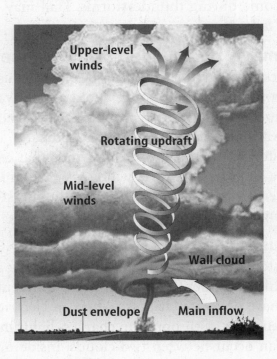

Upper-level winds

Rotating updraft

Mid-level winds

Wall cloud

Dust envelope   Main inflow

Picture This

8. Identify Find the updraft and trace over it with your pencil.

How much damage can a tornado do?

Winds from tornadoes can rip apart buildings and tear trees from the ground. If the winds of a tornado blow through a house, they can lift off the roof and blow out the walls. It can look as though the building exploded. In the center of a tornado is a powerful updraft. The updraft can lift animals, cars, and even houses into the air. Tornados do not last long, but they are very destructive. In May of 1999, thunderstorms produced more than 70 tornadoes in Kansas, Oklahoma, and Texas. These tornadoes caused 40 deaths, 100 injuries, and more than $1.2 billion in damage.

How are tornadoes ranked?

As you have read, winds from tornadoes can cause severe damage. Theodore Fujita, a tornado expert, created a scale to describe and rank tornadoes. The scale, named the Fujita Scale after him, is shown below. The Fujita Scale ranks tornadoes based on how much damage they cause. Tornadoes range from F0 which cause only light damage to F5 which cause incredible damage. Luckily, only about one percent of all tornadoes are in the category of F4 and F5.

The Fujita Scale

Rank	Wind speed (km/h)	Damage
F0	<116	Light: broken branches and chimneys
F1	116–180	Moderate: roofs damaged, mobile homes upturned
F2	181–253	Considerable: roofs torn off homes, large trees uprooted
F3	254–332	Severe: trains overturned, roofs and walls torn off
F4	333–419	Devastating: houses completely destroyed, cars picked up and carried elsewhere
F5	420–512	Incredible: total demolition

What is a hurricane?

The most powerful storm is a hurricane. A **hurricane** is a large, low-pressure system that forms over the warm Atlantic Ocean and has winds of at least 119 km/h. It is like a machine that turns heat energy from the ocean into wind. Similar storms are called typhoons in the Pacific Ocean and cyclones in the Indian Ocean.

Hurricanes are similar to low-pressure systems over land—only stronger. In the Atlantic and Pacific Oceans, low-pressure systems sometimes develop near the equator. In the northern hemisphere, winds around this low pressure rotate counterclockwise. As the storms move across the ocean, they gain strength from the heat and moisture of warm ocean water.

What happens when a hurricane reaches land?

Hurricanes can strike land with great force. The high winds sometimes produce tornadoes. Heavy rains and high waves cause large amounts of damage. Sometimes floods follow the heavy rains and cause additional damage. Hurricanes can destroy crops, tear down buildings, and kill humans and animals.

Picture This

9. **Determine** Circle the category that describes severe damage.

Indiana Academic Standard Check

6.3.11: Identify and explain the effects of oceans on climate.

✔ **10. Identify** What are two storms similar to hurricanes?

_____

_____

What happens to the hurricane on land?

As long as the hurricane remains over water, it gets energy from the warm moist air rising from the ocean. In the figure below, small rising arrows show the movement of warm air from the water below. Cool air goes down through the eye, or center, of the hurricane. The storm needs this energy from the ocean water. When a hurricane reaches land, it loses its energy supply and the storm loses its power.

Picture This

11. **Identify** Highlight all the arrows moving counterclockwise.

Outflow

Descending air

Warm moist air

Eye

Spiral rain bands

What is a blizzard?

Severe storms also can occur in the winter. If you live in the northern United States, you may have experienced the howling wind and blowing snow of a blizzard. A **blizzard** is a winter storm with conditions that include very cold temperatures, high winds, and blowing snow that makes it difficult to see. A blizzard usually lasts at least three hours.

How can you stay safe during severe storms?

When severe weather approaches, the National Weather Service issues a watch or a warning. A watch tells you that even though the weather isn't dangerous yet, it may become dangerous soon. During a watch, stay tuned to a radio or television station that is reporting the weather. ☑

When a warning is given, the weather is already severe. During a severe thunderstorm or tornado warning, go to a basement or to a room in the middle of the house away from windows. When a hurricane or flood watch is given, be prepared to leave home. During a blizzard, stay indoors.

Reading Check

12. **Explain** What does a weather watch tell you?

_____

_____

_____

● After You Read

Mini Glossary

air mass: large body of air that has the same characteristics of temperature and moisture content as the area where it formed

blizzard: severe winter storm with temperatures below −12° C, winds of at least 50 km/h, and blowing snow that causes poor visibility that lasts at least three hours

front: boundary between two air masses with different temperature, density, or moisture

hurricane: large, severe storm that forms over tropical oceans and has winds of at least 119 km/h

tornado: violently rotating column of air in contact with the ground

1. Review the terms and their definitions in the Mini Glossary. Then write a sentence explaining how hurricanes get and keep their strength.

_____

_____

_____

2. Write the name of the correct weather front above each description.

warm front, stationary front, occluded front, cold front

_____   _____

Cold air goes under warm air.   **3 air masses: cold, cool, warm**
Warm air is lifted.   **Warm air closed off from Earth.**

_____   _____

Neither warm nor cold air is moving.   **Lighter, warmer air moves over cold air.**

3. Did highlighting key terms and their meanings help you learn the information about weather patterns? Would you use this study strategy again?

_____

_____

_____

 Science Online   Visit **in6.msscience.com** to access your textbook, interactive games, and projects to help you learn more about weather patterns.

End of Section

chapter 4 Weather

section ❸ Weather Forecasts

> **Standard—6.1.7:** Explain that technology is essential to science ....
> **Also covers:** 6.1.5, 6.2.6

What You'll Learn

- how data are collected for weather maps and forecasts
- what symbols are used on a weather map

Study Coach

Sticky Notes As you read this section, mark the pages you find interesting or where you have a question. Share these pages with another student or with the teacher.

FOLDABLES™

❻ Organize Make a Foldable like the one shown below to help you learn about weather forecasts.

Meteorologist	Weather Symbols
Weather Map	Weather Instruments

● Before You Read

How good are you at predicting the weather? On the lines below, list things you consider when you're deciding what the day's weather might be like.

_____

_____

_____

● Read to Learn

Weather Observations

By looking at the thermometer or at clouds in the sky, you can tell things about the weather. Certain things about weather you know just from where you live. For example, if you live in Florida, you know that it will probably be warm and sunny.

What does a meteorologist do?

A **meteorologist** (mee tee uh RAH luh jist) studies the weather. A meteorologist gathers information about temperature, air pressure, wind, humidity and precipitation. By using tools like computers, Doppler radar, satellites, and weather balloons, a meteorologist makes weather maps and forecasts the weather.

Forecasting Weather

Meteorologists gather information and make predictions about weather in the future. Because storms can be dangerous, it is important to know if a storm is coming. The National Weather Service uses two sources to predict the weather. They collect information, or data, from the upper atmosphere. They also collect data from Earth's surface.

Station Models Meteorologists gather data from Earth's surface. Then this data is recorded on a map. A **station model** shows weather conditions at a specific location using symbols on a map. Information coming from station models and from instruments in Earth's atmosphere is put into computers and helps forecast weather. ☑

How do maps show temperature and pressure?

Weather maps have lines that connect locations with the same temperature or the same pressure. An **isotherm** (I suh thurm) is a line that connects places with the same temperature. Iso means "same." Therm means "temperature." You may have seen isotherms on weather maps on TV.

Weather maps, like the one below, also have isobars. An **isobar** is a line that connects two places with the same atmospheric pressure. Isobars show how fast wind is blowing in an area. When isobars are drawn close together, there is a big difference in air pressure. This means a strong wind is blowing. When isobars are drawn farther apart, there is little difference in pressure. Winds in this area are gentler. Isobars also show locations of high- and low-pressure areas.

On the weather map below, the pressure areas are drawn as circles with the word *High* or *Low* in the middle of the circle. Fronts are drawn as lines and symbols. This information helps meteorologists forecast the weather.

☑ **Reading Check**

1. **Describe** What does a station model show?

_____

_____

_____

Picture This

2. **Locate** Find the low pressure area by Portland and trace over the circle.

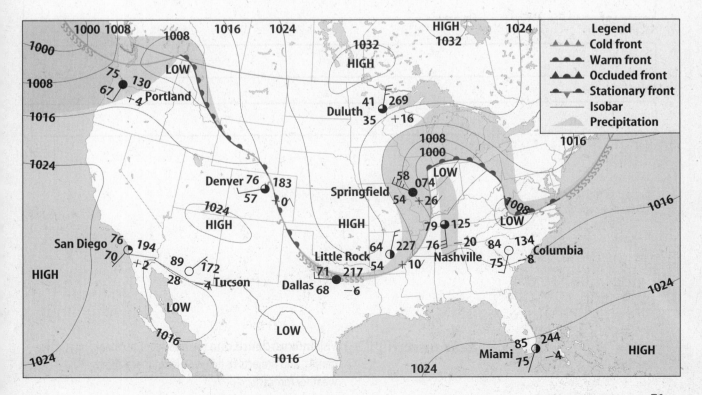

After You Read

Mini Glossary

isobar: line drawn on a weather map that connects two places with the same atmospheric pressure

isotherm: line drawn on a weather map that connects locations with the same temperature

meteorologist: person who studies the weather and uses information from Doppler radar, weather satellites, computers, and other instruments to make weather maps and provide forecasts

station model: indicates weather conditions at a specific location by using symbols on a map

1. Review the terms and their definitions in the Mini Glossary. Then write a sentence explaining the difference between an isobar and an isotherm.

   _____

   _____

2. Arrange the following events in order to show how a meteorologist studies weather and uses information.

   A meteorologist:
   forecasts weather
   gathers data on weather conditions
   makes weather maps

   First

   [   ]

   Second

   [   ]

   Third

   [   ]

 Visit **in6.msscience.com** to access your textbook, interactive games, and projects to help you learn more about weather forecasts.

Air Pollution

section ❶ Types and Causes of Air Pollution

Standard—6.3.13: Identify, explain, and discuss some effects human activities, such as the creation of pollution, have on weather and the atmosphere. Also covers: 6.2.5, 6.3.16

● Before You Read

Think about a day when the air where you live did not look clear. Describe what it looked like on the lines below.

_____

_____

_____

What You'll Learn

■ what the sources of air pollution are
■ how air pollution affects air quality

● Read to Learn

What causes air pollution?

The air you breathe contains oxygen and other gases necessary for life. The air also contains pollutants (puh LOOT ntz). Pollutants are harmful substances that contaminate the environment.

Air pollution comes from both natural events and human activities. Erupting volcanoes are natural events that spew ash and toxic gases. Kilauea Volcano on Hawaii is erupting and emitting toxic gases. People who live downwind report having health problems. Forest fires and grass fires also fill the air with toxic smoke. Human activities that cause pollution include industry, construction, power generation, transportation, and agriculture.

What are primary and secondary pollutants?

Substances that are released directly into the air in a harmful form are called **primary pollutants**. Examples of primary pollutants are ash from volcanoes, soot from trucks, and smoke from smokestacks. Not all pollutants are released directly into the air. **Secondary pollutants** form in Earth's atmosphere. Most of the brown haze, or smog, that you see near cities is caused by secondary pollutants.

Study Coach

Two-Column Notes As you read, organize your notes in two columns. In the left column, write the main idea of each paragraph. Next to it, in the right column, write details about it.

FOLDABLES™

Ⓐ **Identify** Make a two-tab Foldable to identify the characteristics of primary pollutants and secondary pollutants.

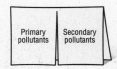

Smog

The smog you see near cities is called photochemical smog. **<u>Photochemical smog</u>** is the brown haze formed when secondary pollutants react with sunlight. Vehicles, some factories, and power plants release nitrogen and organic compounds into the air. These substances react to form nitrogen dioxide. Nitrogen dioxide is a reddish-brown gas that adds to the color of haze. Nitrogen dioxide reacts with sunlight to form ozone, a secondary pollutant. Ozone is a major component of smog.

How does nature affect smog formation?

In many cities, smog isn't a problem because winds scatter the pollutants. But, some areas have mountains which block winds. This occurs in Los Angeles, California, where mountains surround the city and trap the air. As a result, pollutants cannot be blown away by wind. Los Angeles is often sunny and dry. When nitrogen compounds are added to the air and exposed to sunlight for long periods of time, thick blankets of smog can develop. ☑

What is a temperature inversion?

Atmospheric changes can affect the formation of smog. Normally, temperatures are warmest near Earth's surface. Cooler air above the warm air carries away pollutants. However, a temperature inversion sometimes occurs. During an inversion, warm air overlies cool air, trapping the cool air near Earth's surface. A temperature inversion reduces the amount of mixing in the atmosphere. This can cause pollutants to build up near Earth's surface, as shown in the figure.

✔ **Reading Check**

1. **Identify** Which natural features affect smog formation in Los Angeles?

_____

_____

Picture This

2. **Use Models** Using colored pencils, color warm air red and cool air blue in each figure.

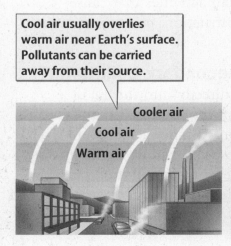

Cool air usually overlies warm air near Earth's surface. Pollutants can be carried away from their source.

Cooler air
Cool air
Warm air

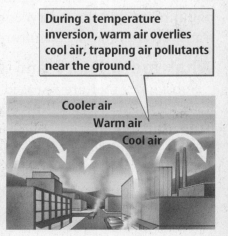

During a temperature inversion, warm air overlies cool air, trapping air pollutants near the ground.

Cooler air
Warm air
Cool air

Acid Rain

Acids and bases are two terms that describe substances. A substance that is neither an acid nor a base is neutral. The pH scale below shows how acidic or basic a substance is. A pH of 7 is neutral. Substances with a pH lower than 7 are acids. Substances with a pH above 7 are bases.

Natural lakes and streams have a pH between 6 and 8. **Acid rain** is precipitation with a pH below 5.6. It can harm plant and animal life. When acid rain falls into lakes and streams, it can lower the pH of the water.

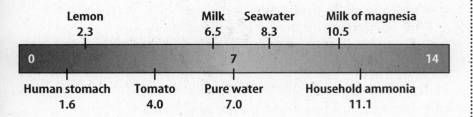

Lemon 2.3		Milk 6.5	Seawater 8.3	Milk of magnesia 10.5
0		7		14
Human stomach 1.6	Tomato 4.0	Pure water 7.0	Household ammonia 11.1	

Picture This

3. **Interpret** Look at the pH scale. Are tomatoes acidic or basic?

_____

What causes acid rain to form?

Power plants burn fuels, like coal and oil, to produce the electricity needed to light homes and power computers. Fuels are also burned to power vehicles and heat buildings. When fuels are burned, they release primary pollutants into the air.

These primary pollutants, including sulfur dioxide and nitrogen oxides, rise into the atmosphere. There, they combine with moisture in the air to form secondary pollutants such as sulfuric and nitric acids. Winds carry these acids long distances. They return to Earth as precipitation in the form of acid rain. Acid rain can discolor painted surfaces, corrode metals, and damage concrete structures.

Which areas are most affected by acid rain?

The average pH of precipitation varies across the United States. However, precipitation in the northeastern United States is more acidic than in other areas. Winds in the upper atmosphere blow toward the northeast, carrying sulfur dioxides and nitrogen oxides produced in the midwest. The acids that form in the atmosphere return to Earth as acid rain. Acid rain lowers the pH of bodies of water in the northeast more than the midwest because soil and rocks in the midwest are naturally more basic. Many northeastern lakes are too acidic for many types of fish. ☑

Reading Check

4. **Identify** Where do most of the pollutants come from that produce acid rain in the northeast?

_____

Particulate Pollution

The solid particles and liquid droplets suspended in air are called **particulate matter**. Some particles, such as smoke from fireplaces, enter the air directly. They are primary pollutants. Other particles, such as liquid droplets, can form from nitrogen or sulfur oxides as they combine with water in the air. ☑

How do coarse and fine particulates differ?

Coarse particulate matter is carried by the wind from unpaved roads and construction sites. Individual particulates are not very large. Each coarse particulate is only about one-seventh the diameter of a human hair. You can see coarse particulate matter easily if a lot of it is in the air.

Fine particulate matter is much smaller—only about one-fourth the size of coarse particulate matter. Fine particulates are released into the air from fires, vehicle exhaust, factories, and power plants. Both coarse and fine particulates can damage buildings and plants and harm the lungs.

Toxic Pollutants and Carbon Monoxide

Toxic air pollutants are substances released into the air that can cause health problems such as cancer. Toxic pollutants also can damage plants and animals. Most toxic air pollution is released by human activities. The circle graph below shows what percentage comes from each major source. Some pollutants are released from natural events.

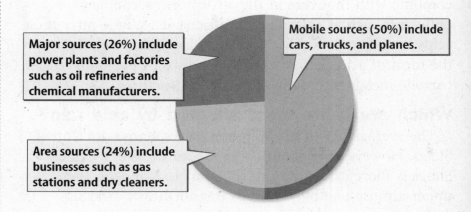

Mobile sources (50%) include cars, trucks, and planes.

Major sources (26%) include power plants and factories such as oil refineries and chemical manufacturers.

Area sources (24%) include businesses such as gas stations and dry cleaners.

When fossil fuels are not completely burned, they form a gas called carbon monoxide. In a typical U.S. city, as much as 95 percent of the carbon monoxide in the air comes from the exhaust pipes of cars and other vehicles. Carbon monoxide is a colorless, odorless gas. High levels of it are poisonous.

☑ Reading Check

5. Define What is particulate matter?

_____

_____

_____

Picture This

6. Interpret Data What percent of toxic pollutants comes from cars, trucks, and planes?

_____

Chlorofluorocarbons

Chlorofluorocarbons (KLOR uh floor oh kar buhns), or CFCs, are compounds used in air conditioners, refrigerators, and aerosol sprays. For many years after they were discovered in 1928, they were thought to be ideal. They don't burn. They are easy to manufacture. They aren't toxic. They have many uses.

Millions of tons of CFCs were manufactured and sold. In 1974, two scientists began to wonder where all the CFCs ended up. Mario Molina and F. Sherwood Roland of the University of California had a theory. They theorized the CFCs could end up high in Earth's atmosphere and damage the ozone layer.

What is the function of the ozone layer?

The ozone layer is about 20 km above Earth's surface. The **ozone layer** is a protective atmospheric layer that absorbs some of the Sun's harmful rays. Ozone is a molecule made up of three oxygen atoms, just like the ozone in smog. However, unlike smog, the ozone at high altitudes of the atmosphere has a positive role. It protects Earth's organisms by absorbing some of the Sun's harmful rays.

What is ozone depletion?

In the mid-1980s, a severe depletion of ozone appeared over Antarctica. The ozone layer seemed to grow smaller. In attempting to find the cause, scientists discovered that CFCs can destroy ozone molecules. If ozone molecules are destroyed, more harmful radiation could reach Earth. ☑

Can ozone depletion be stopped?

In 1987, governments around the world agreed to gradually reduce the use of CFCs. By 1996, all industrialized nations had stopped producing CFCs. Measurements of CFCs in the upper atmosphere show that the level of CFCs is beginning to decrease. However, scientists don't expect the ozone layer to recover for at least 50 more years.

FOLDABLES™

B Organize Use a quarter-sheet of notebook paper to record information on CFCs.

CFCs

Reading Check

7. Identify What are destroyed by CFCs?

_____

◉ After You Read

Mini Glossary

acid rain: precipitation with a pH below 5.6 that can harm plant and animal life

ozone layer: protective atmospheric layer that absorbs some of the Sun's harmful rays

particulate matter: solid particles and liquid droplets suspended in air

photochemical smog: brown haze formed when secondary pollutants interact with sunlight

primary pollutants: substances that are released directly into the air in harmful form

secondary pollutants: substances that pollute the air after first reacting with other substances in Earth's atmosphere

toxic air pollutants: substances released into the air that can cause health problems such as cancer

1. Review the terms and their definitions in the Mini Glossary. Then write a sentence that explains how pollutants are harmful to the environment.

_____

_____

_____

2. Label one figure *Normal Temperature Pattern*. Label the other figure *Temperature Inversion*. Add these labels in the correct places on each figure: *cool air, cooler air, warm air.*

How Temperature Inversion Occurs

 Visit **in6.msscience.com** to access your textbook, interactive games, and projects to help you learn more about what causes air pollution.

Air Pollution

section 2 Effects of Air Pollution

Standard—6.3.16: Explain that human activities, such as ... have changed the capacity of the environment to support some life forms.

● Before You Read

Think about a time that you sneezed even though you did not have a cold. What do you think made you sneeze? Write about it on the lines below.

_____

_____

_____

What You'll Learn

- how air pollution affects the health of humans
- how air pollution affects Earth's organisms
- how air pollution damages buildings

● Read to Learn

Air Pollution and Your Health

More than 133 million people in the United States live in areas where pollution makes the air they breathe unhealthy. Polluted air can have short-term effects and long-term effects. Short-term effects include watery eyes, sore throat, headache, and shortness of breath. The long-term effects of polluted air are more serious. They include diseases of the heart, kidney, liver, lungs, and brain.

Who is most affected by air pollution?

The effects of air pollution on health depend on how long a person is exposed to pollutants and how much pollution is in the air. Children and older people suffer the most effects. Since young children's organs are still developing, they are at great risk. Older people are at risk because they have been breathing pollutants for a long time.

What are the effects of smog?

Compounds in smog can cause eyes to water and sting. Breathing smog-filled air for a long time can cause coughing and chest pains. It also can cause lung infections and make breathing difficult.

Study Coach

Think-Pair-Share Work with a partner. As you read the text, discuss what you already know about the topic and what you learn from the text.

FOLDABLES

C Cause and Effect Make a Foldable using two sheets of paper to create a layered book on air pollution.

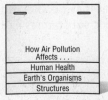

How Air Pollution Affects . . .
Human Health
Earth's Organisms
Structures

What are the effects of carbon monoxide?

Carbon monoxide affects the blood's ability to carry oxygen to the cells. Exposure to high levels of this gas can affect your vision and your ability to concentrate. It can also affect coordination. Very high levels of carbon monoxide can cause death.

What are the effects of particulates?

Do you sneeze when you shake out a dusty rug? Sneezing forces most of the dust out of your respiratory system. Recall that the respiratory system consists of organs that take in oxygen and release carbon dioxide. The respiratory system cannot eliminate all dust, however. Small particles can travel deep into the lungs. The small dust particles irritate the lungs and cause them to become inflamed. Over time, breathing in dust or other small particulates can cause permanent lung damage. This damage makes it harder to breathe and forces the heart to work harder than it should. The figure below shows particles lodged deep in the lungs where they can cause damage to the air sacs.

Small particles

Air sacs

What are the effects of toxic pollutants?

Toxic pollutants in the air, such as cigarette smoke, can damage many body systems. These harmful pollutants can affect the nervous system, the respiratory system, and the reproductive system. They also can increase the risk for cancer. ☑

Exposure to large amounts of toxic air pollution over a short period can be deadly. In 1984, an accident occurred at a pesticide factory in India. Pesticides are chemicals used to kill insects and other pests. A cloud of toxic gas was released, killing more than 4,000 people. Over 200,000 people suffered permanent injuries such as blindness and heart disease.

Picture This

1. **Explain** What might happen to the air sacs in the lungs if a person breathes in small particulates over a long period of time?

_____

_____

_____

Reading Check

2. **Identify** one body system that may be affected by toxic substances in the air.

_____

How does acid rain affect health?

When a person inhales humid air from acid rain, acid can be deposited deep inside the lungs. Acid irritates the lungs' sensitive tissues and reduces the ability to fight infections. The lungs are responsible for moving oxygen into the blood. Once damaged, they can no longer transfer oxygen to the blood easily. To make up for this, the heart works harder to pump oxygen to body cells. Over time, this extra work stresses and weakens the heart.

What is ultraviolet radiation?

Harmful rays from the Sun, called **ultraviolet radiation**, are linked to health problems. Some of these harmful rays are blocked by the ozone layer. Each spring, an ozone hole forms over Antarctica. The hole is an area of the ozone layer that is thinning. The size of the hole changes from year to year because of changing temperatures in the atmosphere. Because of the ozone hole, more ultraviolet radiation reaches Earth's surface.

How does ultraviolet radiation affect humans?

Increased exposure to ultraviolet radiation can cause skin cancer. One type of skin cancer is particularly deadly. Malignant melanoma accounts for only four percent of skin cancer cases but causes 79 percent of deaths from skin cancer. In the United States, about 54,000 people are diagnosed with malignant melanoma each year. Nearly 7,600 people die from it. The number of new cases of diagnosed malignant melanoma has more than doubled since 1973.

The Sun's harmful rays can affect more than a person's skin. Ultraviolet radiation also can cause cataracts. **Cataracts** are a form of eye damage that makes the lens of the eye cloudy. Ultraviolet radiation can also weaken the immune system, which helps the body fight illness.

Can you protect yourself from ultraviolet rays?

There are ways to protect yourself from too much ultraviolet radiation. Avoid outdoor activities during the middle of the day when the sun is hottest. If you must go outdoors, wear a wide-brimmed hat, sunglasses, and a long-sleeved shirt. Applying sunscreen to the skin also helps to block the Sun's harmful ultraviolet rays.

FOLDABLES

D **Take Notes** Make a half-book Foldable as shown to take notes on the ozone layer.

The Ozone Layer

Think it Over

3. **Explain** Why are there more cases of skin cancer now than in the 1970s?

_____

_____

_____

Effects on Earth's Organisms

Like people, animals inhale gases and small particles when they breathe. They also drink pollutants carried in rain and snow that have fallen into lakes and streams. Animals drink the water and eat other animals that have had the water. In this way, pollutants get into animals' food.

Some soft-bodied animals can absorb pollutants directly into their skin. Soft-bodied animals include earthworms or animals with thin, moist skins such as amphibians.

How much damage is done by pollutants?

Just like humans, young animals are not able to stand the same amount of pollution as adult animals can. The damage done by a pollutant depends on three things: the kind of pollutant, the length of time the animal was exposed to the pollutant, and the amount of pollutant that was eaten or absorbed by the animal.

What is biomagnification?

The amount of pollution in the air might not be high enough to cause a problem. But some pollutants stay in animal tissues for a long time. When these animals are eaten by other animals, the pollutants are passed on to the predator. **Biomagnification** (BI oh mag nuh fuh KAY shun) is the process in which pollutant levels increase through the food chain.

Pollutants from the air, such as mercury, can end up in high concentrations in animals due to biomagification. Pollutants often are measured in parts per million, or ppm. The figure below shows how pollutant levels increase through the food chain.

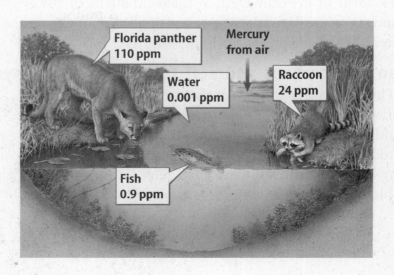

Think it Over

4. Infer Why can earthworms absorb pollutants through their skin?

_____

_____

_____

Picture This

5. Interpret Which animal has the highest concentration of pollutants in its body?

_____

How does acid rain affect lakes and rivers?

Recall that a lower pH level means a substance is more acidic. Acid rain falling into lakes, streams, and rivers can lower their pH levels, making it unhealthy for organisms that live there. ☑

In some streams and lakes in the United States and Canada, acid rain has eliminated certain fish species, such as brook trout. Because of acid rain, hundreds of lakes in the Adirondack Mountains in New York are too acidic for fish to survive. According to the Canadian government, more than 14,000 lakes in eastern Canada are acidic.

Acid rain is an even greater problem when snow melts. Sudden changes in pH levels due to melting snow can kill fish and other organisms. If a large amount of acidic snow falls in the winter and then melts quickly in the spring, a sudden rush of acids flows into lakes and streams. Many fish and other organisms have been killed because of these sudden pH changes.

How does acid rain affect plants and soils?

Acid rain also damages plants. At higher elevations, trees often are surrounded by fog. Trees surrounded by acidic fog suffer injury and are less able to resists pests and diseases. Some stands of evergreen trees in the Great Smoky Mountain National Park have died from exposure to the acidic environment.

Acid rain also can affect soils. As acid rain moves through soil, it can strip away many of the nutrients that trees and other plants need to grow. Some regions of the United States have naturally basic soils. In those regions, acid rains might not affect plant growth as noticeably. The higher pH of basic soils can help raise the pH of acid rain after it falls to the ground.

How does smog affect plants?

Smog is another form of air pollution that is harmful to plants. Over a long period of time, smog breaks away the waxy coating on the leaves of plants. When the coating is lost, plants lose water though their leaves. They are less able to resist pests, diseases, drought, and frost. Scientists estimate that smog formed by exhaust from cars and trucks damages millions of dollars worth of crops in California every year.

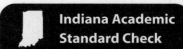
💡 **Think it Over**

7. Explain Describe one way acid rain affects Earth.

_____

_____

How does ozone depletion affect organisms?

As the ozone layer thins, Earth's organisms receive more ultraviolet radiation. Small organisms called phytoplankton (fi tuh PLANG tun) live in Earth's freshwater and oceans. Using carbon dioxide, water, and the Sun's energy, they make their food. As the figure below shows, depletion of the ozone layer increases the amount of ultraviolet radiation reaching Earth's surface. This reduces the phytoplankton's ability to make food. As a result, there are fewer phytoplankton. Although they are tiny, phytoplankton are important because they are the first link in the food chain.

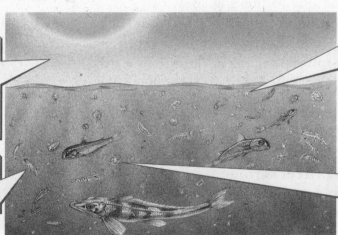

A Ozone depletion causes an increase in the amount of ultraviolet radiation reaching Earth's surface.

B Phytoplankton use the Sun's energy to make food. Ultraviolet radiation weakens phytoplankton and affects how they reproduce.

C Animal plankton eat phytoplankton. As phytoplankton numbers decrease, animal plankton populations will decrease.

D Fewer animal plankton means less food for fish.

Picture This

8. Determine What do animal plankton eat?

_____

How does ozone depletion affect agriculture?

Ultraviolet radiation may affect agricultural crops such as rice by decreasing the plant's ability to fight diseases and pests. This might reduce the amount of rice grown. Since rice is a major food source for more than half the world's population, this could be a serious problem.

Damage to Materials and Structures

Air pollution damages many materials. Acid rain corrodes metal and damages stone and paint. Smoke and soot settle on buildings, bridges, and outdoor works of art. The pyramids in Egypt have survived sun, wind, and sandstorms for more than 4,000 years. In the last 50 years, air pollution has increased the damage to the pyramids and other historic structures.

● After You Read

Mini Glossary

biomagnification (BI oh mag nuh fuh KAY shun) : process by which pollutant levels increase as they are passed through the food chain

cataracts: form of eye damage that makes the lens of the eye cloudy

ultraviolet radiation: harmful rays from the Sun that are linked to health problems

1. Review the terms and their definitions in the Mini Glossary. Choose one of the terms and explain what the term means in your own words.

_____

_____

_____

2. Choose one of the questions in the Read to Learn section. Write the question in the space below. Then write your answer to that question on the lines that follow.

```
Write your question here.



```

_____

_____

_____

3. You and your partner talked about the effects of air pollution. How did this help you understand what you read?

_____

_____

_____

Sciencenline Visit **in6.msscience.com** to access your textbook, interactive games, and projects to help you learn more about the effects of air pollution.

End of Section

Reading Essentials **85**

chapter 5 Air Pollution

section ❸ Solutions to Air Pollution

Standard—6.3.13: Identify, explain, and discuss some effects human activities, such as the creation of pollution, have on weather and the atmosphere.

What You'll Learn

- what the air pollution laws are in the United States
- how you can reduce air pollution

Mark the Text

Identify the Main Point
Highlight the main point in each paragraph. Highlight in a different color a detail or example that helps to explain the main point.

☑ **Reading Check**

1. Identify What is the surrounding air that you breathe called?

_____

_____

● Before You Read

You have learned about the effects of air pollution. On the lines below, write why it's important to find solutions to the problems caused by air pollution.

_____

_____

_____

● Read to Learn

Clean Air Laws

Between 1900 and 1970, factories and cars polluted the air in many parts of the country. Nitrogen oxides, which help form smog and acid rain, increased almost 1,000 percent during this period.

In 1955, the U.S. Congress began passing laws to protect the air. The Clean Air Act of 1963 was one of the most important laws. It was the first federal law to set rules about air pollution. Because of this act and two that followed in 1970 and 1990, companies that exceed air pollution limits may be fined. Car exhaust is checked in areas where the air pollution levels are high.

What is ambient air?

The surrounding air that you breathe is called **ambient** (AM bee unt) **air**. The purpose of air pollution laws is to keep ambient air clean. Scientists constantly test the quality of ambient air. They check the amounts of particulate matter, carbon monoxide, sulfur dioxide, nitrogen dioxide, lead, and ozone. An **air quality standard** is the maximum level of a pollutant that can be carried in ambient air. ☑

What are emissions?

__Emissions__ (ee MIH shunz) are pollutants released into the air from a particular source. Emissions are measured at industry smokestacks and at the tailpipes of automobiles. If these emissions are higher than the air quality standards, emissions must be reduced. ☑

How can emissions be reduced?

One way to reduce emissions is by using devices that capture pollutants before they enter the air. On cars, devices called catalytic (ka tuh LIH tihk) converters change most of the harmful gases to carbon dioxide and water before releasing them into the air.

Another way to reduce emissions is to limit the amount of pollutants produced. Alcohol can be added to gasoline to reduce tailpipe emissions. Since the 1990 Clean Air Act was enacted, only clean-burning gasoline can be sold in the smoggiest areas of the country.

You Can Help

Laws and new technologies help reduce air pollution. You can help, too. Turn off lights and appliances you are not using. Turn down the thermostat in winter and wear a sweater to keep warm. Instead of using an air conditioner, open windows. Using less electricity reduces the amount of fuel that power plants have to burn to create electricity. When less fuel is burned, power plant smokestacks release less pollution. Other ways to reduce pollution are riding a bicycle, car-pooling, and riding buses.

Improving Air Quality

Air quality in the United States has improved since 1990. This has happened even though more cars are on the road and more energy is being used. Strict controls on the sources of pollution have improved the quality of ambient air. ☑

The levels of most air pollutants are decreasing, but the levels of others are increasing. For example, nitrogen dioxide levels are rising. There is more smog in rural areas. Haze is a problem in some national parks. High levels of pollutants in some bodies of water make the fish unsafe to eat. Great progress has been made to reduce pollution, but much remains to be done.

☑ **Reading Check**

2. **Define** What are emissions?

_____

_____

_____

FOLDABLES™

Ⓔ **Organize** Make a half-book Foldable to record ways to reduce air pollution.

Ways to reduce air pollution

☑ **Reading Check**

3. **Determine** What has improved the quality of ambient air in the United States?

_____

_____

● After You Read

Mini Glossary

air quality standard: sets the maximum level of a pollutant that can be carried in ambient air

ambient air: surrounding air that you breathe

emissions: pollutants released into the air from a particular source

1. Review the terms and their definitions in the Mini Glossary. Why are air quality standards important?

   _____

   _____

2. Think of three ways to reduce air pollution at the national level and at a personal level. Fill in the blanks provided.

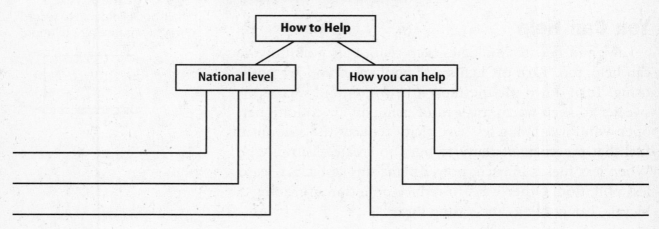

Solutions to Air Pollution

How to Help

National level

How you can help

3. You highlighted the main point in each paragraph. Then you highlighted details and examples. How did this help you understand the solutions to air pollution?

   _____

   _____

   _____

End of Section

 **Science Online** Visit **in6.msscience.com** to access your textbook, interactive games, and projects to help you learn more about solutions to air pollution.

Water

section ❶ The Nature of Water

> **Standard—6.2.5:** Organize information in simple tables and graphs and identify relationships they reveal. Use tables and graphs as examples of ....
> **Also covers: 6.2.7**

● Before You Read

What do you know about water? On the lines below, write what you know about how water affects our daily lives.

_____

_____

_____

● Read to Learn

Forms of Water

You use water every day. When you drink a glass of water, you use water in liquid form. When you put ice in a drink, you're using water in solid form. Even when you breathe, you are using water. Along with the oxygen and other gases in Earth's atmosphere, you inhale gaseous water with every breath you take.

What is water?

Water is a simple molecule composed of two hydrogen atoms bonded to one oxygen atom. The fact that water exists on Earth as a liquid, a solid, and a gas is one of its unique properties. Without water, Earth would be a different place.

What causes water to change form?

Water changes states. Ice melts on the sidewalk and the water in the puddle evaporates. Ice generally melts at 0°C. Liquid water can become gas at many temperatures. Water evaporates from oceans, lakes, and rivers to enter Earth's atmosphere. Water also changes to gas when it boils at 100°C.

What You'll Learn

- the three states of water on Earth
- several unique properties of water
- why water is a polar molecule

Study Coach

Sticky-Note Discussions
As you read this section, use sticky notes to mark the pages where you have questions. When you finish reading, review each marked page to make sure you have answers to your questions.

FOLDABLES™

Ⓐ **Find Main Ideas** Make the following three-tab Foldable to help you understand some of the physical properties of water.

Forms of Water

Heat Energy and Water

Polar Molecule

Absorbing Energy Water molecules are connected by weak bonds. To change from a solid to a liquid or from a liquid to a gas, these bonds must be broken. Breaking bonds requires energy. When water changes to steam, the water molecules absorb energy in the form of heat. The figure below shows water molecules in liquid water and in steam.

Releasing Energy When the state changes go in the other direction, water releases energy as heat. The same amount of heat needed to change liquid to gas is given off when the gas changes back to liquid.

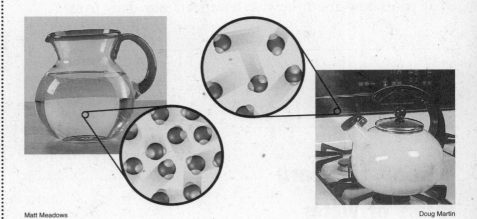

Matt Meadows   Doug Martin

Latent Heat

A pot of water would never boil over a candle flame. A candle does not give off enough heat to boil the water. Water molecules are attracted weakly to each other. The attraction means that you need a lot of heat to boil a pot of water. Energy is needed to separate the molecules. The heat energy needed to change water from a solid to a liquid is called the latent heat of fusion. Heat can be measured using a unit called the joule. It takes about 335 joules to melt a single gram of ice at 0°C. On the other hand, 335 joules of heat will escape when a single gram of water freezes into ice at 0°C. However, the temperature doesn't change during melting or freezing. The energy changes the state of the water but not the temperature.

How long does water take to change states?

Water won't freeze the instant it is put into the freezer. Ice won't melt the minute you place an ice cube on the counter. Ice is a stable form of water. A large amount of heat loss must occur to make ice in the first place. After water is frozen, it takes far more energy to melt the ice than it does to heat the liquid water to almost boiling.

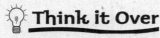

What is the latent heat of vaporization?

It takes even more heat energy to change liquid water to gas, or water vapor. The amount of heat needed to change water from liquid to gas is called the latent heat of vaporization. Each gram of liquid water needs 2,260 joules of heat to change to water vapor at 100°C. Each gram of water vapor that changes back to a liquid releases 2,260 joules of heat. Either way, only the state changes during these processes—not the temperature of the water.

You might have experienced latent heat of vaporization. Have you ever felt a chill after getting out of a swimming pool? When you first leave the pool, your skin is covered with water. As the water evaporates into the air and becomes water vapor, it takes heat from your body and you feel cold.

What is the density of water?

Which has more mass—a kilogram of plastic foam or a kilogram of lead? They have the same mass, of course, but you need a much bigger container to hold the plastic foam. The volume of the lead is smaller because lead has more mass for its size than plastic foam. The lead has a greater density. **Density** is the amount of mass in a unit of volume. The density of pure water is 1.0 g/cm³ at 4°C. Adding another substance to water, such as salt, changes its density. Freshwater will float on top of denser salt water, just as olive oil floats on top of the denser vinegar in salad dressing.

This situation also is found in nature when a freshwater river flows into the salty water of the ocean. The freshwater stays on top until waves and currents mix it with the seawater.

How does temperature affect water density?

As freshwater heats above 4°C, the water molecules gain energy and move apart. For the same volume of water, warm water has fewer molecules than cold water. Warm water has lower density than cold water.

Warm water will float on top of cold water because warm water is less dense. You might have experienced this while swimming in a lake during the summer. The water on top is fairly warm. If you dive down, you feel the colder, denser water below. The difference in density between warm and cold water in the ocean causes currents in the water.

3. Analyze Suppose 670 joules of heat are required to melt 2 grams of ice. How many joules would be released when the 2 grams of water freeze?

_____

Reading Check

4. Determine What happens to the density of water when you add salt to it?

_____

_____

A Polar Molecule

Picture a dripping faucet. A drop of water can hang from the faucet and slowly bulge until it falls into the sink. That's due to another unique property of water called cohesion. **Cohesion** is the attraction between water molecules. This attraction is what allows water molecules to form into drops. Cohesion also helps keep water liquid at room temperature. If not for cohesion, water molecules would quickly evaporate into the air. Not all molecules have this property. Nitrogen and carbon dioxide, which are close in mass to water molecules, completely vaporize at room temperature. If water molecules behaved this way, Earth would be a different, drier place. ☑

How does cohesion work?

Recall that water is made of two hydrogen atoms and one oxygen atom. These atoms share their electrons in covalent bonds. But the oxygen atom pulls more powerfully on the negatively charged electrons than the hydrogen atoms do. This gives the oxygen end of the molecule a partial negative charge and the hydrogen side of the molecule a partial positive charge. As a result, the molecule acts like a tiny magnet. It attracts other water molecules into weak bonds. The figure below shows the weak charges attracting opposites and the bonding of the molecules.

Polar Molecules Because of this behavior, the water molecule is considered a polar molecule. A **polar molecule** has a slightly positive end and a slightly negative end because electrons are shared unequally. The polarity of the water molecule explains many of its unique properties.

✔ Reading Check

5. Determine Which property of water helps keep it liquid at room temperature?

Picture This

6. Identify Circle the bonds between the water molecules. Label the ends of one water molecule as positive (+) or negative (−).

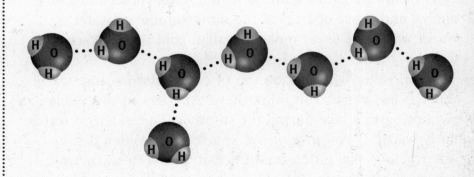

What are some other properties of water?

The polarity of water molecules causes water to have other properties. Water is great for dissolving other substances, such as sea salts or substances that travel through your body. Because of polarity, ice will float on liquid water. As water freezes, the weak bonds between the molecules form an open arrangement of molecules, as shown in the figure below.

Molecules are farther apart when they are frozen than when they are in liquid. As a result, ice has a lower density than liquid water, letting it float on water.

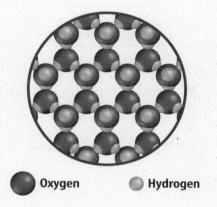

● Oxygen ● Hydrogen

Picture This

7. Determine Why does ice have a lower density than water?

_____

_____

_____

What is specific heat?

You can burn your feet walking on hot sand on the beach. Yet the same hot Sun that is shining on the sand is shining on the water, too. Why is the sand hot and the water cool? One reason is water's high specific heat. <u>Specific heat</u> is the amount of energy that is needed to raise the temperature of 1 kg of a substance 1°C. The same amount of energy raises the temperature of the sand much more than the temperature of the water. When comparing water with most other naturally occurring materials, it will increase its temperature the least when heat is added. This gives water one of the highest values of specific heat.

High specific heat means that water also will cool off more slowly when the energy is taken away. At night, the water in the ocean feels warmer than the sand.

High specific heat is the reason water often is used as a coolant. Water in a car's radiator cools the engine by carrying away heat without becoming too hot itself.

Think it Over

8. Analyze Why does water stay cooler than sand on a hot, summer day?

_____

_____

● After You Read

Mini Glossary

cohesion: attraction between water molecules that allows water to form drops and remain liquid at room temperature

density: amount of mass in a unit of volume

polar molecule: molecule with a slightly positive end and a slightly negative end as a result of electrons being shared unequally

specific heat: amount of energy needed to raise the temperature of 1 kg of a substance by 1°C

1. Review the terms and their definitions in the Mini Glossary. Use one of the words in a sentence to explain one property of water.

_____

_____

2. Complete the graphic organizer below to help you understand how polarity affects water molecules.

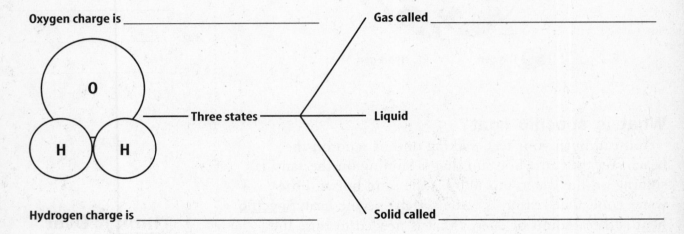

Oxygen charge is _____

Three states

Gas called _____

Liquid

Hydrogen charge is _____

Solid called _____

3. As you read this section, you put sticky notes near the ideas that were difficult to understand. How did using the sticky notes help you understand the information in this section?

_____

_____

_____

End of Section

Science Online Visit **in6.msscience.com** to access your textbook, interactive games, and projects to help you learn more about the nature of water.

Water

section ❷ Why is water necessary?

 Standard—6.3.8: Explain that fresh water ... is essential for life and also for most industrial processes. Understand that this resource can be depleted ....

● Before You Read

What are some ways that water allows you to live more comfortably? What can you do to conserve this resource?

_____

_____

_____

What You'll Learn

- why water is essential for life on Earth
- ways that society uses water
- methods for conserving freshwater

● Read to Learn

Water and Life

Everyone knows that humans can't survive long without water to drink. Even more than food, water is critical to your survival. Water is all around you and all through you. About 70 percent of your body is water. Water fills and surrounds body cells, making many body processes possible. Water helps move nutrients throughout the body. Water helps control the body's temperature, eliminate wastes, digest food, and lubricate joints. When you feel thirsty, your body is telling you that you need more water.

Why is water essential to all life on Earth?

Water is important to all life on Earth. The oceans, streams, rivers, and lakes provide habitats for organisms within and around them.

Plants also need water. The properties of water allow plants to get water from soil. Remember that water molecules are attracted to other polar molecules. Together with cohesion, this provides the capillary action that draws water upward through narrow tubes inside plant stems. Thus, water moves from the soil to the plant leaves, where photosynthesis occurs.

Study Coach

Think-Pair-Share Choose a topic in this section that you find interesting or confusing. Summarize this topic for one of your classmates. Make a list of any unanswered questions or additional information you and your partner learned about this topic.

FOLDABLES™

❸ Organize Information Make the following quarter-sheet Foldables to organize information about why water is important and the conservation of water.

Conserving Water | Ways Water Is Important to Life

Water and Society

Cities around the world often are located near large bodies of water. Water is extremely important to society.

How is water used?

Industry uses water for many purposes, such as processing and cooling during the production of paper, chemicals, steel, and other products. Water also is necessary for transporting manufactured goods. Large amounts of water are used in the mining and refining of Earth's natural resources. The graph below shows how water is used in the United States. In general, communities located near water attract industry and have productive economies.

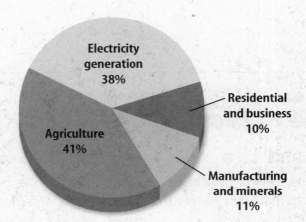

Agriculture uses about 41 percent of all the water used in the United States, mostly for irrigating farmland. **Irrigation** means piping in water from elsewhere and using it to grow crops. The water could come from a nearby lake, river, or reservoir, or it might be pumped from the ground.

Transportation Today travel by car or by air is more common than travel by water. However, water still remains valuable for transportation. Ferries move people, cars, and freight across bays and rivers. Cruise ships are popular for vacations. Large ships are still the least expensive way to move cargo within the country or across the ocean.

Recreation Water also plays a role in recreation. Many people enjoy spending time in the water—fishing, swimming, scuba diving, waterskiing, and boating. Sailors, canoeists, kayakers, and whitewater rafters all spend recreation time on the water. ✔

Picture This

1. **Interpret Scientific Illustrations** How much greater is the percent of water used to generate electricity in the United States than to manufacture goods and process minerals?

_____

_____

2. **Identify** What are two ways people use water for recreation?

_____

_____

Water Use

Water clearly is an important natural resource that must be conserved and protected. Not only is clean water important for use in homes and by society, it is also necessary for maintaining the ecological balance in nature.

Bodies of water must be clean to support the animals and plants that live in them. If too much pollution enters rivers, lakes, or ponds, wildlife might be harmed. Oceans also must be kept clean of pollutants such as oil, chemicals, and litter. ☑

How can water be conserved?

Earth is a watery planet. Yet less than one percent of Earth's water is the freshwater that people and other organisms need to live. It is important to conserve the freshwater on Earth. **Water conservation** is the careful use and protection of water. There are many ways to conserve freshwater.

Much of the water used for irrigation is lost to evaporation. So instead of flooding fields, farmers can use overhead sprinklers. Overhead sprinklers use less water than flooding fields does. Some farmers install tubing that slowly drips water directly above the roots of plants. Sensors installed in the ground and connected to a computer can signal when crops need to be watered. In residential and commercial areas, mulching the ground around the plants helps prevent water loss.

Industries also can conserve water by treating and recycling the water used in factories. New manufacturing processes that conserve water also might increase plant productivity.

What can you do to help?

Everyone can conserve water. You can conserve water in your shower. Turn the water off while soaping up and then use the water just for rinsing. Do the same while brushing your teeth and washing your hands. The average toilet uses 19 L of water per flush. Newer toilets use only 6 L. Find out if your home uses a low-flow toilet system.

✔ Reading Check

3. **Explain** Why must bodies of water be kept clean?

_____

_____

_____

💡 Think it Over

4. **Think Critically** Name two more things you can do to conserve water.

_____

_____

_____

● After You Read

Mini Glossary

irrigation: process of piping water from somewhere else to grow crops

water conservation: the careful use and protection of water

1. Review the terms and their definitions in the Mini Glossary. Write a sentence using one of the terms to explain how you can save water.

_____

_____

_____

2. Use the graph and information from this section to complete the table below. In the first column, list the ways water is used in the United States. In the second column, list some ways that water can be conserved or kept clean by each of these users. You can list methods described in this section, or suggest your own ideas.

Ways Water Is Used in the U.S.	Ways Water Can Be Conserved or Kept Clean

End of Section

 Visit **in6.msscience.com** to access your textbook, interactive games, and projects to help you learn more about why water is necessary for life.

 **Water**

section ❸ **Recycling Water**

 Standard—6.3.8: Explain that fresh water ... is essential for life and also for most industrial processes. Understand that this resource can be ....
Also covers: 6.2.5, 6.2.6 ,6.2.7, 6.3.9

● Before You Read

Where do you think freshwater is found on Earth? Where is salt water found?

_____

_____

_____

What You'll Learn

- to identify Earth's water reservoirs
- to describe natural sources of freshwater
- how water is recycled

● Read to Learn

Earth's Water Reservoirs

About 70 percent of Earth's surface is covered by water, but only a small portion is available for human use. About 97 percent of Earth's water is salty ocean water. Only about three percent of Earth's water is freshwater, and more than three-quarters of that is frozen in glaciers. Of the less than one percent of Earth's total water supply that is available for human use, much of it lies beneath Earth's surface.

Can humans use ocean water?

Ocean water is plentiful on Earth, but it's salty. To use it for drinking, bathing, or watering crops, the salt would have to be removed. Removing salt from salt water usually isn't practical and is done in only a few very dry regions.

Where is most of Earth's ice?

Glaciers occur in Earth's polar regions. Large areas of Greenland and Antarctica are covered by ice. These ice sheets lock up a high percentage of Earth's freshwater. A little over two percent of the Earth's water is ice, but that is 77 percent of Earth's freshwater supply. Melting ice into usable water is not practical.

Study Coach

Make Flash Cards As you read this section, make flash cards to help you remember each type of reservoir on Earth. On one side, name the reservoir type. On the back of the card, describe that reservoir.

Applying Math

1. **Estimate** About how much freshwater on Earth is not frozen and is available for use by people and other land animals?

_____

6.3.9: Illustrate that the cycling of water in and out of the atmosphere plays an important role in determining climatic patterns.

✔ **2. Summarize** How is the water that goes into wells purified?

_____

_____

Picture This

3. Identify Circle the well in the figure. To what layer does it extend?

_____

What is groundwater?

What happens to rain after it falls? A bucket left out in the rain can fill quickly with water. Where does the water that lands on the ground go? Some of it runs off the land and flows into streams, and some evaporates. A large amount soaks into the ground. **Groundwater** is water that is held underground in layers of rock and sediment. The part of groundwater that is held within openings in the soil is called **soil water.** It keeps plants and crops alive. People who get their water from wells are drinking groundwater. Groundwater is purified naturally as it soaks through layers of sediment and rock. But if groundwater does become polluted, it can be extremely hard to clean it. ☑

What is an aquifer?

An **aquifer** is a layer of rock or sediment that holds usable groundwater. Water collects in the open spaces between rock particles. This water flows slowly from one open space to another at rates of a few meters per year. Sometimes aquifers are used to supply water to towns and farms, as shown in the figure below. The water is pumped to Earth's surface through a well. Aquifers are found at different depths below the surface. Sometimes Earth's surface dips below the level where groundwater would be. This is where natural lakes and rivers often are located.

What is surface water?

Surface water is water at Earth's surface. It is found in streams, rivers, ponds, lakes, and reservoirs. You can easily see and use surface water.

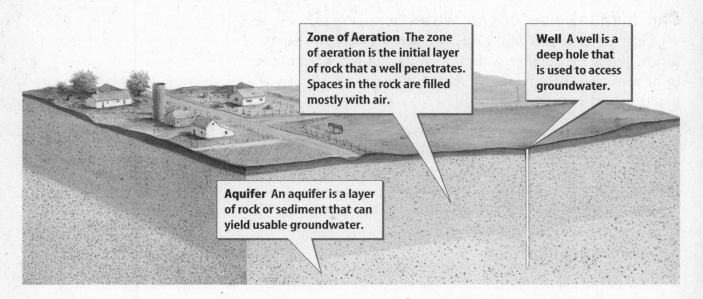

Zone of Aeration The zone of aeration is the initial layer of rock that a well penetrates. Spaces in the rock are filled mostly with air.

Well A well is a deep hole that is used to access groundwater.

Aquifer An aquifer is a layer of rock or sediment that can yield usable groundwater.

Is there water in the atmosphere?

Air holds water, too. Earth's atmosphere can hold from near zero to about four percent water vapor by volume. Water vapor in Earth's atmosphere has several important roles. Clouds need water vapor to form. Therefore, water vapor is the source of rain, sleet, and snow.

Each time water undergoes a change of state, it gives off heat or absorbs heat. For example, heat is given off when water vapor condenses to form water droplets in clouds. Heat is absorbed when water evaporates to form water vapor. That's why you feel cold when you are soaking wet. The atmosphere uses these heating and cooling properties of water to move energy around the planet. This process generates wind and may create storms and even hurricanes.

Water vapor serves another important function in the atmosphere. Water vapor in the atmosphere absorbs heat and acts as a blanket to help keep Earth warm and support life.

The Water Cycle

The water on Earth constantly is recycled through the water cycle. Water evaporates from lakes, rivers, oceans, puddles, and even the soil. It then rises into Earth's atmosphere as water vapor. Eventually, the water vapor condenses to form the droplets and ice crystals in clouds. When the water droplets or ice crystals become heavy enough, they fall back to Earth as rain, snow, or sleet. Rainwater soaks into or runs off the surface to rivers, lakes, and finally the ocean. Then the cycle repeats. The water cycle is shown in the figure below.

FOLDABLES

C Sequence Make a drawing on a sheet of notebook paper to show how water constantly cycles.

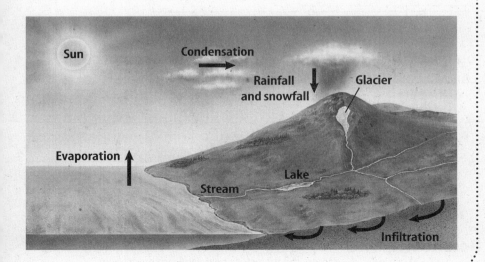

Picture This

4. Apply Use a pencil to trace the path of water as it moves through the water cycle.

● After You Read

Mini Glossary

aquifer: layer of rock or sediment that allows groundwater to flow easily through its connecting openings

groundwater: water that is held underground in layers of rock and sediment

soil water: groundwater that is trapped within openings in the soil and keeps plants and crops alive

surface water: all the freshwater at Earth's surface, including streams, rivers, lakes, and reservoirs

1. Review the terms and their definitions in the Mini Glossary. Then write a sentence describing where one of these water sources could be found.

   _____

   _____

2. Use the words below to complete the chart.

   groundwater   snow   condenses   rain   evaporates

   Water _____ from surface water.

   Water vapor rises into the atmosphere, where it _____.

   The Water Cycle

   The water can soak into the ground to become _____ or run off to become surface water.

   Water falls back to Earth as _____ or _____.

3. As you read this section, you made flashcards to learn more about Earth's water reservoirs. How did this help you understand the information in this section?

   _____

   _____

End of Section

Science Online Visit **in6.msscience.com** to access your textbook, interactive games, and projects to help you learn more about recycling water.

 **Oceans**

section ❶ Ocean Water

Standard—6.3.7: Understand and describe the scales involved in characterizing Earth and its atmosphere. Describe that Earth is ....
Also covers: 6.2.7

● Before You Read

What is the first thing you notice when you look at a globe? Earth has been called "The Water Planet." Why do you suppose that is?

_____

_____

_____

● Read to Learn

Importance of Oceans

Oceans cover almost three-fourths of Earth's surface. Oceans affect all living things and are important to life. They provide a place for many organisms to live. Oceans transport seeds and animals. Materials are shipped across the world on oceans. Oceans also provide humans with resources such as food, medicines and salt. For example, sea sponges are used in medicines for treating cancer and asthma. Fish and other sea creatures provide food. Salt is obtained by evaporating seawater. The water for most of Earth's rain and snow comes from evaporated ocean water. Just as important, 70 percent of the oxygen on Earth is given off by ocean organisms.

Formation of Oceans

When Earth was still a young planet, active volcanoes were everywhere. They erupted regularly, releasing lava, ash, and gases from deep within Earth. The volcanic gases entered Earth's atmosphere. One of the gases was water vapor. Scientists hypothesize that water vapor began gathering in the atmosphere about 4 billion years ago.

What You'll Learn

- why Earth's oceans are important
- how Earth's oceans formed
- the composition of seawater
- how temperature and pressure change with depth

Mark the Text

Identify the Main Point
Highlight the main point in each paragraph. Use a different color to highlight a detail or example that helps explain the main point.

FOLDABLES™

Ⓐ Organize Information
Make the following three-tab Foldable to help you organize information about oceans.

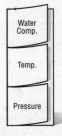

How did water vapor help form oceans?

Over millions of years, the water vapor cooled enough to condense and form clouds. Heavy rains began to fall. With each rainfall, more water collected in the lowest parts of Earth's surface. As more rain fell, more land was covered. Eventually, much of the land was covered by water that formed oceans. Evidence suggests that Earth's oceans formed more than 3 billion years ago.

Composition of Ocean Water

Seawater does not taste like the water you drink. In fact, drinking seawater can make you sick. The salty taste is caused by dissolved substances. Rivers and groundwater dissolve elements like calcium and sodium and carry them to the ocean. Erupting volcanoes add elements like bromine and chlorine to ocean water.

The diagram shows that sodium and chlorine are the most common elements dissolved in seawater. When seawater evaporates, sodium and chloride ions combine to form halite. Halite is the salt used to flavor foods. ☑

☑ Reading Check

1. **Explain** How does seawater provide the salt used to flavor foods?

_____

_____

_____

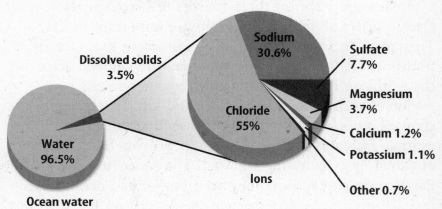

Composition of Ocean Water

Dissolved solids 3.5%

Sodium 30.6%

Sulfate 7.7%

Magnesium 3.7%

Calcium 1.2%

Potassium 1.1%

Chloride 55%

Other 0.7%

Water 96.5%

Ocean water

Ions

Picture This

2. **Interpret Scientific Illustrations** What are the two most common solids dissolved in ocean water?

_____

_____

What is salinity?

<u>Salinity</u> (say LIH nuh tee) is a measure of the amount of dissolved solids, or salts, in seawater. Salinity is measured in grams of dissolved salt in one kilogram of seawater. One kilogram of ocean water contains about 35 g of dissolved salts, or 3.5 percent salts. Remember that one kilogram is equal to 1,000 g.

How does the ocean stay in balance?

Elements are removed from the ocean at the same rate that they are added to the ocean. This allows the composition of the ocean to stay in balance. Rivers, volcanoes, and the atmosphere constantly add substances to the ocean. Biological processes and chemical reactions remove many of these substances. For example, many marine organisms use calcium ions to make bones or shells. Calcium is also removed from ocean water through chemical reactions, forming sediments on the ocean floor.

What gases are found in seawater?

All of the gases in Earth's atmosphere dissolve in seawater. The three most important gases are carbon dioxide, oxygen, and nitrogen.

Oxygen The greatest concentration of dissolved oxygen is near the surface of the ocean. There, oxygen enters seawater directly from the atmosphere. However, there is another reason so much oxygen is found near the surface. Organisms in the sea produce oxygen by photosynthesis. **Photosynthesis** is the process in which organisms use sunlight, water, and carbon dioxide to make food and oxygen.

Photosynthesis requires sunlight. Organisms that carry on photosynthesis are found only in the upper 200 m of the ocean, where sunlight reaches.

Below 200 m, dissolved oxygen levels drop. Here, many animals use oxygen for respiration and it is not replaced. However, dissolved oxygen is found in very deep water. This cold, deep water began as surface water in polar regions. It moves along the ocean floor to other regions.

Carbon Dioxide Most dissolved carbon dioxide found in seawater comes directly from the atmosphere. Some comes from carbon dioxide given off by ocean organisms during respiration. Carbon dioxide reacts with water molecules to form a weak acid called carbonic acid. Carbonic acid helps control the acidity in oceans.

Nitrogen There is more dissolved nitrogen in the ocean than any other gas. Some types of bacteria combine nitrogen and oxygen to form nitrates. Nitrates are important nutrients for plants. Nitrogen is also one of the important building blocks of plant and animal tissue.

✔ Reading Check

3. **Identify** Name three important gases found dissolved in ocean water.

_____

_____

_____

Think it Over

4. **Draw Conclusions** Kelp needs sunlight to photosynthesize. Would kelp be found above or below 200 m?

_____

_____

Water Temperature and Pressure

Oceans have three temperature layers—the surface layer, the thermocline layer, and the deep-water layer, as shown in the figure. The surface layer is the warmest because it is heated by solar energy. The warmest surface water is near the equator and the coolest surface water is near the poles.

Picture This

5. Interpret Scientific Illustrations At about what depth is the ocean's average temperature 15°C? What layer of the ocean is at this depth?

_____

_____

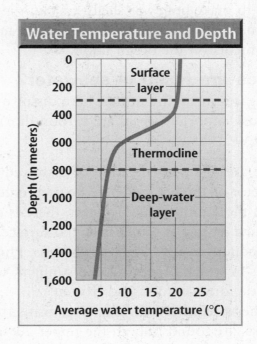

The **thermocline** is the layer of ocean water that begins at a depth of about 200 m. In the thermocline, temperature drops quickly as depth increases. This occurs because solar energy does not reach this deep. Below the thermocline lies the deep-water layer, which contains extremely cold water.

Does pressure increase with ocean depth?

Pressure, or force per unit area, also changes with depth. At sea level, the pressure of the atmosphere pushing down on the ocean is referred to as 1 atmosphere (atm) of pressure. An atmosphere is the pressure placed on a surface at sea level by the column of air above it.

As you go deeper into the ocean, the pressure increases. At the surface, the only pressure is from air. But deeper, there is the added force of the water molecules pushing down. The pressure increases by about 1 atm for each 10 m of depth. For example, a scuba diver at 20 m would feel a pressure of 3 atm (1 atm of air + 2 atm of water).

Applying Math

6. Calculate How much pressure would a scuba diver feel at 40 m?

_____

● After You Read

Mini Glossary

photosynthesis: process by which some organisms use sunlight, water, and carbon dioxide to make food and oxygen

salinity: measure of the amount of dissolved solids, or salts, in seawater

thermocline: layer of ocean water that begins at a depth of about 200 m and becomes colder with increasing depth

1. Review the terms and their definitions in the Mini Glossary above. Write a sentence describing one of the terms in your own words.

   _____

   _____

2. Number the boxes below in the correct order to describe the sequence of events that led to the formation of oceans.

Over millions of years, water vapor in the atmosphere condensed and formed clouds. _____	Volcanoes released lava, ash, and gases including water vapor. _____	Huge amounts of rain fell. _____

Water gathered in the lowest parts of Earth's surface. _____	Much of the land was covered by water that formed oceans. _____

3. As you read, you highlighted the main idea of each paragraph and other important details and examples that helped describe that idea. How did you decide what to highlight in each paragraph?

   _____

   _____

   _____

 Science Online Visit **in6.msscience.com** to access your textbook, interactive games, and projects to help you learn more about ocean water.

End of Section

section 2 Ocean Currents and Climates

 Standard—6.3.11: Identify and explain the effects of oceans on climate.
Also covers: 6.2.7, 6.3.10

What You'll Learn

- how wind and Earth's rotation affect surface currents
- how ocean currents affect weather and climate
- the causes and effects of density currents
- how upwelling occurs

◀ Study Coach

Main Idea-Detail Notes
As you read about different types of currents, write notes in two columns. In the left column, write the type of current. In the right column, write details about that current.

FOLDABLES™

B Understand Cause and Effect Make the following Foldable to help you understand the cause-and-effect relationship of currents.

	cause	effect
currents		
waves		
tides		

● Before You Read

If you filled a bowl with water and gently dropped a scrap of paper onto the water surface, it would float. If you want to make the paper move without touching it or tilting the bowl, how could you do it? What are you creating when you make the paper move without touching it or tilting the bowl?

_____

_____

_____

● Read to Learn

Surface Currents

Ocean water never stands still. Currents move the water from place to place constantly. Ocean currents are like rivers that move within the ocean. They exist at both the ocean's surface and in deeper water.

What causes surface currents?

<u>Surface currents</u> are powered by wind and usually move only the upper few hundred meters of seawater. When the global winds blow on the ocean's surface, they set ocean water in motion. Because of Earth's rotation, the ocean currents that result do not move in straight lines. Earth's rotation causes surface ocean currents in the northern hemisphere to curve to their right. Surface ocean currents in the southern hemisphere curve to their left. You can see this on the map on the next page. The turning of ocean currents is an example of the Coriolis effect. Recall that the Coriolis effect also is observed on winds. Winds curve toward their right in the northern hemisphere and toward their left in the southern hemisphere.

Earth's Global Winds Create Surface Currents

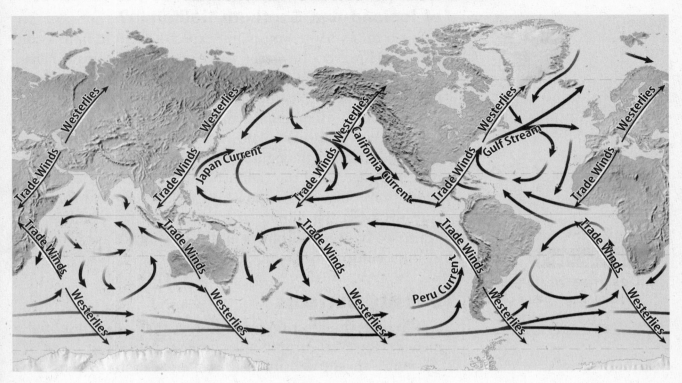

The Gulf Stream Much of what is known about surface currents comes from records kept by early sailors. Sailing ships depended on certain surface currents to carry them west and other currents to carry them east. One of the most important currents for sailing east across the North Atlantic Ocean is the Gulf Stream.

Find the Gulf Stream current on the map above. The Gulf Stream flows from Florida northeastward toward North Carolina. There it curves toward the east and becomes slower and broader.

The Gulf Stream is 100 km wide. It was discovered in the 1500s by Ponce de Leon. In 1770, Benjamin Franklin published a map of the Gulf Stream drawn by Captain Timothy Folger, a Nantucket whaler.

Can currents influence climates?

Since the Gulf Stream begins near the equator, it is a warm current. It carries heat from the equator to other parts of the ocean. Surface currents like the Gulf Stream, on the eastern coasts of continents, tend to be warm. They bring heat from the equator to other areas of Earth. Currents on the western coasts are usually cold. This can influence the climate of regions near these currents.

Picture This

1. **Explain** In the figure, follow a current with your pencil. Which way does your pencil turn, left or right? Why?

_____

_____

_____

How do surface currents affect the climates of Iceland and Southern California?

Based on its name, you might expect Iceland to have a cold climate. However, the warm water of the Gulf Stream helps keep Iceland's climate mild. The current's warm water flows past Iceland and heats the surrounding air. This warm air keeps Iceland's climate mild and its harbors ice-free all year.

Southern California is known for its warmth and sunshine. Look at the figure of surface currents on the previous page. Find the California Current. It carries cold water from polar regions toward the equator. Cold surface currents affect the climate of coastal cities. For example, San Francisco has cool summers and many foggy days because of the California Current. ✓

Density Currents

Wind has no effect on water deeper than a few hundred meters. However, currents may develop because of differences in the density of the water. Seawater becomes more dense as it gets colder or when it becomes more salty. Gravity causes dense seawater to sink beneath less dense seawater. As the mass falls, it spreads to less dense waters of the ocean. This creates a density current. A **density current** is a pattern in the ocean that forms when a mass of dense seawater sinks beneath less dense seawater. Changes in temperature and salinity work together to create density currents. A density current moves very slowly.

How does salinity affect density currents?

One important density current begins in the cold water north of Iceland. When water freezes, dissolved salts are left behind in the unfrozen water. The very salty water that is left behind is more dense and sinks. Slowly, it spreads along the ocean floor toward the equator and the southern Atlantic Ocean. As the water is sinking near Iceland, the warm surface water of the Gulf Stream moves up from the equator to replace it.

Another density current occurs in the Mediterranean Sea. Warm air in the Mediterranean region causes the seawater to evaporate. This leaves salt behind and increases the salinity of the water. The dense, salty water sinks and flows out to the Atlantic Ocean. At the surface, less dense water from the Atlantic Ocean flows into the Mediterranean Sea.

2. Describe What affects the climate of coastal cities?

_____

_____

💡 **Think it Over**

3. Sequence of Events
Number the events to show the order in which a density current forms near Iceland.

____ saltier water sinks and flows

____ warm water replaces the cold water

____ ocean water freezes

How do density currents affect climate?

What if the density currents near Iceland stopped forming? Some scientists hypothesize that this has happened in the past and could happen again. Pollution and population growth could lead to large amounts of carbon dioxide in the atmosphere. The carbon dioxide would trap more of the Sun's heat and raise Earth's temperature. If Earth's temperature rose enough, ice couldn't form easily near the polar regions. Glaciers on land would melt. The freshwater from the glaciers would reduce the salinity of the ocean water. The density currents would weaken or stop. If density currents stopped flowing southward, warm equatorial surface water would no longer flow northward. Earth could face drastic climate changes, including different rainfall patterns and temperatures.

Think it Over

4. **Describe** What might be affected if density currents stopped?

_____

_____

Upwelling

An **upwelling** is a current in the ocean that brings deep, cold water to the ocean surface. The Coriolis effect pushes surface water away from some coastal regions. Cold water from deep in the ocean rises up to replace it. The illustration shows an upwelling of cold water. The cold water is full of nutrients from dead, decayed organisms. Tiny marine organisms thrive in these nutrient-rich areas, which, in turn, attract many fish. As a result, areas of upwelling are important fishing grounds because fish are attracted to the areas to eat the organisms.

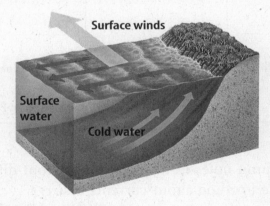

Surface winds

Surface water

Cold water

Picture This

5. **Infer** Why does upwelling around Peru make Peru a rich fishing ground?

_____

_____

What happens during El Niño?

During an El Niño (el NEEN yoh) event, the winds blowing cold water from the coast of Peru slow down. The Eastern Pacific Ocean becomes warmer, and upwelling is reduced or stopped. Without nutrients provided by upwelling, fish and other organisms cannot find food. This disrupts the rich fishing grounds off Peru's coast.

● After You Read

Mini Glossary

density current: current created by the circulation pattern in the ocean that forms when a mass of dense seawater sinks beneath less dense seawater

surface current: ocean current that usually moves only the upper few hundred meters of seawater

upwelling: ocean current that moves cold, deep water to the ocean surface

1. Review the terms and their definitions in the Mini Glossary above. Choose a term and write a sentence in which you provide an example of that term.

   _____

   _____

2. Complete the chart below to organize information from this section.

   ```
                              Ocean
                             Currents
                          /            \
   ```

Density Currents	Surface Currents
• travel in the ocean at a depth of _____. • caused by _____ water sinking below less _____ water.	• travel in the ocean at a depth of _____. • set in motion by global _____ blowing on Earth's surface.

3. Earlier, you created two-column notes to help you learn about different types of currents. How did writing notes make learning about currents easier?

   _____

   _____

   _____

End of Section

Science●**nline** Visit **in6.msscience.com** to access your textbook, interactive games, and projects to help you learn more about ocean currents and climate.

Oceans

section ➌ Waves

Standard—6.3.10: Describe the motions of ocean waters, such as tides, and identify their causes.

Before You Read

Have you ever surfed? Maybe you have seen someone surf. How does a surfer who is out in the ocean return to shore?

_____

_____

_____

What You'll Learn
- how wind can form ocean waves
- how water molecules in a wave move
- how the Moon and Sun cause Earth's tides
- what forces cause shoreline erosion

Read to Learn

Waves Caused by Wind

Surfers catch and ride waves all the way back to the beach. A **wave** in water is a rhythmic movement that carries energy through the water. Waves that surfers ride could have started halfway around the world.

When wind blows across a body of water, friction pushes the water along with the wind. When wind speed is great enough, water will pile up into waves. Three things affect the height of a wave: the wind speed, the length of time the wind blows, and the distance over which the wind blows. As wind continues to blow, the waves become higher. When the wind stops, waves stop forming. But waves that have already formed will still continue to travel for long distances.

What are the parts of a wave?

Each wave has a crest, its highest point, and a trough, its lowest part. The wavelength is the horizontal distance between the crests or troughs of two waves. Wave height is the vertical distance from the trough of a wave to the crest. Most waves in the ocean are between 2 m and 5 m high. Some storms have been known to produce waves taller than a six-story building.

Study Coach

Authentic Questions
Before you begin reading, write down any questions you have about waves. Look for the answers as you read.

FOLDABLES

Ⓑ Understand Cause and Effect Complete the sections for waves and tides on the Foldable you made earlier.

	cause	effect
currents		
waves		
tides		

How do waves move?

When you watch a wave, it looks as if the water is moving forward. But unless the wave is breaking onto the shore, the water is not moving forward. Each molecule of water returns to its original position when a wave passes. The molecule may be pushed forward by the next wave, but it will return to its original position when the wave passes. Water molecules move in circular patterns within a wave. ☑

What are breakers?

A breaker is a collapsing wave. As a wave approaches the shore, it changes shape. The bottom of a wave hits the shallow floor of the ocean and causes friction. This friction slows the bottom of the wave. However, the wave's crest keeps moving at the same speed. Eventually, the bottom of the wave moves too slowly to support the top of the wave. The crest outruns the trough, and the wave collapses. Water tumbles over on itself, and the wave breaks onto the shore. After a wave crashes, gravity pulls the water back to sea. The figure below shows how waves break.

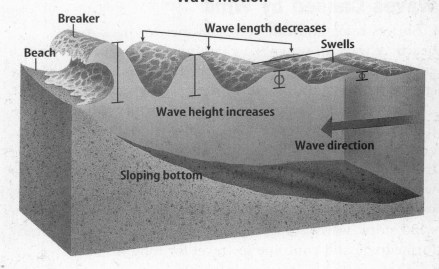

Wave Motion

On coasts that slope gently, waves deposit eroded sediments on shore, forming beaches. Beaches extend inland as far as the tides and waves are able to deposit sediments.

Waves usually hit the shore at slight angles. This creates a longshore current. Longshore currents move sideways, parallel to the shore. As a result, beach sediments are moved sideways. Longshore currents carry many metric tons of loose sediment from one beach to another.

☑ **Reading Check**

1. **Describe** How does a wave affect the position of a water molecule?

_____

_____

_____

Picture This

2. **Describe** What happens to wave lengths and wave heights as waves move toward the shore?

_____

_____

_____

Tides

During the day, the water level at the ocean's edge changes. This rise and fall in sea level is called a **tide.** A tide is a wave that can be thousands of kilometers long but only 1 m to 2 m high in the open ocean. As the crest of this wave approaches the shore, the sea level rises to form high tide. Later in the day, the trough of the wave reaches the shore and the sea level drops to form low tide. The difference between sea level at high tide and low tide is the tidal range. ☑

How are tides created?

Tides are created by the gravitational attraction of Earth and the Moon and of Earth and the Sun. Because the Moon is much closer to Earth, it has a stronger pull. The Moon's gravity pulls at Earth, including its bodies of water. This forms two bulges of water. One is on the side of Earth closest to the Moon, caused by the water's attraction to the Moon's gravitational pull. The other is on the side farthest away, created because the Moon is pulling Earth away from the water. These two places will have high tide. As Earth rotates, the bulges follow the Moon. This results in high tide happening around the world at different times.

What are spring tides and neap tides?

The Sun's gravity can increase or decrease the Moon's pull. When the Moon, Earth, and Sun line up, spring tides are created. During spring tides, high tides are higher and low tides are lower than usual. When the Moon, Earth, and the Sun form a right angle, high tides are lower and low tides are higher than usual. These are called neap tides. The different positions of the Moon, Earth, and the Sun during spring tides and neap tides are illustrated below.

Spring Tide

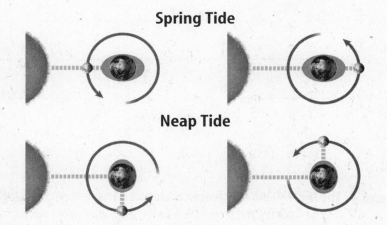

Neap Tide

✔ **Reading Check**

3. **Infer** Is a tide always as high as it is long?

_____

_____

Picture This

4. **Draw Conclusions** There are more floods during a spring tide than there are during a neap tide. Why do you think that is?

_____

_____

After You Read

Mini Glossary

tide: rhythmic rise and fall in sea level created by the gravitational attraction of Earth and the Moon, and Earth and the Sun

wave: in the ocean, the rhythmic movement that carries energy through water

1. Review the terms and their definitions in the Mini Glossary above. Then write a sentence using both vocabulary words.

   _____

   _____

2. Complete the cause-and-effect chart below to describe how the Moon's gravitational pull creates high and low tides.

CAUSE	EFFECT
The Moon is closer to Earth than the Sun.	The gravitational pull of the _____ is stronger than the pull of the _____ on Earth.
The Moon's gravity pulls at Earth.	Two _____ form in the ocean.
As Earth rotates, the bulges follow the Moon.	High _____ happens around _____ at different times.

3. You wrote down any questions you had about waves before you read. Were any of your questions answered in the text? If not, ask the class your questions.

   _____

   _____

   _____

End of
Section

Science Online Visit **in6.msscience.com** to access your textbook, interactive games, and projects to help you learn more about waves and tides.

 Oceans

section ④ Life in the Oceans

> **Standard—6.4.8:** Explain that in all environments ... organisms with similar needs may compete ... for resources, including food, space, and shelter.
> **Also covers:** 6.2.5, 6.2.6, 6.2.7, 6.4.9, 6.7.2

● Before You Read

What do you know about life in the ocean? Name some marine organisms that you've seen or would like to learn more about.

_____

_____

What You'll Learn

- types of plankton, nekton, and bottom dwellers
- the differences between producers, consumers, and decomposers
- ocean food chains

● Read to Learn

Types of Ocean Life

Many different kinds of organisms live in the ocean. Where the organism lives and how it moves classifies it as plankton, nekton, or a bottom dweller.

What are plankton?

<u>Plankton</u> are tiny marine organisms that drift in the surface waters of every ocean. Most plankton are one-celled, microscopic organisms. Eggs of ocean animals, very young fish, and larval jellyfish are plankton. ☑

What are nekton?

<u>Nekton</u> are marine animals that actively swim in ocean waters. Fish, whales, shrimp, turtles, and squid are examples of nekton. Nekton are found in all temperatures and depths of the ocean.

What are bottom dwellers?

Bottom dwellers are animals that live on the ocean floor. Bottom dwellers include crabs, snails, and sea urchins. They can swim or move along the floor searching for food. Some bottom dwellers, such as sponges and anemones, are permanently attached to the ocean floor. They must obtain food by filtering out particles from the seawater.

> **Mark the Text**
>
> **Underline** As you read, underline the definitions for nektons, planktons, and bottom dwellers.

> **Indiana Academic Standard Check**
>
> **6.4.8:** Explain that in all environments ... organisms with similar needs may compete ....
>
> ✔ **1. Define** How many cells do most plankton have?
>
> _____

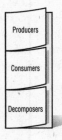

Think it Over

2. Draw Conclusions
Microscopic bacteria feed off decaying matter. Are they consumers or decomposers?

Ocean Ecosystems

No matter where an organism lives, it is part of an ecosystem. An **ecosystem** is a community of organisms, which includes producers, consumers, and decomposers, that interact with each other and their surroundings.

What are producers?

A **producer** is an organism that can make its own food. They are a food source for other organisms. Producers near the surface of the water contain chlorophyll and perform photosynthesis. These producers use sunlight and carbon dioxide to make food and oxygen.

Since sunlight cannot penetrate deep water, producers that live in deep water perform chemosynthesis. **Chemosynthesis** is a process in which bacteria make food from dissolved sulfur compounds. Chemosynthesis occurs most often along mid-ocean ridges. There, water is heated from gases, like sulfur, escaping through Earth's crust. Bacteria use the dissolved sulfur to produce food.

What are consumers and decomposers?

Consumers and decomposers depend on producers for survival. A **consumer** is an organism that gets its energy from eating other organisms. Consumers can use the energy stored in the cells of producers and other consumers. When producers and consumers die, decomposers digest them. **Decomposers** break down tissue and release nutrients and carbon dioxide back into the ecosystem. Bacteria are common decomposers.

What are food chains?

Throughout the ocean, energy is transferred from producers to consumers and decomposers through **food chains.** A food chain can start with microscopic algae. Microscopic animals eat the algae. These consumers are eaten by another consumer, the herring, which is eaten by a cod. Seals eventually feed on the cod. At each stage in the food chain, unused energy is passed from one organism to another. Most food chains are complicated. Usually, a species depends on more than one organism for food. Food chains that are complicated and interconnected are called food webs.

Ocean Nutrients

Nearly everything in an ecosystem is recycled. When organisms respire, or breathe, carbon dioxide is released back into the ecosystem. When organisms get rid of wastes, or die and decompose, nutrients are recycled. All organisms need certain nutrients to survive. Plants need nitrogen and phosphorous. Producer organisms need carbon dioxide to build tissue. These gases move through cycles through the ocean and between the ocean and the atmosphere. For example, carbon cycles through the ocean and between the ocean and the atmosphere. The illustration below shows this carbon cycle.

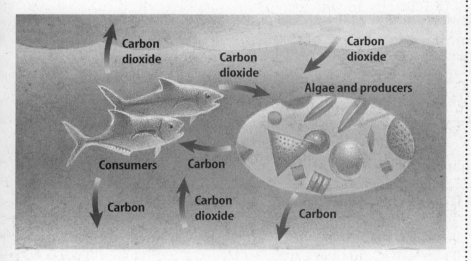

Carbon dioxide

Carbon dioxide

Carbon dioxide

Algae and producers

Consumers

Carbon

Carbon

Carbon dioxide

Carbon

Picture This

3. **Label** the nekton you see in the illustration.

How are nutrients recycled in coral reefs?

Coral reefs are ecosystems that need clear, warm, sunlit water. Each coral animal builds a hard capsule around its body using calcium it removes from seawater. Each capsule then cements to another, and a large colony called a reef is formed. Bottom dwellers and nekton move to the reef. Nearly 25 percent of all marine species and 20 percent of all fish live on coral reefs. Coral reefs can usually be found in tropical regions in water no deeper than 30 m. ☑

A healthy reef is a delicate balance. Producers, consumers, and decomposers all share a reef. They form a complex food web. Energy, nutrients, and gases are cycled among them all.

☑ Reading Check

4. **Define** Where are coral reefs usually found?

_____

_____

_____

● After You Read

Mini Glossary

chemosynthesis: process that occurs in deep ocean water in which bacteria make food from dissolved sulfur compounds

consumer: organism that gets its energy from eating other organisms

decomposer: organism that breaks down tissue and releases nutrients and carbon dioxide back into the ecosystem

ecosystem: community of organisms—producers, consumers, and decomposers—that interact with each other and their surroundings

food chain: series of stages that shows the transfer of energy from producers to consumers and decomposers

nekton: marine animals, such as fish and turtles, that actively swim in ocean waters

plankton: tiny marine organisms, such as eggs of ocean animals, that drift in the surface waters of every ocean

producer: organism that can make its own food by photosynthesis or chemosynthesis

1. Review the terms and their definitions in the Mini Glossary above. Then choose a term and write a sentence that includes an example of that term.

_____

_____

2. Complete the main idea chart below.

Plankton	Nekton	Bottom dwellers
Definition: _____ _____ _____	Definition: _____ _____ _____	Definition: _____ _____ _____
Example: _____	Example: _____	Example: _____

3. Did underlining the definitions for plankton, nekton, and bottom dwellers help you read the text more carefully? Pick a term and try to define it in your own words without looking back at the text. Then reread the text and see how well you did.

_____

_____

 Visit **in6.msscience.com** to access your textbook, interactive games, and projects to help you learn more about life in the oceans.

Rocks and Minerals

section ❶ Minerals—Earth's Jewels

Standard—6.3.14: Give examples of some minerals that are very rare and some that exist in great quantities. Explain how recycling ....
Also covers: 6.2.6

● Before You Read

Think about a gem, such as a diamond, and a rock that you have seen. How are gems and rocks the same and how are they different?

_____

_____

_____

● Read to Learn

What is a mineral?

Suppose you wanted to look for minerals (MIH nuh rulz). Would you have to crawl into a cave or go down into a mine to find them? No. You could find minerals just walking around outdoors. You can even find minerals in your home. Things you use every day, such as pots, glasses, and the salt you sprinkle on food, are all made from minerals. Minerals and products made from them are all around you.

How are minerals defined?

A **mineral** is a solid, inorganic material found in nature. Inorganic means that minerals are not made from living things such as plants or animals. Every mineral has its own particular chemical makeup and its own unique arrangement of atoms. An X-ray of a mineral would reveal the orderly arrangement of its atoms, often seen in the mineral's crystal structure. Every mineral's distinct crystal structure gives it unique properties. These properties can be used to identify minerals. So far, more than 4,000 minerals have been identified. **Rocks** usually are made up of two or more minerals.

What You'll Learn

- how rocks and minerals are different
- what properties are used to identify minerals

Study Coach

Sticky-note Discussions
As you read this section, use sticky notes to mark pages you find interesting or you have a question about. Share the information or question with another student in your class or your teacher.

FOLDABLES

Ⓐ Find Main Ideas Make a layered Foldable from four sheets of paper as shown to help you understand the properties of minerals.

Properties of Minerals
Crystals
cleavage and fracture
color
streak or luster
hardness
specific gravity
other properties

How do minerals form?

Minerals form in several ways. Some minerals form from melted rock inside Earth called magma. As magma cools, atoms combine in orderly patterns to form minerals. Minerals also form when magma reaches Earth's surface. Magma at Earth's surface is called lava.

Some minerals form from evaporation of water. For example, ocean water has salt dissolved in it. If the water evaporates, salt crystals remain. Many kinds of minerals are dissolved in water. When the water evaporates, the minerals form crystals.

Minerals also form from a process called precipitation (prih sih puh TAY shun). Water can hold only a certain amount of dissolved minerals. Any extra minerals separate from the water and fall out of solution. The extra minerals are deposited as crystals. For example, large areas of the ocean floor are covered with manganese nodules that formed in this way. The manganese fell out of solution and formed round deposits of manganese crystals.

What are some clues to mineral formation?

Sometimes just by looking at a mineral you can tell how it formed. Some minerals have large grains that fit together like the pieces of a puzzle. Large mineral grains usually form in open spaces within the rocks. They may have formed in these big spaces as magma cooled very slowly. When magma cools slowly, mineral grains have more time to grow.

Some crystals grow from solutions rich in dissolved minerals. To figure out how a mineral was formed, first look at the size of the mineral crystals, then look at how the crystals fit together.

Properties of Minerals

Imagine you are walking down the street. You think you see a friend walking ahead of you. The person is the same height and weight and has the same hair color as your friend. Is it your friend? Then the person turns around and you see her face and recognize her features right away. You've identified your friend by physical properties that set her apart from other people.

Each mineral also has unique properties. You can identify minerals by their unique properties in the same way you identify friends by their physical properties. ✔

✔ **Reading Check**

2. **Determine** What can be used to identify minerals?

_____

_____

What are crystals?

All minerals have an orderly pattern of atoms. These atoms are arranged in a repeating pattern. A **crystal** is a solid material that has an orderly, repeating pattern of atoms. Sometimes crystals have smooth growth surfaces, called crystal faces.

What are cleavage and fracture?

One clue to a mineral's identity is the way it breaks. Some minerals split into pieces with smooth, flat planes that reflect light. Minerals that break this way have cleavage (KLEE vihj). The mica in the figure below shows cleavage because it splits into thin sheets. ☑

Some minerals do not show cleavage when they break. These minerals break into uneven pieces with rough edges. Minerals that break into uneven chunks have fracture (FRAK chur). The figure below shows the fracture of the mineral flint.

✔ **Reading Check**

3. **Describe** If a mineral has cleavage, how does it break?

_____

_____

Mica

Flint

How does color help identify minerals?

Copper is a mineral that has a reddish-gold color. The reddish-gold color of a penny tells you it is made of copper. Sometimes a mineral's color helps you identify it.

Sometimes, though, a mineral's color can fool you. The common mineral pyrite (PI rite) has a shiny gold color similar to the color of the mineral gold. During the California Gold Rush of the 1800s, miners sometimes thought pyrite was gold. Pyrite has little value, while gold is extremely valuable.

While different minerals may look similar in color, the same mineral may be found in several different colors. For example, the mineral calcite can occur in different colors depending on what other materials are mixed in with it.

Picture This

4. **Compare** How is mica different from flint in the way it breaks?

_____

_____

_____

What are streak and luster?

Scraping a mineral across an unglazed white tile, called a streak plate, produces a streak of color. The color of a mineral's streak is another way to identify it. Oddly, a mineral's streak is not always the same color as the mineral itself. Yet a mineral's streak color is a more accurate way of identifying a mineral. For example, pyrite has a green-black or brown-black streak. Gold has a yellow streak. If the gold miners had used streak tests to identify the minerals they found, they might not have confused pyrite with gold.

Some minerals are shiny. Others are dull. Another property of minerals is luster. A mineral's luster describes how light reflects off its surface. If a mineral shines like metal, the mineral has a metallic (muh TA lihk) luster. A mineral with a nonmetallic luster looks dull, glassy, pearly, or earthy. Together, a mineral's color, streak, and luster help identify it. ☑

How is a mineral's hardness measured?

Some minerals are harder than others. Talc is a mineral that is so soft, it can be scratched with a fingernail. Diamond is the hardest mineral. Diamond can be used to scratch or cut almost anything else.

In 1822, Austrian geologist Friedrich Mohs developed a way to classify mineral hardness. The Mohs scale is shown in the figure below.

☑ **Reading Check**

5. **Identify** What is the term for the way a mineral reflects light?

_____

Picture This

6. **Analyze** Look at the table showing the Mohs scale. If harder minerals can scratch softer minerals, what mineral can gypsum scratch?

_____

Mohs Scale		
Mineral	**Hardness**	**Hardness of Common Objects**
Talc	1 (softest)	
Gypsum	2	fingernail (2.5)
Calcite	3	copper penny (3.0)
Fluorite	4	iron nail (4.5)
Apatite	5	glass (5.5)
Feldspar	6	steel file (6.5)
Quartz	7	streak plate (7)
Topaz	8	
Corundum	9	
Diamond	10 (hardest)	

How is the Mohs scale used?

A mineral with the number 1 on the Mohs scale is the softest mineral, talc. A mineral with the number 10 is the hardest mineral, diamond.

A mineral's hardness is determined by scratching it with other minerals. For example, fluorite (number 4 on the Mohs scale) will scratch calcite (number 3 on the Mohs scale). But fluorite cannot scratch apatite (number 5 on the Mohs scale).

You can use objects you have at home to determine a mineral's hardness. Look at the table on the previous page. The hardness of several common objects is listed. Using common objects can help you determine the hardness of the mineral. Knowing a mineral's hardness will help you identify that mineral.

What is specific gravity?

Imagine two 3 cm cubes. One is made out of wood and the other is made out of lead. Which one is heavier? Though both cubes are the same size, the lead cube is much heavier than the wooden cube. Some minerals are much heavier for their size than others. Specific gravity compares the weight of a mineral with the weight of an equal volume of water. For example, pyrite is about five times heavier than water. Pure gold is more than 19 times heavier than water. You could feel the difference by holding each one in your hand. Measuring specific gravity is another way you can identify minerals. ☑

What other properties help identify minerals?

Some minerals have other unusual properties that can help identify them. For example, the mineral magnetite acts like a magnet. A piece of magnetite will attract metal paper clips just like a magnet.

The mineral calcite has two unusual properties. When it comes into contact with an acid like dilute HCl, calcite begins to fizz. Calcite also changes a single ray of light into a double ray of light. If you look through a piece of calcite, you will see a double image.

Halite is a mineral that has a salty taste. Scientists sometimes use taste to identify a mineral. You should not do this because some minerals are harmful to the body. ☑

Together, all the properties you have read about are used to identify minerals. Learn to use them and you can identify most minerals you find.

✔ **Reading Check**

7. **Determine** Specific gravity compares the weight of a mineral with what ?

_____

_____

✔ **Reading Check**

8. **Identify** What unusual property does the mineral halite have?

_____

Common Minerals

Rocks that make up huge mountain ranges are made of minerals. But of the 4,000 known minerals, only a few make up most of the rocks. These minerals are known as the rock-forming minerals. If you learn to recognize these common minerals, you will be able to identify most rocks.

What are silicates?

Most rock-forming minerals are silicates (SIH luh kaytz). Silicates contain the elements silicon and oxygen. Quartz is a mineral that is pure silica (SiO_2). Feldspar is a silicate mineral in which silica is combined with iron. More than half of the minerals in Earth's crust are types of feldspar. ☑

What are carbonates?

Other important rock-forming minerals are carbonates. Carbonates are compounds containing the elements carbon and oxygen. The carbonate mineral calcite makes up most of the common rock limestone.

Other common minerals can be found in rocks formed on the bottom of ancient seas. When these seas evaporated, the mineral gypsum remained. Rocks that contain the mineral gypsum are found in many places.

The mineral halite, or rock salt, is found beneath the surface of much of the Midwest. The mineral halite formed when the ancient seas that covered the Midwest evaporated.

What are gems?

Which type of ring would you rather have—a quartz ring or a diamond ring? Of course, you would rather have a diamond ring. Diamond is a gem that is often used in jewelry. A **gem** is a rare, valuable mineral that can be cut and polished, giving it a beautiful appearance. To have the quality of a gem, a mineral must be clear. It should not have any flaws, defects, or cracks. A gem must also have a beautiful luster or color. Few minerals meet these high standards. That is why the ones that do are rare and valuable.

Why are gems so rare?

Gems are rare because they are made under special conditions. Scientists have learned to make synthetic diamonds by using very high pressure. This pressure is greater than any found in Earth's crust. For this reason, scientists think diamonds form deep inside Earth's mantle.

💡 **Think it Over**

10. Classify What qualities must a mineral have in order to be considered a gem?

_____

_____

_____

What are ores?

An <u>ore</u> is a mineral that contains enough of a useful substance that it can be mined and sold for a profit. Many metals that humans use every day come from ores. For example, the iron used to make steel comes from the mineral hematite. The lead used in batteries comes from galena, and the magnesium in vitamins comes from dolomite.

Ores of these useful metals must be removed from Earth in a process called mining. Mining is an expensive process. To offset the costs and be profitable, ores must be found in large deposits or rich veins.

How can minerals be conserved?

Because minerals often take millions of years to form, there are limited amounts of them in Earth's crust. As a result, minerals are considered a nonrenewable resource. For this reason, scrap metal is often reused or recycled. Old, used metal products are melted down and made into new products. Conserving metal in this way decreases the need for mining and saves mineral resources. Recycling also limits the amount of land that is disturbed by mining. Do you recycle? The figure below shows some common items collected and recycled.

How are ores processed?

After an ore is mined, it must be processed to remove the useful mineral or element. Smelting is the process used to obtain copper. In the smelting process, the ore is melted and unwanted materials are removed. After smelting, the copper is refined, or purified. Then it is made into many types of products used in homes, businesses, and industry. Copper products include electrical wiring, pots and pans, and most electronics. ✓

💡 **Think it Over**

11. **Apply** Why is it important to recycle metal products?

_____

_____

_____

✓ **Reading Check**

12. Name one everyday product that contains copper.

_____

● After You Read

Mini Glossary

crystal: solid material with atoms arranged in an orderly, repeating pattern

gem: rare, valuable mineral that can be cut and polished

mineral: solid, inorganic material found in nature that always has the same chemical makeup, atoms arranged in an orderly pattern, and unique properties

ore: material that contains enough of a useful metal that it can be mined and sold for a profit

rock: solid inorganic material that is usually made up of two or more minerals

1. Review the terms and their definitions in the Mini Glossary. Write one sentence about minerals. Use at least two terms in your sentence.

_____

_____

_____

2. Compare minerals and gems using this Venn diagram.

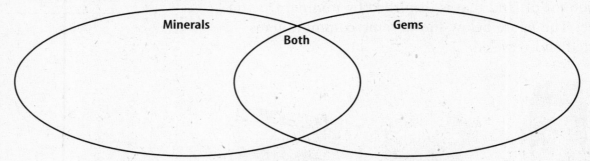

Minerals   Both   Gems

3. As you read, you used sticky notes to mark interesting pages or questions. How did this strategy help you understand the information you learned about minerals?

_____

_____

End of Section

Science Online Visit **in6.msscience.com** to access your textbook, interactive games, and projects to help you learn more about minerals.

section ❷ Igneous and Sedimentary Rocks

> **Standard—6.3.14:** Give examples of some minerals that are very rare and some that exist in great quantities. Explain how recycling ....

● Before You Read

Think about an erupting volcano. Often, there is red-hot material exploding out of it. What do you think happens to the material when it cools?

_____

_____

● Read to Learn

Igneous Rock

Rocks are constantly changing. Slowly, over time, rocks are worn away and new rocks form. These processes produce the three main kinds of rocks—igneous, sedimentary, and metamorphic.

Deep inside Earth, it is hot enough to melt rock. **Igneous** (IHG nee us) **rock** forms when melted rock from inside Earth cools and hardens. When melted rock material cools on Earth's surface, it is called **extrusive** (ehk STREW sihv) igneous rock. When melted rock material cools beneath Earth's surface, it is called **intrusive** (ihn TREW sihv) igneous rock.

What is igneous rock made from?

The chemicals in the melted rock determine the color of the rock that forms. Melted rock that contains a lot of silica will produce an igneous rock with a light color. Light-colored igneous rocks are call granitic (gra NIH tihk) rocks. Melted rock that contains more iron, magnesium, or calcium, will produce an igneous rock that has a dark color. Dark-colored igneous rocks are called basaltic (buh SAWL tihk) rocks. Intrusive igneous rocks are often granitic. Extrusive igneous rocks are often basaltic.

What You'll Learn

- how intrusive and extrusive igneous rocks are different
- how different types of sedimentary rocks form

▸ **Study Coach**

Two Column Notes As you read, organize your notes in two columns. In the left column, write the main ideas of each paragraph. Next to it, in the right column, write details about it.

FOLDABLES™

Ⓑ Classify Make the following Foldable to help you organize information about rocks made from lava and magma.

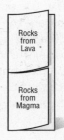

Rocks from Lava

Rocks from Magma

How do rocks form from lava?

When melted rock reaches Earth's surface, it is called lava. Extrusive igneous rocks form from lava that cools on Earth's surface. Since lava cools quickly, large mineral crystals, or grains, do not have time to form. As a result, extrusive igneous rocks usually have small mineral crystals that are hard to see and a smooth, sometimes glassy, appearance.

Extrusive igneous rocks can form in two ways. They may form when a volcano erupts and shoots lava and ash into the air or onto the surface. Extrusive igneous rocks also may form from cracks in Earth's crust called fissures (FIH shurz). When a fissure opens, lava oozes out onto the ground or into water. This is called a lava flow.

How do rocks form from magma?

Melted rock inside Earth is called magma. Intrusive igneous rock forms when magma cools below the surface of Earth. They form when a huge glob of magma inside Earth is forced upward but never reaches the surface. The glob of magma sits under the surface and cools slowly. Over millions of years, the magma cools and hardens into igneous rock. The cooling process is so slow, minerals in the magma have time to form large crystals. The figure below shows where intrusive and extrusive igneous rocks form around a volcano.

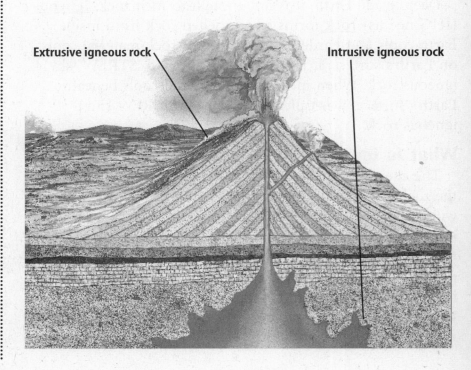

Extrusive igneous rock

Intrusive igneous rock

Think it Over

1. **Describe** What would you look for to determine if a rock is an intrusive or an extrusive igneous rock?

_____

_____

_____

Picture This

2. **Identify** Use a blue pencil to trace the path of the magma to the area where the extrusive igneous rock forms. Use a red pencil to circle the area where the intrusive igneous rock forms.

Sedimentary Rocks

Tiny pieces of rock, shells, mineral grains, and other materials are called sediment (SE duh munt). For example, the sand at the beach is a type of sediment.

Sediment is made and transported in several ways. Wind, water, and ice break down pieces of rock or rock mineral grains. Wind, water, and ice can also carry these sediments from one place to another. When the sediments settle, they form a thin layer. **Sedimentary** (sed uh MEN tuh ree) **rock** is made from sediment that collected in layers to form rock layers. It takes many thousands or even millions of years for sedimentary rock to form. Because rock is being worn away all the time, sedimentary rock forms continuously. There are three main categories of sedimentary rock—detrital, chemical, and organic.

How are detrital rocks formed?

Some sedimentary rocks are made of mineral grains or tiny pieces of rocks that have been worn away by wind, water, or ice. Sedimentary rocks that form from tiny mineral grains or other rock particles are called detrital (dih TRI tuhl) sedimentary rocks. Wind, gravity, ice, or water carry these tiny particles of sediment and deposit them in layers. Layer upon layer of mineral grain sediment is deposited. As the layers pile up, top layers press down, or compact, lower layers. Other minerals dissolved in water act like cement to bind the layers of sediment together into rock. Sandstone is a common detrital sedimentary rock.

How are detrital rocks identified?

To identify detrital sedimentary rock, you use the size of the grains that make up the rock. The smallest, clay-sized grains feel slippery when they are wet. These clay-sized grains make up a rock called shale.

Silt-sized grains are slightly larger than clay-sized grains and feel rough. Siltstone is a detrital sedimentary rock made up of silt-sized grains.

Sand-sized grains are even larger. Rough sedimentary rocks, such as sandstone, are made of sand-sized grains.

The roughest detrital sedimentary rock is made up of pebbles. Pebbles that are mixed and cemented together with other sediments form detrital rocks called conglomerates (kun GLAHM ruts).

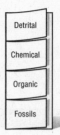
Think it Over

3. **Classify** Write the four grain sizes in order from smallest to largest.

_____

_____

_____

_____

How do chemical sedimentary rocks form?

Chemical sedimentary rocks can form in different ways. Sometimes chemical sedimentary rocks form from ocean water that is rich in minerals. When the water evaporates, mineral layers are left behind. Over time, the layers form chemical sedimentary rock.

Some chemical rocks form from geysers or hot springs. At a geyser or hot spring, hot, mineral-rich water reaches the surface from deep underground. As the hot water evaporates on the surface, layers of minerals are left behind. Eventually, the layers of minerals form chemical sedimentary rocks. ✔

Have you ever sat in the Sun after swimming in the ocean? If you have, you may have noticed tiny crystals forming on your skin as the Sun warms and dries you. When the ocean water on your skin evaporated, it left behind crystals of salt, or halite. The halite was dissolved in the ocean water. When the water evaporated, mineral crystals remained.

How do organic sedimentary rocks form?

Think about the chalk your teacher uses to write on the chalkboard. Did you know that chalk may also be a sedimentary rock? Another sedimentary rock is the coal that is used as a fuel to produce electricity.

Chalk and coal are examples of organic sedimentary rocks. When living matter dies, the remains pile up in layers. Over millions of years, the layers are pressed together to form rock. If the rock is formed from layers of dead plant material, then coal forms. If the rock is formed from layers of dead animal material, such as bits of seashells, then chalk may form. Organic sedimentary rock made from seashells in the ocean can also form limestone. ✔

Are fossils found in sedimentary rocks?

Chalk, limestone, and other types of organic sedimentary rocks are made from the fossils of millions of tiny organisms. Fossils are the remains or traces of once-living plants and animals. Often, the fossils in organic sedimentary rock are extremely small. But sometimes, the fossils are large and reveal much of the body of the once-living plant or animal. For example, dinosaur bones and footprints are fossils that have been found in sedimentary rocks.

✔ **Reading Check**

4. Draw Conclusions
What must happen to water in order for its dissolved minerals to be deposited?

_____

_____

✔ **Reading Check**

5. Identify What organic material forms coal?

_____

_____

● After You Read

Mini Glossary

extrusive: igneous rocks that have small or no crystals and form when melted rock cools quickly on Earth's surface

igneous rock: intrusive or extrusive rock that forms when melted rock from inside Earth cools and hardens

intrusive: igneous rocks that usually contain large crystals and form when magma cools slowly beneath Earth's surface

sedimentary rock: type of rock made from pieces of other rocks, dissolved minerals, or plant and animal matter that collect to form rock layers

1. Review the terms and their definitions in the Mini Glossary. Then write one sentence about igneous rock and one sentence about sedimentary rock.

_____

_____

_____

2. Fill in the blanks in the boxes below.

```
                        ┌──────────────────────┐
                        │  TWO TYPES OF ROCK   │
                        └──────────────────────┘
        ┌─────────────────────────┐        ┌─────────────────────────┐
        │ _____ │        │ _____ │
        │ rock forms from magma   │        │ rock forms from layers  │
        │ deep inside Earth.      │        │ of sediment.            │
        └─────────────────────────┘        └─────────────────────────┘
```

| _____ _____ forms from cooling lava on the surface. | _____ _____ forms from cooling magma underground. | _____ _____ forms from mineral grains or tiny parts of rock. | _____ _____ forms from mineral dissolved in water that evaporates. | _____ _____ forms from the remains of once-living plants and animals. |

3. Did the two column notes you made help you understand the information about sedimentary rock? Would you use this strategy again to learn new information?

_____

_____

Science Online Visit **in6.msscience.com** to access your textbook, interactive games, and projects to help you learn more about igneous and sedimentary rocks.

End of Section

Rocks and Minerals

section ❸ Metamorphic Rocks and the Rock Cycle

Standard—6.2.5: Organize information in simple tables and graphs and identify relationships they reveal. Use tables and graphs ....

What You'll Learn
- the conditions needed for metamorphic rock to form
- that all rocks are linked by the rock cycle

● Before You Read

Imagine that someone leaves a hat on a chair and you accidentally sit on it. Describe how the pressure of your body changes the hat.

_____

_____

_____

Mark the Text

Underline As you read, underline the key words and ideas in each paragraph to help you understand new information.

● Read to Learn

New Rock from Old Rock

Rocks on Earth are constantly changing because of different physical processes. Sedimentary rocks are formed by low temperature processes that break down and wear away bits of rock. Igneous rocks are formed by high temperature conditions that form molten rock material. There are other conditions on Earth that also produce new rocks.

How do pressure and temperature change rock?

Deep inside Earth, rock is under great pressure. Just as the pressure of your body can change a hat you sit on, pressure inside Earth can cause certain changes in rock. Changes in pressure and temperature can change the chemicals that make up rock and the size of the mineral grains in rock.

It can take millions of years for rocks to change. It may take that long for pressure to build up while rocks are buried deeply or continents collide. Sometimes rocks are cooked by magma moving up into Earth's crust. The heat of the magma doesn't melt the rock, but it does change the rock's mineral crystals. All these events make new rock out of old rock.

FOLDABLES

D Organize Make the following Foldable to help you understand how rocks change.

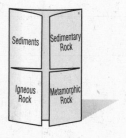

How do metamorphic rocks form?

Do you recycle your plastic milk jugs? Have you ever thought about what happens to these jugs after you put them in the recycling bin? First the jugs are collected, sorted, and cleaned. Then they are heated and squeezed into pellets. The pellets later can be made into useful new products.

Rocks are recycled too, in a process that takes millions of years. Most rocks are recycled deep inside Earth, where great pressure and high temperatures process them into new rocks. **Metamorphic** (me tuh MOR fihk) **rock** is new rock that forms when existing rock is heated or squeezed, but not melted. The new rock that forms not only looks different, but it might be chemically changed, too. Sometimes the minerals in the new rock line up in a distinct way. ☑

The word *metamorphic* means "change of form." This is a good word for rocks that get a new look when they are under great pressure and high temperature.

How are metamorphic rocks grouped?

New metamorphic rocks can form from any other type of rock—sedimentary, igneous, or even other metamorphic rock. One way to identify and group rock is by its texture. A rock's texture is a physical property that refers to how the rock looks. Texture helps to divide metamorphic rock into two main groups—foliated (FOH lee ay tud) and nonfoliated.

What are foliated rocks?

Foliated rocks have visible layers of minerals. The word *foliated* comes from a Latin word that means "leafy." Foliated minerals have been heated and squeezed into layers, like the pages, or leaves, of a book. Many foliated rocks have bands of different-colored minerals. Slate, gneiss (NISE), phyllite (FIH lite), and schist (SHIHST) are examples of foliated rocks. Some walkways and roofs are made of slate, a foliated metamorphic rock. ☑

What are nonfoliated rocks?

Nonfoliated rocks do not have distinct layers or bands. They are usually more evenly colored than foliated rocks. Often mineral grains can't be seen in nonfoliated rocks. If the mineral grains are visible at all, they are not lined up in any particular way. Soapstone and marble are nonfoliated rocks. Quartzite is a nonfoliated rock made from quartz sand grains. When the sand grains are squeezed and heated, they form the new kind of crystals found in quartzite.

✔ **Reading Check**

1. **Identify** What type of rock forms when existing rock is heated or squeezed?

_____

✔ **Reading Check**

2. **Identify** What would you look for to identify a foliated rock?

_____

_____

The Rock Cycle

Rocks are constantly changing from one type to another. Scientists have made a model to show how all rocks are related to one another and how different processes constantly change rocks. The **rock cycle** is the model that shows the slow continuing process of rocks changing from one type to another. Every rock on Earth is on an endless journey through the rock cycle. A rock's trip through the rock cycle can take millions of years. The rock cycle is shown below.

Picture This

3. Circle the three types of rock in the Rock Cycle.

The Rock Cycle

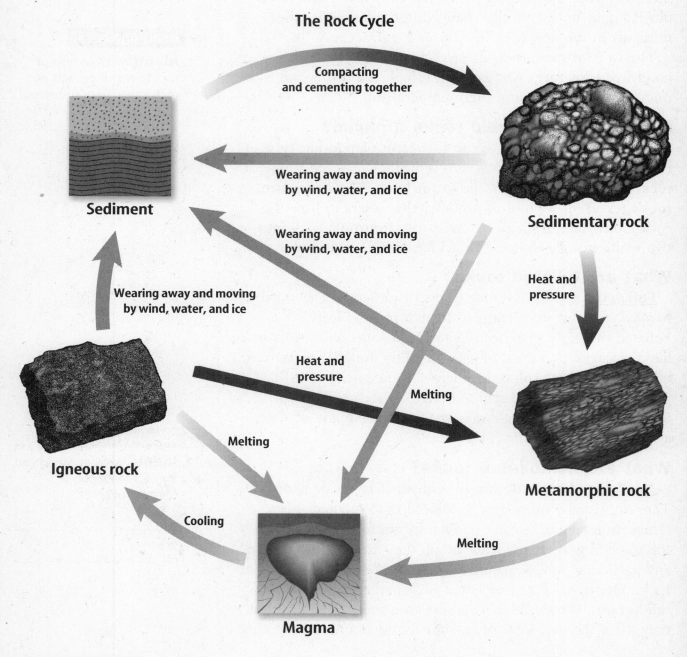

Compacting and cementing together

Sediment

Wearing away and moving by wind, water, and ice

Wearing away and moving by wind, water, and ice

Sedimentary rock

Heat and pressure

Wearing away and moving by wind, water, and ice

Heat and pressure

Melting

Igneous rock

Melting

Cooling

Melting

Metamorphic rock

Magma

What is the journey of a rock?

Look at the figure of the rock cycle on the previous page. Pick any spot on the rock cycle model. What form of rock is on the spot you chose? From that spot, follow the rock through the rock cycle. Notice the processes that act on the rock and change it. These processes include heat and pressure, wearing away, moving, melting, cooling, compacting, and cementing together. Look at the types of rock they become through these different processes. You can see that any rock can turn into any other type of rock.

What forms from magma?

Now start tracing the rock cycle from the magma at the bottom of the figure. The magma rises to the surface as a glob of lava. The lava cools and forms an igneous rock.

What changes igneous rock?

Wind, rain, and ice slowly wear away bits of the igneous rock, breaking off some of its tiny mineral grains, or sediment. The sediment is carried by the wind or by a river or maybe even by ice. Eventually, the sediment is deposited in thin layers. Over time, the layers build up. The weight of the top layers presses down on lower layers compacting them. The pressure acts like glue, cementing the layers together to form a sedimentary rock.

What other changes occur?

Deep inside Earth, the sedimentary rock is under great pressure and high temperature. Slowly, over millions of years, the sedimentary rock is changed into metamorphic rock. The metamorphic rock may eventually be melted to form magma. When magma cools below Earth's surface, intrusive igneous rock forms. When magma explodes out of a volcano and lava flows onto Earth's surface, extrusive igneous rock forms.

The cycle of change continues. The processes that are part of the rock cycle change rocks slowly over time. These processes are taking place right now.

Think it Over

4. **Think Critically** Is magma the source of all rocks on Earth? Explain your answer.

_____

_____

_____

Think it Over

5. **Predict** How can one sedimentary rock be changed into another sedimentary rock?

_____

_____

_____

● After You Read

Mini Glossary

foliated: metamorphic rocks that have visible layers of mineral
metamorphic rock: new rock that forms when existing rock is heated or squeezed

nonfoliated: metamorphic rocks that do not have distinct layers or bands
rock cycle: model that shows the slow continuing process of rocks changing from one type to another

1. Review the terms and their definitions in the Mini Glossary. Then write one sentence about metamorphic rocks. Use at least two vocabulary words in your sentences.

_____

_____

2. Fill in the blanks in the chart below to show how rocks change.

The Rock Cycle

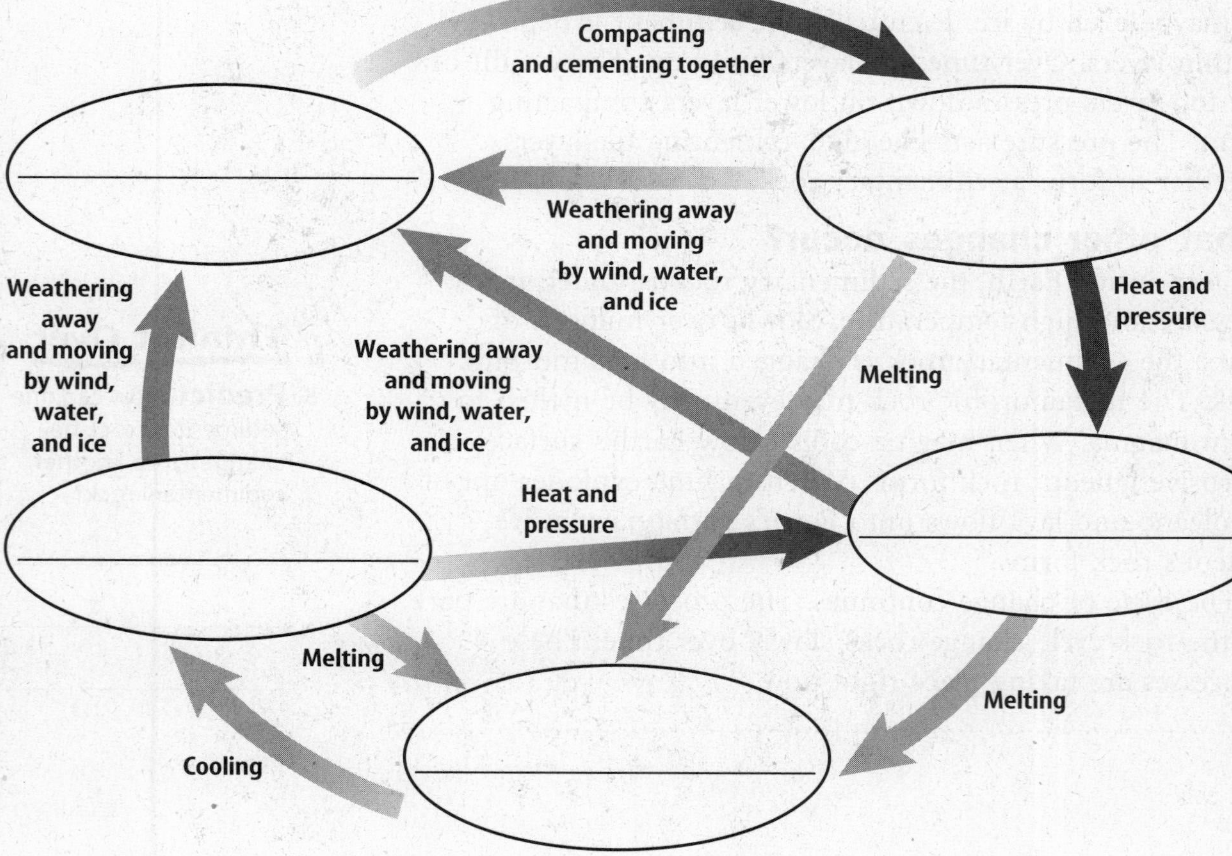

Compacting and cementing together

Weathering away and moving by wind, water, and ice

Weathering away and moving by wind, water, and ice

Weathering away and moving by wind, water, and ice

Heat and pressure

Melting

Heat and pressure

Melting

Melting

Cooling

Science Online Visit **in6.msscience.com** to access your textbook, interactive games, and projects to help you learn more about metamorphic rocks and the rock cycle.

Weathering and Erosion

section ❶ Weathering and Soil Formation

 Standard—6.3.15: ... the composition and texture of soil and its fertility and resistance to erosion are greatly influenced by plant roots and debris ....

⬤ Before You Read

Have you ever heard someone describe something as weathered? On the lines below, describe how a weathered object might look.

_____

_____

_____

⬤ Read to Learn

Weathering

Have you seen potholes in roadways and broken concrete in sidewalks and curbs? Potholes in roads and broken side-walks are proof that solid materials can be changed by nature. **Weathering** is a mechanical or chemical process that causes rocks to change by breaking them down into smaller pieces. Rocks can be changed by freezing and thawing, by oxygen in the air, and even sometimes by plants and animals. These things cause rocks to weather and, in some cases, to become soils.

Mechanical Weathering

When a sidewalk breaks apart, a large slab of concrete is broken into many small pieces. The concrete looks the same. It's just broken apart. This is like mechanical weathering of rocks. **Mechanical weathering** is a process that breaks rocks into smaller pieces without changing them chemically. The small pieces of rock are the same as the original rock. There are many causes for mechanical weathering, including ice wedging and living organisms.

What You'll Learn
- processes that break rock apart
- processes that chemically change rock
- how soil forms

Mark the Text

Highlight Highlight the key terms and their meanings as you read this section.

FOLDABLES

A Compare Make a two-tab Foldable as shown below to compare weathering and erosion.

Mechanical Weathering

Chemical Weathering

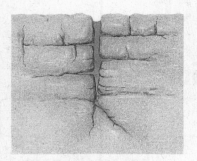
1. Water seeps into cracks.

2. Water freezes and expands, opening cracks.

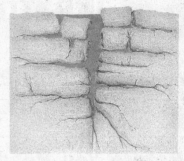
3. Ice melts and the process repeats.

Picture This

1. **Highlight** the areas in each figure where water fills in the cracks. What do you notice about the spaces between the rocks in figures 1 and 3?

_____

_____

_____

What is ice wedging?

In some parts of the world, air temperature drops low enough to freeze water. Then, when the temperature rises, the ice thaws. This freezing and thawing cycle breaks up rocks. How can this happen? The figure above shows this process. When it rains or snow melts, water seeps into cracks in rocks. If the temperature drops below freezing, ice forms. As the ice forms, its takes up more space than the water did. That's because water expands when it freezes. As it expands, it puts pressure on the rocks. With enough force, the rocks will crack more. In time, they will break apart. Ice wedging causes potholes to form in roadways.

How do plants and animals cause weathering?

Plants and animals can cause mechanical weathering, too. Plants can grow in the most unlikely places. Sometimes their roots grow deep into cracks in rock where water collects. This puts pressure inside the rock and slowly wedges the rock apart.

Gophers, prairie dogs, and other animals that dig in the ground also cause mechanical weathering. As they burrow through sediment or soft sedimentary rock, these animals break rock apart. Sometimes as they dig, they push rock and sediment to the surface. At the surface, another kind of weathering, called chemical weathering, takes place.

Chemical Weathering

<u>Chemical weathering</u> is a process in which the chemical makeup of rock is changed. This kind of weathering is rapid in tropical areas where it is moist and warm most of the time. On the other hand, in areas that are dry or cold, chemical weathering occurs slowly. ☑

☑ **Reading Check**

2. **Identify** What does chemical weathering change in rock?

_____

Rates of Weathering	
Climate	Chemical Weathering
Hot and dry	Slow
Hot and wet	Fast
Cold and dry	Slow
Cold and wet	Slow

Think it Over

3. **Explain** What two conditions speed up the process of chemical weathering?

_____

_____

What causes chemical weathering?

The table above shows the rates of chemical weathering in areas with different climates. You have read that temperature and rainfall are important factors in how quickly chemical weathering occurs. But what causes the process of chemical weathering to begin? Two main causes of chemical weathering are natural acids and oxygen.

How do natural acids affect rocks?

Some rocks react with natural acids in the environment. For example, when water mixes with carbon dioxide in the air or soil, carbonic acid forms. Carbonic acid can change the chemical makeup of rocks. Even though carbonic acid is weak, it reacts with many rocks. When carbonic acid comes in contact with rocks like limestone, dolomite, and marble, they dissolve. Other rocks also weather when exposed to carbonic acid.

How do plant acids affect rocks?

Plant roots also produce acid that reacts with rocks. Many plants produce a substance called tannin. When water and tannin mix, they form tannic acid. This acid dissolves some minerals in rock. When that happens, the rest of the rock is weakened. Over time, it can break into smaller pieces.

How does oxygen affect rocks?

When you see rusty cars, red soil, or red stains on rocks, you are seeing oxidation. Oxidation is the effects of chemical changes caused by oxygen. Oxygen reacts with iron in materials like steel, causing these materials to rust and weaken. Rocks chemically weather in a similar way. When some iron-containing minerals are exposed to oxygen, they can weather into minerals that are like rust. This leaves the rock weakened, and it can break apart. ☑

Reading Check

4. **Identify** What can oxygen do to materials that have iron in them?

_____

_____

6.3.15: … the composition and texture of soil and its fertility and resistance to erosion are greatly influenced by plant roots ….

✔ **5. Identify** What does soil contain besides rock, water, and air?

_____

Picture This

6. Explain Do you think mountaintops have rich soil or poor soil? Why?

_____

_____

_____

FOLDABLES

B Explain Make a half-book Foldable from notebook paper to explain soil formation and types of soil.

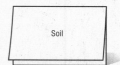

Soil

Is soil just dirt under your feet, or does it have more value? <u>Soil</u> is a mixture of weathered rock, organic matter, water, and air that supports the growth of plant life. Organic matter is rotted leaves, twigs, roots, and other material. Many things affect the way soil forms including the parent rock, the slope of the land, time, climate, and organisms. ☑

How does parent rock affect soil?

One factor that affects soil formation is the type of parent rock, or original rock, that is being weathered. For example, in places where limestone is chemically weathered, clay soil is common. That's because clay is left behind when the limestone dissolves. In places where sandstone is weathered, sandy soil forms.

How does the slope of the land affect soil?

The <u>topography,</u> or surface features, of the land also influence the types of soils that form. On steep hillsides, like those in the figure below, soil has little chance of forming. That's because rock fragments move downhill all of the time. However, in areas where the land is flat, wind and water deposit fine sediments that help form thick soils.

How does time affect soil?

It takes time for rocks to weather. It can take thousands of years for some soils to form. As soils develop, they become less like the rock from which they formed. In young soils, the parent rock determines the characteristics of the soil. As weathering goes on, however, the soil is less and less like the parent rock. Deep, rich soils are found in some places where the weathering has gone on for a long time. For deep soils to form, soil materials must build up slowly on the land and not be eroded.

How does climate affect soil?

Climate affects soil changes, too. If rock weathers rapidly, deep soils can form quickly. This is more likely to happen in tropical areas where the climate is warm and moist.

Climate also affects the amount of organic material in soil. In desert climates, soils contain little organic material. But in warm, humid climates, there is a lot of organic material.

When plants and animals die, they begin to decay. Eventually, humus is formed. Humus is a dark material that helps soil hold water and provides nutrients for plants. A humus-rich soil layer is shown in the figure below.

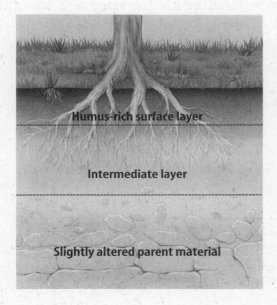

Humus-rich surface layer

Intermediate layer

Slightly altered parent material

Picture This

7. Identify Circle the layer of humus in the figure.

How do organisms affect soil?

Organisms also affect how soil forms. Lichens are small organisms that consist of an alga and a fungus. You may have seen lichens as colorful patches on trees or rocks. Lichens can grow directly on rock. As they grow, they take nutrients from the rock that they are breaking down and form a thin soil. After soil has formed, many other plants can grow, including trees and grasses. ☑

The roots of the plants break down more of the parent rock. Dead plant material, such as leaves, builds up. This adds organic matter to the soil. Some plants provide more organic matter to soil than others. Soil under grassy areas often is richer than soil in forests. Much of the midwestern United States used to be grasslands. This is why it is now some of the best farmland in the country.

☑ Reading Check

8. Explain If lichens grow directly on rock, where do they get nutrients?

_____

_____

_____

● After You Read

Mini Glossary

chemical weathering: process in which the chemical makeup of rock is changed

mechanical weathering: process that breaks rocks into smaller pieces without changing them chemically

soil: mixture of weathered rock, organic matter, water, and air that supports the growth of plant life

topography: surface features of the land that influence the types of soils that form

weathering: mechanical or chemical process that causes rocks to change by breaking them down into smaller pieces

1. Review the terms and their definitions in the Mini Glossary. Then write two sentences explaining how mechanical and chemical weathering are the same and how they are different.

_____

_____

_____

2. Complete the following table by adding the missing information.

Factors That Affect Soil	Mechanical Weathering	Chemical Weathering
Ice wedging		No
Plants		Yes
Animals	Yes	
Natural acids	No	
Plant acids		Yes
Oxygen		

End of Section

Science Online Visit **in6.msscience.com** to access your textbook, interactive games, and projects to help you learn more about weathering and soil.

Weathering and Erosion

section ❷ Erosion of Earth's Surface

 Standard—6.2.7: Locate information in reference books, back issues of newspapers and magazines, CD-ROMs, and computer databases.

● Before You Read

Have you ever seen a flood or a picture of a flood? On the lines below, describe how the water looked.

_____

_____

_____

● Read to Learn

Agents of Erosion

Imagine looking over the rim of the Grand Canyon. Far below is the winding Colorado River. Imagine watching a sunset over Utah's famous arches. These stunning views are examples of Earth's natural beauty. But how do canyons and arches form in solid rock?

These and other landforms are a result of erosion of Earth's surface. **Erosion** is the movement of rock or soil by forces like gravity, ice, wind, and water.

Gravity

Gravity is a force that pulls objects toward other objects. Gravity pulls everything on Earth toward Earth's center. As a result, water flows down hills. Rocks tumble down slopes. When gravity alone causes rock or sediment to move down a slope, the erosion is called **mass movement.**

Mass movements can occur anywhere there are hills or mountains. One place they often occur is near volcanoes. Creep, slump, rock slides, and mudflows are four types of mass movements. They are all caused by gravity.

What You'll Learn

■ what causes erosion
■ the effects of erosion

Study Coach

Make Flash Cards As you read this section, make flash cards for each vocabulary term or unknown word. On one side of the card, write the term or word. On the other side of the card, write the definition.

FOLDABLES

C **Compare and Contrast** Make the four-tab Foldable as shown below. Use it to record information on causes of erosion.

What is creep?

<u>Creep</u> is the process in which sediments move slowly downhill. Creep is common where freezing and thawing occur. As ice expands in soil, it pushes sediments up. Then as soil thaws, the sediments move farther down the slope. The figure below shows how creep can move large amounts of sediment down a slope. Sometimes, creep causes damage to structures.

Picture This

1. Trace over the arrow that shows the direction the soil and sediment are moving.

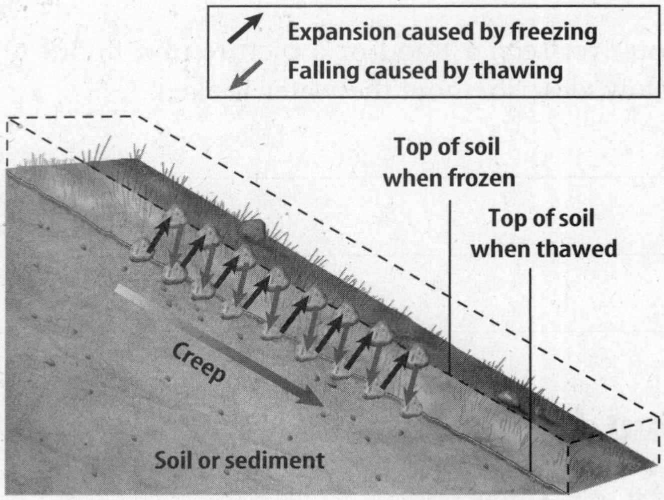

↗ Expansion caused by freezing
↙ Falling caused by thawing

Top of soil when frozen

Top of soil when thawed

Creep

Soil or sediment

What is slump?

A <u>slump</u> occurs when a mass of rock or sediment moves downhill along a curved surface. Slumps are most common in thick layers of loose sediment. They also can form in sedimentary rock. Slumps often occur on slopes that have been worn away by erosion. This often happens at the base of cliffs that have been worn away by waves. Slumps of this kind are common along the coast of Southern California, where they threaten to destroy homes and other buildings. ☑

What is a rock slide?

Can you imagine millions of cubic meters of rock roaring down a mountain at speeds faster than 250 km/h? That is about as fast as a small plane flies. This can happen when a rock slide occurs. During a rock slide, layers of rock break loose from slopes and slide to the bottom. The rock layers often bounce and break apart as they move. This makes a huge, jumbled pile of rocks at the bottom of the slope. Rock slides can destroy whole villages and cause hazards on mountain roads.

2. Identify What occurs when a mass of rock or sediment moves downhill along a curved surface?

What are mudflows?

Mudflows can occur where heavy rains or melting snow and ice soak the soil. A mudflow is a mass of wet sediment that flows downhill on top of the ground. Some mudflows are thick. As a result, they flow slowly and only move a few meters per day. Other mudflows are more fluid and move downhill at speeds close to 160 km/h. Fast-moving mudflows are common on some volcanoes.

Ice

In some parts of the world, ice causes erosion. In cold regions, more snow might fall than melt. Over many years, the snow can build up to form large, deep masses of ice called glaciers. When the ice in a glacier becomes thick enough, its own weight makes it flow downhill. It moves because of gravity. As glaciers move over the land, they erode materials from some areas and deposit them in other areas.

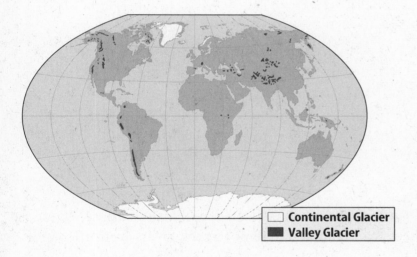

☐ **Continental Glacier**
■ **Valley Glacier**

The figure above shows where two kinds of glaciers, continental glaciers and valley glaciers, are found. Continental glaciers are huge ice sheets that can bury whole mountains. They once covered wide areas of Earth, but today they are found just in polar regions. Continental glaciers cover about ten percent of the land. ☑

Valley glaciers are much smaller. They are found in high mountains where the temperature isn't warm enough to melt the ice sheets. Most of the time, these ice sheets only move 0.01 to 2.0 meters per day. But at times, they can flow up to 100 meters per day.

Applying Math

3. Calculate A rock slide may move 250 km/h. A mudflow may move 160 km/h. How much faster might a rock slide be than a mudflow?

_____

_____

Picture This

4. Locate and Infer Outline areas where continental glaciers are found. Why do you think these are the only areas that have continental glaciers?

_____

_____

✔ **Reading Check**

5. Identify Name the two kinds of glaciers.

_____

_____

How do glaciers cause erosion?

Glaciers can erode rocks in two ways. If the rock under the glacier has cracks in it, the ice can pull out pieces of rock. This causes the rock to erode slowly. Loose pieces of rock freeze into the bottom of the glacier and are dragged along as the glacier moves.

As the rock fragments are dragged over Earth's surface, they scratch the rock below like sheets of sandpaper. This scratching is the second way that glaciers can erode rock. Scratching makes grooves in the rock underneath and can wear rock into a fine powder called rock flour.

How do glaciers change the land?

Glacial erosion is a powerful force that shapes the land. In mountains, valley glaciers can move rock from mountaintops. This forms large bowls, called cirques (SURKS), and steep peaks. When a valley glacier moves into a stream valley, it erodes rock along the valley sides. That makes a wider, U-shaped valley. These features are shown in the figure below.

Picture This

6. Identify Circle the cirque in the figure. Highlight the U-shaped valley.

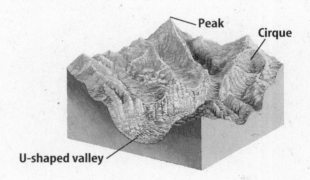

Peak

Cirque

U-shaped valley

Continental glaciers also shape Earth's surface. These ice sheets can completely remove rock layers from the land.

What do glaciers deposit?

Glaciers can deposit sediments. When ice melts from a glacier, the sediment it was carrying gets left behind. This sediment dropped from the ice is called till. Till is a mix of soil and rock particles, ranging in size from small bits of clay to large boulders. ☑

In summer, a lot of melting occurs around glaciers. So much ice can melt that streams often flow away from the glacier. These streams carry and drop sediment. The sand and gravel dropped by streams flowing from glaciers are called outwash. Unlike till, outwash usually is made up of particles of rock that are all about the same size.

Reading Check

7. Identify What is the term for sediment that is dropped from the ice of a glacier?

_____

Wind

If you've had sand blow into your eyes, you understand wind as a cause of erosion. When wind blows across loose sediment, it lifts and carries it. Wind leaves behind particles that are too heavy to move. The erosion of the land by wind is called **deflation**. Deflation can lower the land's surface by several meters.

Wind that is carrying sediment can wear down rocks. It works just like a sandblaster. **Abrasion** is a form of erosion that occurs when wind blows sediments into rocks, makes pits in the rocks, and produces smooth, polished surfaces. ☑️

How does wind deposit sediment?

When wind blows around an object, like a rock or plant, it slows down. As the wind slows, it drops the sand it was carrying. If this sand deposit keeps growing, a sand dune might form. Sand dunes move, as shown in the figure, when wind carries sand up one side of the dune and it flows down the other side.

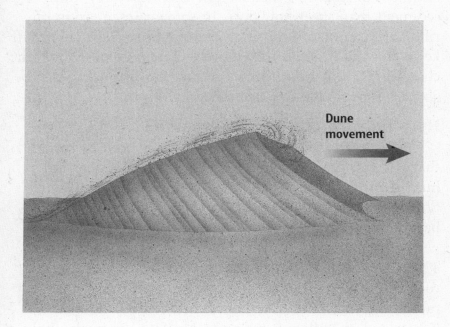

Dune movement

✔ **Reading Check**

8. Identify What form of erosion produces smooth, polished surfaces?

_____

Picture This

9. Draw red arrows on the sand dune to show the direction of the wind against it. Draw blue arrows to show how the sand moves over the top of the sand dune and flows down the other side.

Sometimes, wind carries only fine sediment called silt. When silt is deposited and blankets the surface, it is called loess (LOOS). Loess is as fine as talcum powder. Loess is often dropped downwind of large deserts and glacial outwash deposits.

Water

You probably have seen muddy water running down a street after a heavy rain. Water that flows over the ground is called **runoff**. Runoff is a key force in erosion, especially if the water is moving fast. The faster water moves, the more material it can carry. Water can flow over the land in a few different ways.

What is sheet flow?

When raindrops hit the ground, they break up clumps of soil and loosen small bits of sediment. If these raindrops fall on a slope, a thin sheet of water might start to move downhill. You have seen something similar if you've ever washed a car and seen sheets of water flowing over the hood. When water flows down a hill as a thin sheet, it is called sheet flow. This thin sheet of water can carry loose sediment with it, causing a type of erosion called sheet erosion. ☑

What are rills and gullies?

Where a sheet of water flows around objects and becomes deeper, rills can form. Rills are small channels cut into sediment on Earth's surface. These channels carry more sediment than sheet flow does. In some cases, a group of rills can form on a slope after just one heavy rain. As runoff keeps flowing through rills, more sediment erodes. Soon, the channel gets wider and deeper. When the channels get to be about 0.5 m across, they are called gullies.

How do streams cause erosion?

Gullies often connect to streams. Streams can be so small that you can jump to the other side or large enough for huge river barges to use them. Most streams have water flowing through them all the time, but some streams only have water part of the year.

In mountains and hills, streams flow down steep slopes. These streams have lots of energy. They often cut into the rock below them. This type of stream often has white-water rapids and may have waterfalls. When streams flow on flatter land, they flow more smoothly. Streams might snake back and forth across their valley, washing away and depositing sediment along their sides. In the end, all streams flow into an ocean or a lake where they drop their load of water and sediment. The level of water in the ocean or lake determines how deeply a river can erode.

10. Identify What type of erosion is caused by sheet flow?

_____

💡 **Think it Over**

11. Evaluate Which factors affect the speed of the water in a stream?

_____

_____

How do streams shape the land?

Streams are the main cause of erosion on Earth. The figure above shows the flow of a stream shaping land. Streams shape more of the land than ice, wind, or gravity. Over time, water moving in a stream can cut canyons into solid rock. Many streams together can shape the land over a wide area, forming valleys and leaving some rock as hills.

Streams also shape the land by depositing sediment. They can form sandbars along their path and build up sheets of sand across their valleys. When rivers enter an ocean or lake, the water slows. Then sediment is deposited, sometimes forming large deposits called deltas. The city of New Orleans is built on a delta formed by the Mississippi River. ☑

Effects of Erosion

All types of erosion change the land. Rock and sediment are removed from some areas and deposited in other areas. Where rock is removed, canyons, valleys, and mountain cirques can form. Where sediment is deposited, deltas, sandbars, sand dunes, and other land features can form.

<u>Picture This</u>

12. **Draw** arrows to show the direction in which the water is moving. Put an X at the spot where the stream flows into the lake and deposits sediment.

☑ **Reading Check**

13. **Identify** What forms when water slows and deposits sediment where a river enters a lake?

_____

● After You Read

Mini Glossary

abrasion: form of erosion that occurs when wind blows sediments into rocks, makes pits in the rocks, and produces smooth, polished surfaces

creep: process in which sediments move slowly downhill

deflation: erosion of land that occurs when wind blows loose sediments and carries them away, leaving behind particles that are too heavy to move

erosion: movement of rock or soil by forces like gravity, ice, wind, and water

mass movement: occurs when gravity alone causes rock or sediment to move down a slope

runoff: water that flows over the ground

slump: occurs when a mass of rock or sediment moves downhill along a curved surface

1. Review the terms and their definitions in the Mini Glossary. Write two sentences explaining the difference between deflation and abrasion.

_____

_____

_____

2. Complete the following table to compare different types of erosion.

Type of Erosion	Mass Movement?	Caused by What Force?	Affects What?
Abrasion	No	Wind	Exposed rock
Creep			
Deflation	No		
Glacier			
Runoff			
Slump		Gravity	
Stream			

3. In this section you made flash cards. How was this helpful in learning about weathering and erosion?

_____

End of Section

Science **O**nline Visit **in6.msscience.com** to access your textbook, interactive games, and projects to help you learn more about erosion of Earth's surface.

chapter 10 · Resources

section ❶ Energy Resources

> **Standard—6.3.17:** Recognize and describe that energy is a property of many objects and is associated with heat, light, electricity . . .

● Before You Read

Energy resources are used to make electricity, run cars, and heat homes. On the lines below, list four ways you use energy resources every day.

_____

_____

● Read to Learn

Generating Energy

Energy is the ability to change things, such as the temperature, speed, and direction of an object. When energy is used to change things, energy often changes from one form to another. The chemical energy in wood changes to heat and light energy when wood is burned.

What are fossil fuels?

In the United States, power plants burn fossil fuels to provide energy for homes and factories. A **fossil fuel** is an energy resource formed from the buried remains of ancient plants and other organisms. Coal, oil, and natural gas are examples of fossil fuels.

How is coal formed?

Coal used today formed millions of years ago from plants in swampy regions. After the plants died, they were covered by layers of mud, sand, and more dead plants. Over time, microorganisms changed the dead plant material into a substance called peat. As the weight of overlying layers pressed down on the peat, heat was generated. Heat and pressure changed the peat into a soft, brown coal called lignite. After more years of heat and pressure, the lignite changed into harder forms of coal such as bituminous coal and anthracite.

What You'll Learn

- the advantages and disadvantages of using fossil fuels
- how nonrenewable resources are formed and used

Study Coach

Create-a-Quiz As you read the text, create a quiz question for each topic. When you have finished reading, see if you can answer your own questions correctly.

FOLDABLES

Ⓐ Find Main Ideas Make the following three-tab Foldable to identify the main ideas about fossil fuels.

How Formed | Pollution | How Much Left

How are oil and natural gas formed?

Oil and natural gas formed over millions of years from the partial decay of algae and other microscopic ocean organisms called plankton. The organisms died and fell to the seafloor. Over long periods of time, the decaying organisms built up in ocean sediment. They were buried under thick layers of sand and mud. Heat was given off as the dead organisms decayed and pressure increased with the weight of more layers of sand and mud. The heat and pressure caused chemical changes in the remains of the dead organisms. After millions of years, the buried material formed oil and natural gas. ☑

Where are oil and natural gas found?

After oil and natural gas have formed, they move upward. This happens because they are less dense than both the surrounding rock and the water contained within small spaces in the rock, called pores. Oil and natural gas rise until they reach a layer of rock they cannot pass through. The oil and natural gas become trapped beneath it. Since natural gas is less dense than oil, it usually is found above oil. The figure below shows oil and natural gas trapped underground. Engineers drill through the rock layers to reach underground deposits of oil and natural gas.

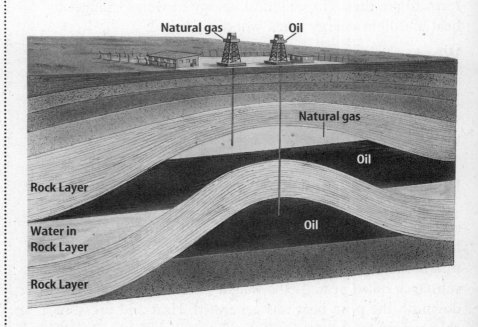

1. **Explain** What kind of organisms formed oil and natural gas?

_____

_____

Picture This

2. **Apply** Draw another well that drills into the topmost deposit of oil.

Pollution and Fossil Fuels

Fossil fuels are important resources. However, burning fossil fuels can cause environmental problems. When fossil fuels are burned in cars, power plants, homes, and factories, gases such as nitrogen oxide and sulfur oxide and tiny bits of soot and dust are released into the air. These substances contribute to pollution. **Pollution** is harmful waste products, chemicals, and substances found in the environment.

Air pollution can make your throat feel dry or your eyes sting. Many people have trouble breathing when air pollution levels are high. For the elderly and people with lung or heart problems, air pollution can be deadly. In the United States, about 60,000 deaths each year are linked to air pollution.

Plants and trees can be harmed by pollution. **Acid rain** is produced when gases released by burning oil and coal mix with water in the air to form acidic rain or snow. When acid rain reaches the soil, it affects the growth of plants and trees. As pollution levels increase, the ability of the environment to support different life-forms suffers. ☑

How can air pollution be reduced?

Reducing the number of pollutants released into the air is easier than cleaning pollutants from the air. Today, cars have catalytic converters, shown in the figure below, that reduce the amount of pollutants released.

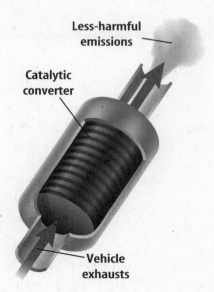

Less-harmful emissions

Catalytic converter

Vehicle exhausts

Think it Over

3. **Analyze** What is one disadvantage of burning fossil fuels?

_____

_____

Reading Check

4. **Summarize** How does acid rain affect the environment?

_____

_____

Picture This

5. **Identify** Mark an X where exhaust emissions contain the most pollutants. Circle the area where emissions have fewer pollutants.

Are fossil fuels running out?

Pollution isn't the only problem with fossil fuels. If the population continues to grow or if people continue to consume more energy, then the demand for energy will increase. Remember that the process of fossil fuel formation took millions of years. There is only a limited amount of fossil fuels in Earth. Plants and other organisms that die today will not become fossil fuels for millions of years.

What are nonrenewable resources?

Some energy resources are being used faster than natural processes can replace them. <u>Nonrenewable</u> resources are resources that cannot be replaced by natural processes in less than about 100 years. Fossil fuels, which take millions of years to form, are nonrenewable resources. This means that humans could run out of these important sources of energy someday.

How much is left?

At current levels of usage, coal provides about 26 percent of the world's energy needs, and oil and natural gas provide almost 64 percent. Scientists estimate that there are enough coal reserves to last 200 to 300 years at present rates of usage. Available oil reserves could be used up within 30 to 40 years. It is estimated that natural gas reserves will last about 60 more years. The figure below shows the estimated time that coal, oil, and natural gas will last at current rates of use.

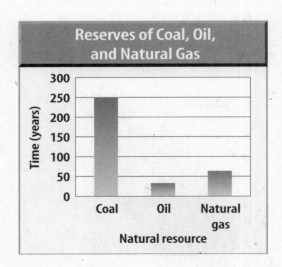

Using less electricity and driving a fuel-efficient car help reduce fossil fuel use. This helps reduce pollution and makes the fossil fuels we have last longer.

💡 **Think it Over**

6. **Analyze** Why should humans limit their use of fossil fuels and work to find other energy sources?

_____

_____

Applying Math

7. **Interpret Data** Which of the three fossil fuels is estimated to last the longest?

_____

● After You Read

Mini Glossary

acid rain: damaging rain or snow formed when gases released by burning oil and coal mix with water in the air

fossil fuel: nonrenewable energy resource, such as coal, oil, and gas, formed from the buried remains of ancient plants and animals

nonrenewable: energy resource that cannot be replaced by natural processes in less than about 100 years

pollution: harmful waste products, chemicals, and substances found in the environment

1. Review the terms and their definitions in the Mini Glossary. Choose two related terms and use them in a sentence about fossil fuels or pollution.

_____

_____

2. Complete the following Venn diagram to show how the formation of coal and the formation of oil and natural gas are similar and how they are different.

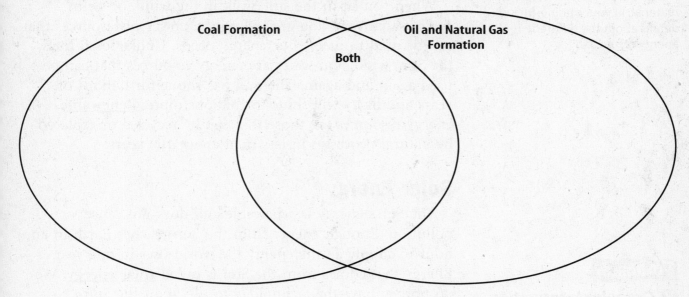

Coal Formation

Oil and Natural Gas Formation

Both

3. You created quiz questions as you read this section. How did this help you understand the information in this section?

_____

_____

 Visit **in6.msscience.com** to access your textbook, interactive games, and projects to help you learn more about fossil fuels.

End of Section

Reading Essentials **157**

Resources

section ❷ Alternative Energy Resources

Standard—6.1.5: Identify places where scientists work, including ... farms, factories, and natural field settings ranging from space to the ocean floor.
Also covers: 6.2.7

What You'll Learn

■ the advantages and disadvantages of alternative energy resources

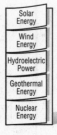

FOLDABLES

Ⓑ Organize Information
Make the following Foldable to organize information about alternative energy sources.

| Solar Energy |
| Wind Energy |
| Hydroelectric Power |
| Geothermal Energy |
| Nuclear Energy |

● Before You Read

What do you think of when you hear the word *renew*? Write one example of something that can be renewed.

● Read to Learn

Other Sources of Energy

When you sit in the sun, walk in the wind, or swim against a current, you are feeling the power of resources that can be used to meet your energy needs. Unlike fossil fuels, the Sun, wind, and water are energy resources that can be used again and again. The Sun has shone for billions of years and likely will shine for billions more. **Renewable** energy resources are those that can be recycled or replaced by natural processes in less than about 100 years.

Solar Energy

The Sun's energy is renewable and does not cause pollution. Enough energy from the Sun reaches Earth in an hour to supply all the energy the world uses in one year. Energy that comes from the Sun is called **solar energy**. We do not yet have the technology to use all of the Sun's energy, but we can use some of it.

What are solar cells?

Solar cells collect light and change it into electricity. In a solar cell, thin layers of the element silicon are sandwiched together and attached to tiny wires. Light striking the different layers produces an electric current. Solar cells can be used to power calculators or to supply electricity to remote areas. Solar cells are expensive, so they are not widely used.

Is solar energy the answer?

Solar energy does not cause pollution. It is renewable and available in large amounts. However, there are some disadvantages to using solar energy. It is available only when the Sun is shining, so solar cells can't work at night. In addition, different parts of Earth receive different amounts of solar energy. If you live in an area that often is cloudy, solar energy probably cannot meet all of your energy needs. It also is expensive to harness and store enough of the Sun's energy. Some scientists think the best solution to our energy problems might be to use fossil fuels and solar energy along with other energy sources. ☑

Energy from Wind

Wind energy lets you fly a kite or sail a sailboat. The first large-scale use of wind energy was developed in Vermont during World War II. Today windmills are used around the world to generate electricity. In the United States, many regions have been identified as having wind conditions well-suited to using wind power. European countries such as Denmark and Finland also use wind power. When a large number of windmills, shown in the figure below, are placed in one area for the purpose of generating electricity, the area is called a wind farm.

Like all forms of energy, energy from the wind has advantages and disadvantages. Wind is nonpolluting and renewable. It does not harm the environment or produce waste. However, only a few areas of the world have winds strong enough to generate lots of electricity. Also, wind isn't steady. Sometimes it blows too hard, and sometimes it stops altogether.

✔ **Reading Check**

1. **List** What are two advantages of using solar energy?

_____

_____

Picture This

2. **Think Critically** Why is having a steady wind that blows every day better for producing energy from the windmills shown in the figure than having a strong wind that blows only occasionally?

_____

_____

Hydroelectric Power

Energy from moving water also can generate electricity. **Hydroelectric power** is the production of electricity using water. In areas where there are waterfalls, water can be used to generate electricity. Niagara Falls generates hydroelectric power for a large number of cities in northeastern North America.

In places without waterfalls, concrete dams may be built to produce hydroelectric power. The river water that backs up behind a dam creates a reservoir, or large storage area, of water. Many large reservoirs are considered lakes. Pipes from this reservoir carry water to a turbine. The water in the pipes is under great pressure as it falls to the turbines. The pressure of the water turns the turbines that drive the electric generators in the power plant. The figure below shows how a dam and a hydroelectric power plant work to generate electricity.

Picture This

3. **Apply** Trace the path of the water from the reservoir, through the dam, to the discharge.

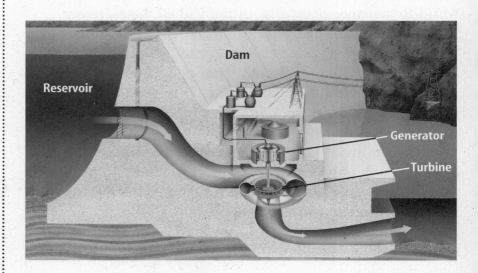

4. **Describe** What can happen to a reservoir after a dam is built?

_____

_____

Are there problems with hydroelectric power?

Like solar power and energy from the wind, hydroelectric power does not cause pollution and is renewable. But this energy resource has its problems. When dams are built, the reservoir located behind the dam can fill with sediment. Downstream from the dam, increased erosion can occur. Land above the dam is flooded, and wildlife habitats are disturbed. In addition, dams and power plants already have been built near most rivers suitable for generating hydroelectricity. ☑

Energy from Earth

Another renewable energy resource exists beneath Earth's surface near bodies of hot, molten rock called magma. **Geothermal energy** is the energy from the heat of magma and hot rock that surrounds it that can be used to generate electricity.

Groundwater heated by the hot rocks turns to steam and forms a geyser. The steam, along with hot groundwater, spurts through openings in Earth's crust. Geysers are a form of geothermal energy from magma that is located close to Earth's surface. Some people in Iceland and California use the hot water and steam from geysers to heat their homes.

Sometimes magma is far below Earth's surface, but engineers can drill wells to reach heated rock. Water injected into the rock turns to steam and rises to Earth's surface. The rising steam is used to generate electricity.

Does geothermal energy have disadvantages?

Geothermal energy has its disadvantages. Using geothermal energy can release hot, salty water at Earth's surface, which can be harmful to nearby plants and animals. Also, only a few places on Earth have magma near the surface. In most places, deep wells must be drilled, which are expensive and can disrupt nearby habitats.

Nuclear Energy

Atoms are the basic units of matter. Each atom contains a nucleus, which contains energy. Scientists have found a way to get energy from atoms. **Nuclear energy** is produced by splitting the nuclei of certain elements. In this process, known as fission, energy is released. This energy is used to change water into steam. The steam is used to drive a turbine to generate electricity for homes and industries. ☑

What fuel is used?

The most commonly used fuel in nuclear power plants is uranium. Uranium has a nucleus that can be split easily. Mined uranium ore is refined and placed in long, metal pipes called fuel rods. The fuel rods sit in a pool of cooling water within a nuclear reactor. Energy is released when neutrons given off by the uranium split a nucleus of another uranium atom. This releases more neutrons and more energy. This process is known as a chain reaction.

5. Apply What areas are best suited to use geothermal energy?

_____

_____

Reading Check

6. Identify What part of an atom is involved in nuclear energy?

_____

What are the disadvantages of nuclear energy?

Nuclear energy produces more than electricity. It also produces radioactive nuclear waste. This waste contains materials that can cause cancer or harm living things. Some nuclear waste remains radioactive for more than 10,000 years. Nuclear waste must be handled and stored carefully to keep it from harming living things and from entering the environment. Nuclear fuels are also nonrenewable. ☑

Why is the use of nuclear energy limited?

Because of potential problems in storing nuclear waste, nuclear energy has seen limited use in the United States. Electricity generated from nuclear power makes up only eight percent of total U.S. energy use. Worldwide, about 30 countries use nuclear energy to generate electricity, with France and Japan using the most. Almost 80 percent of France's energy needs are met by nuclear power.

Today, the use of nuclear power and renewable energy resources is limited. Improvements in technology might make these resources, particularly the Sun, major sources of energy in the future.

How does the world meet its energy needs?

In 1998, the United States met 85 percent of its energy needs using fossil fuels. The figure below shows the percentage of energy obtained from different sources in the United States, which closely matches global use. Ninety percent of the world's energy comes from fossil fuels. Nuclear power provides seven percent of the world's energy needs, and hydroelectric power provides three percent. That leaves less than one percent for the remaining sources of energy—solar, geothermal, and wind combined.

Picture This

8. Interpret Data What percentage of energy in the U.S. comes from sources other than fossil fuels?
 a. 15%
 b. 23%
 c. 39%
 d. 64%

Energy Use in the United States, 1998

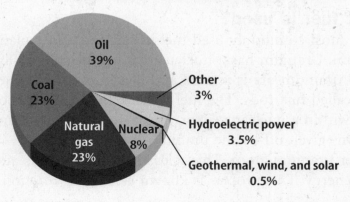

- Oil 39%
- Coal 23%
- Natural gas 23%
- Nuclear 8%
- Other 3%
- Hydroelectric power 3.5%
- Geothermal, wind, and solar 0.5%

● After You Read

Mini Glossary

geothermal energy: the heat energy from magma and hot rock that surrounds it

hydroelectric power: electricity produced from moving water

nuclear energy: energy produced by splitting the nuclei of certain elements

renewable: energy resource that can be recycled or replaced by natural processes in less than about 100 years

solar energy: energy from the Sun

1. Review the terms and their definitions in the Mini Glossary. Choose one term and write a sentence explaining one advantage of this energy resource.

   _____

   _____

2. Complete the table below with an advantage and a disadvantage of each renewable and nonrenewable energy resource.

ENERGY RESOURCES		
	Advantages	**Disadvantages**
Solar power		
Energy from wind		
Hydroelectric power		
Geothermal energy		
Nuclear energy		

 Science Online Visit **in6.msscience.com** to access your textbook, interactive games, and projects to help you learn more about renewable energy sources

End of Section

Resources

section ❸ Water

> **Standard—6.3.8:** Explain that fresh water ... is essential for life and also for most industrial processes. Understand that this resource can be depleted ....
> Also covers: 6.1.7, 6.2.7

What You'll Learn

- how water is important to living things
- different sources of water

Study Coach

Make Flash Cards Think of a quiz question for each paragraph. Write the question on one side of the flash card and the answer on the other side. Keep quizzing yourself until you know all of the answers.

FOLDABLES

ⓒ Find Main Ideas Make the following Foldable to help you identify the main ideas or major topics on water.

Water as a Resource

● Before You Read

List three ways you use water every day.

_____

_____

● Read to Learn

Water—A Vital Resource

Earth has a vast amount of water. About 70 percent of Earth is covered by water. This water moves continually through the water cycle. Water is needed for life by all living organisms. Without water, living organisms could not carry out important life processes, such as growth. Water may be Earth's most valuable resource.

How much water is usable?

Only a small portion of Earth's water is available for human use. About 97 percent of the world's total water supply is salty ocean water. Only three percent is freshwater, and more than three-fourths of that is frozen in glaciers and ice caps. Less than one percent of Earth's water is available for humans to use. This small percentage is found underground or in lakes, streams, and rivers.

Groundwater

Some freshwater lies under Earth's surface. **Groundwater** is water that soaks into the ground and collects in small spaces between bits of soil and rock. If these spaces are connected, water can flow through layers of soil and rock. People drill wells into the layers. Water is pumped to the surface. The water is used as drinking water, in factories, and in agriculture.

Is groundwater a renewable resource?

In the United States, groundwater provides 40 percent of public water supplies. Industries and farms also use groundwater. In many farming areas, groundwater is the only source of water available. Groundwater is sometimes considered renewable because it is part of the water cycle, as seen in the figure below. However, it takes a long time for groundwater to accumulate. Therefore, it can take a long time to clean groundwater if it becomes polluted. That's why clean, usable groundwater should be considered a nonrenewable resource. ☑

☑ Reading Check

1. **Explain** Why should clean, usable groundwater be considered a nonrenewable resource?

_____

_____

The Water Cycle

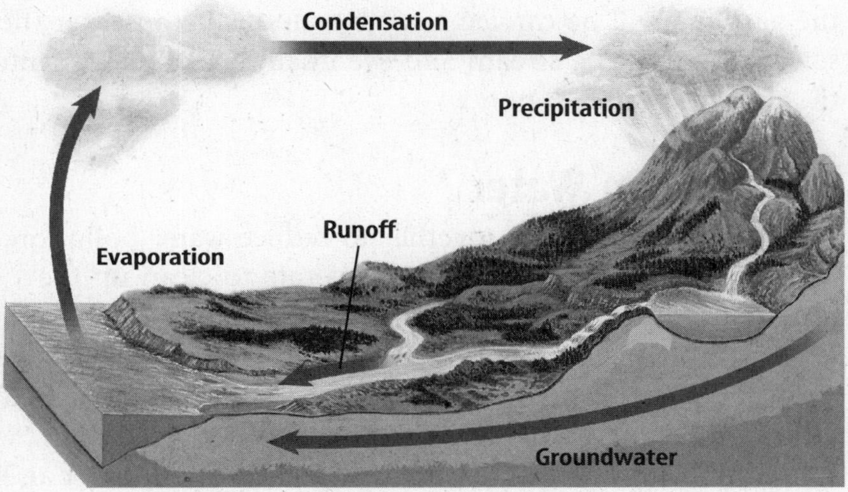

Condensation

Precipitation

Evaporation

Runoff

Groundwater

Picture This

2. **Describe** How does water move from Earth's surface into the atmosphere?

_____

_____

What is surface water?

Not all places get water from underground. Surface water comes from streams, rivers, ponds, lakes, and reservoirs. Surface water is the water you can easily see on Earth.

How is water used?

Your body needs water to survive. People also use water for recreation such as swimming and fishing. People bathe and cook food using water.

Water is used by industry to make products. Boats transport products and people across oceans or along rivers. Farmers use water to irrigate crops.

Many plants and animals live in oceans, lakes, or rivers, where they spend their entire lives.

Water Pollution

Water pollution occurs when harmful chemicals or wastes are added to water. **Point source pollution** is pollution that comes from a single, easily seen source. A factory pipe pouring chemicals into a river is an example of point source pollution. You can see the pollution occurring.

Most pollution is hard to trace to a single source. **Nonpoint source pollution** cannot be traced back to an exact location. Nonpoint sources can be streets, homes, or farms. A farmer may use chemical fertilizers to grow crops. The fertilizers enter streams, lakes, and wetlands where they can damage the environment. Some of the chemicals seep into the ground and can pollute groundwater. You might cause water pollution. If you spill gasoline in your driveway, the gasoline will be carried away by runoff. It can enter the sewage system or a stream and eventually make its way into the drinking water supply.

Cleaning Up Water

Many countries work together to reduce water pollution. The United States and Canada cooperate to clean up the pollution in Lake Erie, which borders both countries. The U.S. government has passed laws to help keep water supplies clean. The Safe Drinking Water Act sets standards designed to keep drinking water safe. The Clean Water Act helps states build water-treatment plants to clean water to be used for drinking and other purposes. ☑

How is water purified?

To purify water, it first is run through a settling basin. Large particles of sediment settle out. Smaller particles are filtered out by sand and gravel. The water then is pumped into a tank where chemicals are added to kill microorganisms. In most water-purification plants, chlorine is used to treat the water. After it has been purified, the clean water is pumped to consumers.

Water Distribution

Water is vital to all living things. People often build cities near shorelines and along rivers. To better manage water resources, many countries have passed laws to reduce water pollution and to monitor the quality of the water supply.

● After You Read

Mini Glossary

groundwater: water that soaks into the ground and collects in small spaces between bits of soil and rock

nonpoint source pollution: pollution that cannot be traced to a single source

point source pollution: pollution that can be traced to a single, identifiable source

1. Review the terms and their definitions in the Mini Glossary. Use the term *groundwater* in a sentence to describe why water resources are important.

_____

_____

2. Complete the Venn diagram below to explain how point source pollution and nonpoint source pollution are similar and how they are different. Give an example of each.

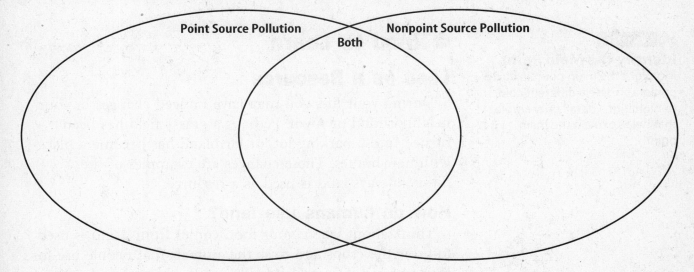

Point Source Pollution   Both   Nonpoint Source Pollution

3. You made flash cards with quiz questions as you read this section. How did the questions help you understand the information in this section?

_____

_____

_____

 **Science** ●nline Visit **in6.msscience.com** to access your textbook, interactive games, and projects to help you learn more about water.

End of Section

 **Resources**

section ❹ Land

> **Standard—6.3.16:** Explain that human activities, such as reducing the amount of forest cover, ... have changed the capacity of the environment ....
> **Also covers:** 6.2.5, 6.2.6, 6.2.7

What You'll Learn

- why land is a renewable resource
- how forests and minerals are used as resources

Mark the Text

Identify the Main Point
Highlight the main point in each paragraph. Use a different color to highlight a detail or example that helps explain the main point.

FOLDABLES™

ⓓ Find Main Ideas Make the following Foldable to help you identify the main ideas or major topics on land.

Land as a Resource

● Before You Read

Why do you think land is considered a valuable resource that must be used wisely?

_____

_____

_____

● Read to Learn

Land as a Resource

During your life, you may have noticed changes in your neighborhood or town. Perhaps a grassy field has been turned into a parking lot, or farmland has become a place with new homes. These changes are examples of the different ways land is used as a resource.

How do humans use land?

Think about where your food comes from. Land is used to grow the crops and raise the animals that people use for food. A peanut butter and jelly sandwich requires land to grow the wheat used in bread, land to grow peanuts for the peanut butter, and land to grow the sugarcane and fruit for the jelly. Land is needed to raise cattle and to grow the grain the cattle eat so you can eat hamburgers.

Think about your home, your school, and other places you go, like a park or shopping mall. Things you buy at the mall come from factories. Malls and factories take up space. Every time a house, a mall, or a factory is built, more land is used. Land is a renewable resource because it usually can be used over and over again. But one look at a globe will show you that the amount of usable land is limited. Therefore, wise choices need to be made when it comes to land use.

Why must land be used wisely?

People need food, clothing, jobs, and a place to live. Each of these things take space. But preserving natural habitats is also important. Recall that a habitat is the place where organisms live. Ponds, wetlands, and forests are examples of natural habitats. If a wetland is filled in to build an apartment building, an important natural habitat is lost.

Laws help control habitat loss and help people use land wisely. Before building can occur in a natural area, the land must be studied to determine the impact building will have on the living things, the soil, and the water in the area. If endangered plants or animals live in the area, building might not be allowed. ✔

Problems can arise when people use land for farming or grazing animals. If these activities are not done properly, soil can be eroded, causing its quality to be reduced.

Resources From Land

People use land to grow crops, to raise animals, and to live on. In addition to meeting human needs for food and shelter, land provides two other important resources—forests and minerals.

How do forests help people?

Look around your classroom. Do you see books, paper, desks, and pencils? These products are made of wood. Wood comes from trees in a forest, like the one below, that were cut down and taken to a lumberyard to be processed into boards and other wood products.

✔ Reading Check

1. **Think Critically** Why does a study of the land have to be done before buildings are put up?

_____

_____

Picture This

2. **Explain** Why might trees be considered a renewable resource?

_____

_____

_____

How do forests affect the atmosphere?

In addition to providing much-needed wood, forests have an important effect on Earth's atmosphere. During the process of photosynthesis, trees and other plants use carbon dioxide, water, and sunlight to produce oxygen and sugars. As forests grow, they take in carbon dioxide and store carbon. If a forest is cut down, it can no longer take in carbon dioxide. Therefore, more carbon dioxide is left in the atmosphere. Increases in atmospheric carbon dioxide might cause global warming. Global warming is an increase in world temperatures. Global warming could lead to changes in climate that would affect natural habitats all over Earth. ☑

☑ **Reading Check**

3. Cause and Effect How might cutting down forests increase global warming?

_____

_____

Forest Conservation

Because forests are such a valuable resource, they must be used with care. **Conservation** is the careful use of resources with the goal of reducing damage to the environment.

There are two ways forests can be conserved during harvesting. In select-cutting, a limited number of older trees are cut. New trees are planted in their place. The young trees grow among the older trees. By the time all of the original trees have been cut, a new forest has grown.

In clear-cutting, all of the trees in a specific area are cut down. New trees are planted on the cleared area. One advantage of this method is that trees in a specific area of a forest are of the same age and can be removed more easily. However, clear-cutting often harms wildlife and causes soil erosion.

Are trees renewable or nonrenewable?

Some trees take many years to mature. However, trees can be viewed as a renewable resource because after one tree is cut, another can be planted in its place.

Some forests are nonrenewable. Individual trees can be replanted, but these forests are complex ecosystems that support countless living things. These ecosystems take a long time to develop. If many or all of the trees are removed, it could take centuries for the forest ecosystem to develop again. When such forests are cut, some animals, like the golden lion tamarin monkey shown on the next page, may disappear forever.

💡 **Think it Over**

4. Infer How might clear-cutting affect the plants and animals that lived in the area of forest cut down?

_____

_____

Picture This

5. **Predict** This monkey lives only in a narrow strip of forest in Brazil. What would happen to the monkey if all the forest's trees were cut down?

_____

_____

_____

Mineral Resources

Minerals are another type of resource that is obtained from land. Metal objects come from mineral resources, which are found in rock. Generally, it costs more to get those minerals out of the rock than the minerals are worth. But sometimes large deposits of valuable minerals are found in one place. These minerals can be classified as ores. An **ore** is a mineral resource that can be mined at a profit.

What are some problems with using ores?

Ores, like fossil fuels, are resources found under Earth's surface. To get to ores, large quantities of soil and rock often must be moved. This process is called mining. Mines can look unsightly, and the waste produced by mines can pollute surface water. Air pollution also is produced when industrial plants process the ores. Dust and soot particles are released into the air. Care must be taken to mine and use the ores in ways that do not harm water resources, living things, and natural habitats. ☑

How can the way one resource is used affect other resources?

Using each type of resource has advantages and disadvantages. In addition, the way one resource is used often affects another. For example, burning too many fossil fuels can cause air and water pollution. Trees can be replanted to conserve a forest, but the trees might die if they're exposed to acid rain caused by burning fossil fuels. A farmer can manage a farm carefully to lessen soil erosion. But if the water supply is polluted from chemical runoff caused by mines, the crops will suffer. Successful resource management is possible only if everyone uses all of Earth's resources wisely.

☑ **Reading Check**

6. **Summarize** Why must special care be taken during the mining of ores?

_____

_____

_____

● After You Read

Mini Glossary

conservation: careful use of resources so that damage to the environment is reduced

ore: mineral resource that can be mined for profit

1. Review the terms and their definitions in the Mini Glossary. Write a sentence explaining why forest conservation is important.

_____

_____

2. Complete the table below with examples of wise land use.

Wise Use	
Farming	
Mining	
Forests	
Building	

3. As you read this section, you highlighted details that supported the main ideas. How did this help you understand the information in this section?

_____

_____

_____

End of Section

Science **Online** Visit **in6.msscience.com** to access your textbook, interactive games, and projects to help you learn more about land.

Cells—The Units of Life

section ❶ The World of Cells

 Standard—6.4.5: Investigate and explain that all living things are composed of cells whose details are usually visible only through a microscope.
Also covers: 6.4.6, 6.4.7

● Before You Read

What did you use as a small child to build with? What did you make? In this section, you will learn about cells, the building blocks of life.

_____

_____

_____

_____

● Read to Learn

Importance of Cells

The cell is the smallest unit of life in all living things. Cells are organized structures that help living things carry on the activities of life. They help living things move, grow, reproduce, and break down food. Different cells have different jobs. In the human body, for example, white blood cells help fight disease. Red blood cells carry oxygen to different parts of the body. Even though different cells have different jobs, all cells are alike in many ways.

What is the cell theory?

Cells were not observed until microscopes were invented. In 1665, scientist Robert Hooke made a microscope and used it to observe tiny, boxlike objects in a slice of cork. He called the objects cells because they reminded him of small rooms, called cells, where monks lived.

Throughout the 17th and 18th centuries, scientists continued to observe many living things under microscopes. Their observations led to the development of the cell theory.

What You'll Learn
- what the cell theory is
- the parts of animal and plant cells
- the functions of different cell parts

Study Coach

Identify the Main Point
Read each subhead. Then work with a partner to write questions about the information in each subhead. Take turns asking and answering the questions. Use the questions as a study guide about cells.

FOLDABLES™

Ⓐ **List** Make a layered-look Foldable, as shown below. List the three main ideas of the cell theory on the tabs.

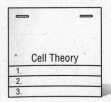

Cell Theory
1.
2.
3.

B Define Make a vocabulary Foldable using notebook paper, as shown below. List each of the terms in this section on one of the tabs. Write the definition of the term on the inside of the tab.

Ideas of the Cell Theory There are three main ideas of the cell theory.

- All living things are made of one or more cells.

- The cell is the basic unit of life. All the activities of life take place inside cells.

- All cells come from cells that already exist.

How many cells do living things have?

The smallest organisms on Earth are **bacteria**. Bacteria are one-celled organisms, meaning they are made up of only one cell. Larger organisms are made of many cells. The human body, for example, is made up of more than 10 trillion (10,000,000,000,000) cells.

How do microscopes help scientists?

Scientists have used microscopes to study cells for more than 300 years. In recent years, better microscopes have helped scientists learn more about the differences between cells and observe the small parts that are inside cells.

Most science classrooms use a microscope called a compound light microscope. In a compound microscope, light passes through the object that you are looking at and then through two or more lenses before it reaches your eye. The lenses make the image of the object look larger.

What are cells made of?

Even though cells are small, they are made of even smaller parts. Each cell part has its own job. Just as every building has walls, every cell has a boundary. All of the cell's activities take place inside this boundary. Some parts of the cell are used as storage areas. Other parts use oxygen, water, minerals, and other nutrients to make substances the cell needs. Still other parts release the energy needed for maintaining life.

What makes up the outside of a cell?

The **cell membrane** is the outer boundary of the cell. It helps hold the cell together, like walls hold a building together. The cell membrane forms a flexible boundary between the cell and its environment. It helps to control what goes into and comes out of the cell. Some kinds of cells, including plant cells, have a rigid **cell wall** that surrounds the cell membrane. The cell wall helps support and protect the cell. Animal cells do not have cell walls. ✓

✓ Reading Check

1. **Explain** one of the roles of the cell membrane.

_____

_____

_____

What makes up the inside of a cell?

The inside of a cell contains a gelatinlike substance called **cytoplasm** (SI tuh pla zum). Water makes up most of the cytoplasm. The cytoplasm also contains many chemicals that are needed by the cell. Most of the cell's activities happen in the cytoplasm.

What are organelles?

Except for bacterial cells, all cells have **organelles** (or guh NELZ). Organelles are specialized cell parts that move around in the cytoplasm. They perform jobs that are necessary for life. Each kind of organelle does a different job. In the figure of the animal cell below, the nucleus, the vacuole, and the mitochondrion are organelles.

What makes up the nucleus?

Every cell contains hereditary material that directs most of the cell's activities. The hereditary material is a chemical called DNA. DNA is contained in the chromosomes (KROH muh zohmz). In the cells of all organisms except bacteria, the chromosomes are contained in an organelle called the **nucleus** (NEW klee us).

Where are substances stored in cells?

Food, water, and other substances are stored in balloonlike organelles called **vacuoles** (VA kyuh wohlz). Some vacuoles store wastes. In plants, most cells contain a large vacuole that stores water and other substances.

💡 Think it Over

2. **Explain** why cells have many different kinds of organelles.

_____

_____

_____

Picture This

3. **Identify** Highlight the name of the cell part that is a storage area. Circle two organelles.

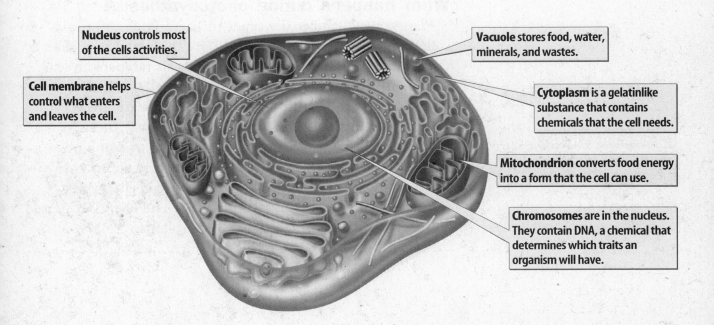

Nucleus controls most of the cells activities.

Cell membrane helps control what enters and leaves the cell.

Vacuole stores food, water, minerals, and wastes.

Cytoplasm is a gelatinlike substance that contains chemicals that the cell needs.

Mitochondrion converts food energy into a form that the cell can use.

Chromosomes are in the nucleus. They contain DNA, a chemical that determines which traits an organism will have.

Energy and the Cell

All cells need energy. Except for bacteria, all cells have organelles called **mitochondria** (mi tuh KAHN dree uh) (singular, *mitochondrion*) that supply the energy the cell needs. Inside the mitochondria, a process called cellular respiration (SEL yuh lur • res puh RAY shun) takes place as shown in the figure below.

Picture This

4. **Identify** Highlight the names of the two materials needed by the mitochondrion to produce energy.

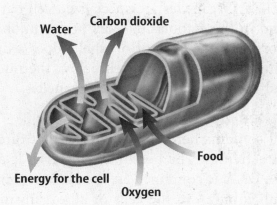

Water

Carbon dioxide

Food

Energy for the cell

Oxygen

Cellular respiration involves chemical reactions that change the energy stored in food into a form of energy the cell can use. This energy is released as food and oxygen combine. The waste products of cellular respiration are carbon dioxide and water. Cells that have mitochondria use energy from cellular respiration to do all of their work.

What happens during photosynthesis?

Plants, algae, and many types of bacteria use a process called **photosynthesis** (foh toh SIHN thuh sus) to make their food. In plants, most photosynthesis happens in leaf cells. Inside the leaf cells are green organelles called **chloroplasts** (KLOR uh plasts). Most leaves are green because of chloroplasts. During plant photosynthesis, chloroplasts take in light energy and use it to combine carbon dioxide from the air with water to make food. Energy is stored in food. As the plant needs energy, its mitochondria release the food's energy. The energy is passed to other organisms when they eat the plants. ☑

 **Reading Check**

5. **Recall** What plant organelle is used in photosynthesis?

● After You Read

Mini Glossary

bacteria: the smallest organisms on Earth; made of single cells

cell membrane: a flexible structure that holds the cell together

cell wall: rigid structure that surrounds the cell membrane; helps support and protect the cell

chloroplasts: green organelles located in leaf cells

cytoplasm: the inside part of a cell in which most of the cell's activities take place

mitochondria: an organelle in which the process of respiration takes place

nucleus: an organelle that contains hereditary material

organelles: specialized cell parts that move around in the cytoplasm and perform activities that are necessary for life

photosynthesis: the process through which plants, algae, and many types of bacteria make food

vacuoles: balloonlike organelles in the cytoplasm in which food, water, and other substances are stored

1. Review the terms and their definitions in the Mini Glossary. Choose two terms and write a sentence that explains how plants make their own food.

   _____

   _____

2. Complete the chart below to identify the job of each of the listed cell parts.

Part of Cell	Part's Job
cell membrane	
	helps support and protect cells of plants
cytoplasm	
nucleus	
	contains DNA

3. How is asking and answering questions with a partner helpful in remembering what you have read?

   _____

   _____

 Visit **in6.msscience.com** to access your textbook, interactive games, and projects to help you learn more about the world of cells.

End of Section

Cells—The Units of Life

section ❷ The Different Jobs of Cells

> **Standard—6.4.3:** Describe some of the great variety of body plans and internal structures animals and plants have that contribute ....
> **Also covers: 6.4.5, 6.4.6**

What You'll Learn
- how different cells have different jobs
- the differences among tissues, organs, and organ systems

⬤ Before You Read

A poster in a store window reads: "We specialize in repairing DVD players." What does the word *specialize* in the poster mean?

_____

_____

Mark the Text

Identify the Main Point
Underline the main point of each paragraph as you read the section.

⬤ Read to Learn

Special Cells for Special Jobs

Cells in many-celled organisms are specialized. A specialized cell does a specific job. Specialized cells work together to perform all the life activities of a many-celled organism.

What types of cells do animals have?

The human body and the bodies of other animals are made up of many types of specialized cells. These cells come in various sizes and shapes. The figure below shows examples of the shapes and sizes of human cells.

Picture This

1. Identify Highlight the part of the description for nerve, muscle, and skin cells that describes their shape. Circle the part of the description that explains what the cells do.

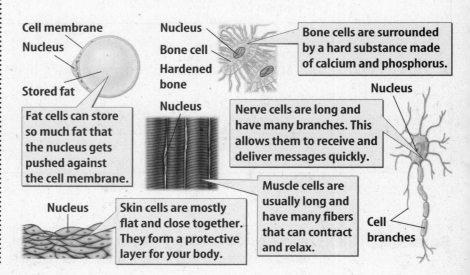

Cell membrane
Nucleus
Stored fat

Fat cells can store so much fat that the nucleus gets pushed against the cell membrane.

Nucleus
Bone cell
Hardened bone

Bone cells are surrounded by a hard substance made of calcium and phosphorus.

Nucleus

Nerve cells are long and have many branches. This allows them to receive and deliver messages quickly.

Nucleus

Cell branches

Nucleus

Skin cells are mostly flat and close together. They form a protective layer for your body.

Muscle cells are usually long and have many fibers that can contract and relax.

What types of cells make up plants?

Plants also are made up of many types of specialized cells. Plants have different types of cells in their leaves, roots, and stems. Each type of cell has a certain job. Some plant cells, such as those in plant stems, are long and tubelike. They form a system through which water, food, and other substances move from one part of the plant to another. Other cells, like those on the outside of a plant stem, are shorter and thicker. They help to make the stem strong. ☑

Cell Organization

The cells of many-celled organisms are not just mixed together in any kind of way. Cells are organized into systems that work together to perform jobs that keep the organism healthy and alive.

How are tissues and organs different?

Cells that are alike are organized into tissues (TIH shewz). **Tissues** are groups of similar cells that all do the same sort of work. For example, bone tissue is made up of bone cells that are organized to form the bones in your body.

Different types of tissues working together can form an **organ** (OR gun). For example, the stomach is an organ that includes muscle tissue, nerve tissue, and blood tissue. The tissues in the stomach work together to help the stomach digest food. The heart and the kidneys are other organs in the human body.

What are organ systems?

A group of organs that work together to do a certain job is called an **organ system.** For example, the mouth, stomach, and intestines are used in digestion. These and other organs make up the digestive system. Other organ systems in the human body include the respiratory system, the circulatory system, the reproductive system, and the nervous system.

Organ systems also work with each other. For example, your muscular system works with your skeletal system to make your body move. Your muscular system is made up of hundreds of muscles that are attached to your bones. The bones make up your skeletal system. The muscles help bones move.

FOLDABLES™

C Organize Make a four-tab Foldable using notebook paper, as shown below. Inside each tab, list facts about each level of cell organization.

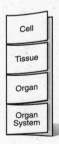

Cell

Tissue

Organ

Organ System

● After You Read

Mini Glossary

organ: structure formed by different types of tissues working together

organ system: a group of organs that work together to do a certain job

tissue: group of similar cells that all do the same sort of work

1. Review the terms and their definitions in the Mini Glossary. Write a sentence that explains how the three terms are related.

_____

_____

_____

2. Choose one of the question headings in the Read to Learn section. Write the question in the space below. Then write your answer to that question on the lines that follow.

Write your question here.

_____

_____

_____

End of Section

Science nline Visit **in6.msscience.com** to access your textbook, interactive games, and projects to help you learn more about the different jobs of cells.

Bacteria, Protists, and Fungi

section ❶ Bacteria

Standard—6.4.2: Give examples of organisms that cannot be neatly classified as either plants or animals, such as fungi and bacteria. **Also covers:** 6.4.5, 6.4.9

● Before You Read

Do you know someone who has had food poisoning? What do you think causes food poisoning?

_____

_____

_____

What You'll Learn

■ the characteristics of bacterial cells
■ the two major groups of bacteria
■ why bacteria are important

● Read to Learn

What are bacteria?

Bacteria are found everywhere. People did not know about bacteria for thousands of years. In the late 1600s, a Dutch merchant, Antonie van Leeuwenhoek (LAY vun hook), used his microscope to look at scrapings from his teeth. He did not know that the organisms he was looking at were bacteria.

Characteristics of Bacteria

Bacteria are one-celled organisms. Bacterial cells are considered to be prokaryotic (proh kar ee AH tihk). The genetic material of prokaryotic cells is not found in the nucleus. Instead, the genetic material floats freely in the cytoplasm. Some bacteria are found as individual cells. Others grow in groups or in long chains of cells.

What are producer and consumer bacteria?

Organisms that can make their own food are called producers. Organisms that cannot make their own food are consumers. Some bacteria are producers, and others are consumers. Some producer bacteria use energy from sunlight to make food. Other producer bacteria use energy from inorganic chemicals to make food. ☑

Study Coach

Identify the Main Idea
Organize your notes into two columns. In the left column, list a main idea about the material in each subhead. In the right column, list the details that support the main idea.

✔ Reading Check

1. **Define** What is a producer?

_____

_____

_____

2. Identify two ways consumer bacteria get food.

_____

_____

_____

Consumer Bacteria Consumer bacteria get food in different ways. Some break down dead organisms to get energy. Others live as parasites, taking nutrients from living organisms. ☑

What is the difference between aerobes and anaerobes?

An organism that uses oxygen for respiration is called an **aerobe** (AR ohb). An organism that can live without oxygen is called an **anaerobe** (A nuh rohb). Humans are aerobic organisms because they need oxygen to live. Most bacteria are aerobes, but some are anaerobes. Bacteria that are anaerobes can live in places with little or no oxygen.

What is the structure and function of bacteria?

Bacterial cells are smaller than plant and animal cells. Bacteria also do not have as many structures inside their cells. A bacterial cell is made up of cytoplasm surrounded by a cell membrane and a cell wall. Some bacteria cells are surrounded by a gel-like capsule that helps protect them. Many bacteria that live in moist places have whiplike tails, called flagella, that allow the bacteria to move.

Endospores Some bacteria can produce a thick wall around themselves when the conditions in the environment are not favorable. Inside this wall, the bacterium changes into a dormant form called an **endospore**. The bacterium can survive this way for hundreds of years.

Shapes of Bacteria The bacteria found in your home and in your body have three kinds of shapes, as shown below. Sphere-shaped bacteria are called cocci (KAW ki). Rod-shaped bacteria are called bacilli (buh SIH li). Spiral-shaped bacteria are called spirilla (spi RIH luh).

Picture This

3. Identify Write *cocci, bacilli,* or *spirilla* on the line under the appropriate picture.

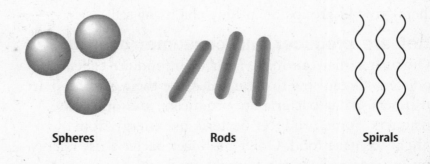

Spheres   Rods   Spirals

_____   _____   _____

Types of Bacteria

The two main groups of bacteria are archaebacteria and eubacteria. Archaebacteria (ar kee bak TIHR ee uh) live in harsh environments where few other kinds of organisms can survive. Eubacteria (YOO bak tihr ee uh) live in less harsh environments. Both groups of bacteria probably have existed for billions of years. ✔

How are eubacteria classified?

The larger of the two groups of bacteria is eubacteria. Most eubacteria are consumers, but some are producers. Some are aerobes, and others are anaerobes. Most eubacteria are helpful, but some eubacteria cause diseases. Eubacteria are classified according to the conditions in which they grow, their chemical makeup, the way they get food, and the waste products they produce.

How are archaebacteria classified?

Archaebacteria are grouped according to the kinds of harsh environments in which they live. Some archaebacteria grow in hot, acidic environments such as hot springs. Other archaebacteria live in evaporation ponds used for salt production. Some even live in the digestive tracts of animals. Archaebacteria are not known to cause any diseases.

Bacteria and Your Health

Some bacteria can be harmful to humans. However, bacteria can help you stay healthy. In fact, you could not survive without some bacteria living on or in your body.

How are bacteria helpful?

Some bacteria produce chemicals called **antibiotics**. Antibiotics limit the growth of other bacteria, or even kill them. For example, one common bacteria found in soil produces the antibiotic streptomycin. Many diseases in people and animals can be treated with antibiotics.

Millions of bacteria live on your skin and other parts of your body. Certain types of bacteria usually are harmless. They often limit the growth of other harmful bacteria. Most bacteria found in your large intestine are harmless to you and help you stay healthy. Some bacteria in your intestine produce vitamin K, which helps make your blood clot.

✔ **Reading Check**

4. **Compare** the environments of the two types of bacteria.

_____

_____

_____

_____

FOLDABLES™

A Classify Make a three-tab Foldable, as shown below. Use the Foldable to describe how bacteria affect your health, industry, and the environment.

What kinds of bacteria are harmful?

Some bacteria are pathogens. A **pathogen** is any organism that causes disease. Tooth decay is a common disease caused by bacteria in your mouth. As shown in the figure below, bacteria grow on the surface of your teeth and use sugar for food. As the bacteria break down the sugar, an acid is produced. The acid can damage the enamel of your teeth. Bacteria then decay the softer parts of your teeth.

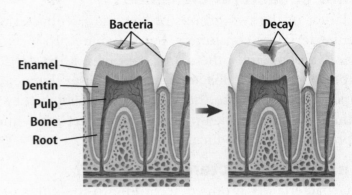

Picture This

5. **Highlight** the name of the part of the tooth that is damaged as bacteria in your mouth break down sugars.

Bacteria also cause diseases such as diphtheria, whooping cough, and tetanus. You have probably been vaccinated against these diseases. A **vaccine** is made from particles taken from the damaged cell walls of disease-causing bacteria or from killed bacteria. The vaccinations you receive keep you from getting diseases caused by those bacteria.

What are toxins?

Many pathogens produce poisons, called toxins, as they grow in your body or in food that you might eat. For example, botulism is a kind of food poisoning. Botulism is caused by a toxin produced by anaerobic bacteria whose endospores can survive in canned food. Most botulism endospores and other bacteria are destroyed by a long-term heat treatment known as sterilization. Most canned food that you buy has been sterilized. ☑

6. **Identify** a toxin that can be destroyed by sterilization.

_____

Bacteria and Industry

Many foods are produced using bacteria. Foods such as yogurt, cheeses, chocolate, and vinegar are all made with the help of bacteria. All food contains some bacteria, unless the food is sterilized. But when food is heated to sterilization temperature, the taste of the food can be changed.

What is pasteurization?

Pasteurization is a process that kills most harmful bacteria with little change in the flavor of the product. Pasteurization increases the length of time that foods can be stored without spoiling. Milk and fruit juices are some foods that usually are pasteurized.

Uses of Bacteria Many industries use bacteria. Bacteria and their by-products can be grown in bioreactors. Bioreactors are used to make medicines, vitamins, adhesives, and other substances.

Some bacteria are used to break down industrial or sewage wastes into simpler, harmless compounds. Sewage-treatment plants use bacteria to process waste. Some bacteria can digest oil and are used to clean up oil spills.

Bacteria and the Environment

Some consumer bacteria are called saprophytes (SAP ruh fites). A **saprophyte** is an organism that uses dead material as a source of food and energy. When saprophytic bacteria digest dead organisms, the nutrients in the dead organisms are made available to other organisms. When you compost kitchen or garden wastes, you use saprophytic bacteria to help turn those wastes into rich soil. Without saprophytic bacteria, layers of dead material would be deeper than you are tall all over Earth's surface. ☑

What is nitrogen fixation?

All living things need nitrogen. However, the nitrogen in Earth's atmosphere is not in a form that most organisms can use. Certain bacteria, called nitrogen-fixing bacteria, can change nitrogen from the air into a form that plants can use. Nitrogen-fixing bacteria are the only organisms that can combine nitrogen with other chemicals so it can be used by plants. Nitrogen-fixing bacteria live on the roots of certain plants, such as peas and soybeans. Animals and other organisms get nitrogen by eating plants that contain fixed nitrogen. These organisms then might be eaten by other organisms. In this way, nitrogen-fixing bacteria are an important part of many food chains.

Think it Over

7. Compare Why are some foods pasteurized rather than sterilized?

_____

_____

_____

Reading Check

8. Explain how saprophytes get energy.

_____

_____

_____

● After You Read

Mini Glossary

aerobe (AR ohb): an organism that uses oxygen for respiration

anaerobe (A nuh rohb): an organism that can live without oxygen

antibiotic: a chemical produced by bacteria that limits the growth of or kills other bacteria

endospore: a dormant form of bacteria

pasteurization: a process that is used to kill most harmful bacteria with little effect on the flavor of the product

pathogen: any organism that causes disease

saprophyte (SAP ruh fite): any organism that uses dead material as a food and energy source

vaccine: a substance made from particles taken from damaged bacterial cell walls or from killed bacteria

1. Review the terms and their definitions in the Mini Glossary. Write a sentence that explains the difference between aerobes and anaerobes.

_____

_____

_____

2. Complete the diagram below by defining each term.

Producers	versus	Consumers
_____		_____
_____		_____
_____		_____

Aerobes	versus	Anaerobes
_____		_____
_____		_____

End of Section

Science Online Visit **in6.msscience.com** to access your textbook, interactive games, and projects to help you learn more about bacteria.

Bacteria, Protists, and Fungi

section ❷ Protists

Standard—6.4.2: Give examples of organisms that cannot be neatly classified as either plants or animals, such as fungi and bacteria.
Also covers: 6.4.5

● Before You Read

Ponds sometimes are covered with green slime. What do you think the green slime is? What does it do?

_____

_____

_____

_____

What You'll Learn

- the characteristics of all protists
- the three protist groups
- the similarities and differences of the three protist groups

● Read to Learn

What is a protist?

A **protist** is a one-celled or many-celled organism that lives in moist or wet surroundings. Unlike bacteria, protists' cells are eukaryotic (yew kar ee AH tihk). Eukaryotic cells have a nucleus surrounded by a membrane. They also have other structures in their cytoplasm that are surrounded by membranes.

Protists are a group of organisms with different characteristics. One group has funguslike characteristics. Another has animal-like characteristics, while another group has plantlike characteristics. Some protists have both plant and animal-like characteristics. Some protists are producers. Others are consumers. Consumer protists include predators, parasites, and saprophytes. ☑

What are funguslike protists?

Funguslike protists spend part of their lives as one-celled organisms and part as many-celled organisms. Examples of funguslike protists are slime molds, water molds, and downy mildews. All funguslike protists are consumers. They are either saprophytes or parasites.

Mark the Text

Identify Main Ideas Skim the section before you read it. Circle the names of the three protist groups. As you read, underline one fact about each of the protist groups.

✔ **Reading Check**

1. **Identify** three types of consumer protists.

_____

_____

_____

What are animal-like protists?

Single-celled animal-like protists are known as **protozoans.** Protozoans live in water, soil, and in living or dead organisms.

Protozoans often are grouped by how they move from place to place. Many move by using whiplike flagella. Others are covered with cilia (SIHL ee uh), which are short, threadlike structures attached to the cell membrane. The motions of the cilia help move the protozoan through its watery environment. Some protozoans also move by making a part of their cytoplasm into a temporary footlike structure called a **pseudopod** (SEW duh pahd). ☑

All protozoans are consumers. Some take in food by using cilia to sweep food into their mouthlike openings. Others use pseudopods to trap food, such as bacteria cells. Some protozoans are saprophytes. Others are parasites that cause disease in animals and humans.

What are plantlike protists?

Plantlike protists are known as **algae** (AL jee). Some algae are one-celled and others are many-celled. The algae you find washed up on a beach are many-celled algae that are sometimes called seaweed.

Algae are grouped by their structure and the pigments, or coloring, they contain. Algae can be red, brown, golden, or different shades of green.

All algae contain the green pigment chlorophyll. Some algae also contain other pigments that cover up the green of the cholorophyll. Like plants, algae use chlorophyll to make their own food and produce oxygen as a waste product. Use the table below to review the important characteristics of three groups of protists.

☑ **Reading Check**

2. **Explain** What characteristic is used to group protozoans?

_____

_____

_____

Picture This

3. **Compare** Highlight the characteristic that funguslike and animal-like protists share.

Characteristics of Protist Groups		
Funguslike	**Animal-like**	**Plantlike**
Consumers; most saprophytes or parasites	Consumers; obtain food in many ways	Producers that contain chlorophyll
Most reproduce using spores, like fungi.	Like animals, most do not have cell walls.	Many have cell walls like plants.
	Most can move from place to place using cilia, flagella, or pseudopods.	Many-celled forms remain attached to surfaces with rootlike structures.

The Importance of Protists

Most protists can be seen only with a microscope. Even though they are small, protists are important to humans and to the environment.

How do protists affect humans?

Protists or their products are used in many everyday items. Algae are used in making toothpaste and ice cream. People in many parts of the world eat some algae. Other algae are used to make fertilizers. Others produce the sparkle that makes road lines visible at night.

Many protozoans are parasites that cause diseases such as malaria. The malaria parasite lives in mosquitoes and is transferred to humans. Malaria kills more than one million people each year.

A water mold is a funguslike protist that caused the Irish potato famine in the 1840s. A famine is an extreme shortage of food. The mold either killed most of the plants or caused the potatoes to rot. More than a million people in Ireland died as a result of the famine.

How do protists affect the environment?

Algae are important as food for animals that live in lakes and other bodies of water. Algae also produce much of the oxygen dissolved in Earth's water. Animals that live in water need oxygen to live. ☑

The algae in water environments can cause problems. Sometimes too much algae grows and the water becomes the color of the algae. This is called an algal bloom. So much algal waste is produced that it could kill fish and other organisms. Humans who drink or swim in the water might get sick.

Termites are able to eat wood because of protozoans that live in their digestive systems. Bacteria that live on and inside the protozoans produce substances that help termites digest wood.

FOLDABLES

B **Describe** Make a two-tab Foldable using notebook paper, as shown below. Use the Foldable to describe the effect protists have on humans and on the environment.

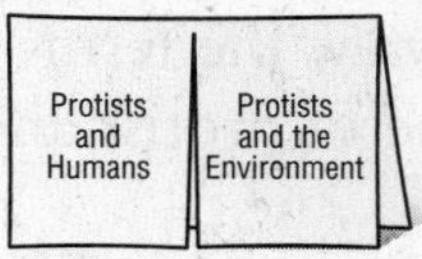

Protists and Humans | Protists and the Environment

✔ Reading Check

4. **Explain** What are two positive effects of protists in the environment?

_____

_____

_____

● After You Read

Mini Glossary

algae (AL jee): plantlike protists

protist: a one- or many-celled organism that lives in moist or wet surroundings

protozoan: a one-celled, animal-like protist

pseudopod (SEW duh pahd): temporary extensions of a protozoan's cytoplasm

1. Review the terms and their definitions in the Mini Glossary. Write a sentence about one type of protist and its characteristics.

_____

_____

_____

2. In the box on the left, write two uses that people have found for protists. In the box on the right, write two problems caused by protists.

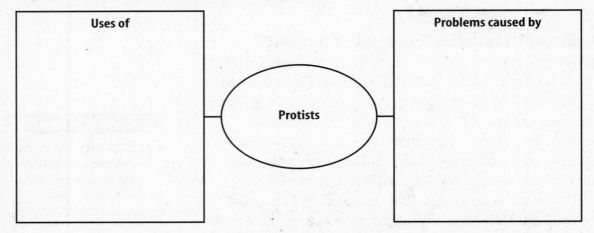

Uses of

Protists

Problems caused by

3. How did marking the text for main ideas help you learn about protists?

_____

_____

_____

End of Section

 **Science Online** Visit **in6.msscience.com** to access your textbook, interactive games, and projects to help you learn more about protists.

190 Bacteria, Protists, and Fungi

chapter 12

Bacteria, Protists, and Fungi

section ❸ Fungi

 Standard—6.4.2: Give examples of organisms that cannot be neatly classified as either plants or animals, such as fungi and bacteria.
Also covers: 6.4.8

● Before You Read

Have you ever eaten raw mushrooms? Have you eaten mushrooms that were cooked in a casserole? On the lines below, describe what a mushroom looks like and how it feels.

_____

_____

_____

● Read to Learn

What are fungi?

Do you ever have mushrooms on your pizza? Mushrooms are a type of fungi. The mushroom you see is only a small part of the organism that produces it. Most of the fungus grows below the mushroom underground or below the surface of the organic material on which it is growing.

What are the characteristics of fungi?

Most kinds of fungi are many-celled. Fungi cells are eukaryotic. Fungi once were thought to be plants. The cells of fungi have cell walls like plants. However, unlike plants, fungi do not have specialized tissues and organs such as leaves and roots. Fungi do not have chlorophyll and cannot make their own food. Most fungi are saprophytes, but some are parasites.

Fungi reproduce through the production of small, waterproof structures called spores. Spores can spread from place to place and grow into a new fungus when conditions are right. Fungi grow best in warm, humid places, such as tropical forests or between your toes. A type of fungus called mildew grows in moist places, like the shower curtain in a bathroom. ☑

What You'll Learn

- the characteristics of all fungi
- how fungi are classified by their methods of reproduction
- the difference between imperfect fungi and all other fungi

Study Coach

Make Flash Cards Think of a quiz question for each paragraph. Write the question on one side of the flash card and the answer on the other side. Keep quizzing yourself until you know all of the answers.

✔ Reading Check

1. Draw Conclusions Why is mildew found in places like shower curtains?

_____

_____

_____

What are the structures and functions of fungi?

The body of a fungus is made up of many-celled, threadlike tubes called **hyphae** (HI fee). In most fungi, the strands of hyphae form fuzzy mats, like those made by mold growing on bread. The hyphae grow, as shown below. Hyphae produce enzymes that help break down the food. The cells of the hyphae then take in the digested food.

Picture This

2. **Highlight** all of the hyphae on the figure. Then underline the name of the substance the hyphae produce.

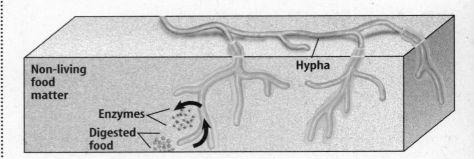

Non-living food matter

Hypha

Enzymes

Digested food

Hyphae also are important in the sexual reproduction of fungi. When fungi reproduce sexually, the hyphae of two different organisms of the same type of fungus join together. A special structure grows where the two hyphae join. Spores are produced in this structure.

Types of Fungi

The structure of a fungus and the kind of reproductive structures it makes are useful characteristics for identifying the different types of fungi. ☑

What are club fungi?

Mushrooms and toadstools are examples of club fungi. The spores of club fungi are made in a club-shaped part found on the reproductive structure.

What are sac fungi?

Yeasts and molds are examples of sac fungi. The spores of sac fungi are made in little sac-like parts of the reproductive structure. Yeasts are one-celled sac fungi.

What are zygospore fungi?

The fuzzy, black mold you sometimes find growing on a piece of fruit is a kind of zygospore fungi. When two zygospore hyphae join together during sexual reproduction, they form a special cell called a zygospore. **Sporangia** (spuh RAN jee uh) are reproductive structures that grow from the zygospore and produce spores.

Indiana Academic Standard Check

6.4.2: Give examples of organisms that cannot be neatly classified as either plants or animals, such as fungi and bacteria.

✔ 3. **Identify** the two characteristics used to classify fungi.

_____

_____

_____

What are other kinds of fungi?

Some fungi do not undergo sexual reproduction. They are called imperfect fungi because they seem to have an imperfect, or incomplete, life cycle.

Fungi in the Environment

Fungi are important in the environment because they break down waste materials. They turn food scraps and dead plants and animals into simpler materials that can then be used by other organisms. Fungi can cause diseases in plants and animals. Dutch elm disease is caused by sac fungi.

What are lichens?

Some fungi live in a close, helpful association with other organisms. A **lichen** (LI kun) is formed when a fungus and either a green alga or a cyanobacterium live together. This living arrangement provides the alga or cyanobacterium with a moist, protected place to live. The fungus gets food made by the alga or cyanobacterium.

Lichens that grow in the cracks of rocks release acids that help break down the rock. Over time, soil forms from the broken-down rock and decaying lichens. Lichens are sensitive to pollution. When lichens disappear from an area, the environment may have pollution problems. ☑

What are mycorrhizae?

Some fungi live in association with plants. Certain fungi form a complex web called **mycorrhizae** (mi kuh RI zee) around the roots of plants. The plants provide food to the fungi and the fungi help the plant roots take in water and nutrients.

Fungi and Humans

Some fungi are important in the production of other foods. The bread you eat probably was made with yeast. Yeasts and other fungi also are used to make some cheeses.

Fungi also can spoil food. You might find a kind of fungus called mold growing on an old loaf of bread or leftover food.

What are helpful and harmful fungi?

Many fungi naturally make antibiotics to prevent bacteria from growing near them. Penicillin is an antibiotic made by fungi. Some types of club fungi damage food crops. Other types of fungi can grow on or in your body and sometimes cause disease, such as athlete's foot.

C **Describe** Make a two-tab Foldable, as shown below. Use it to describe the effect fungi have on the environment and on humans.

Fungi in the Environment

Fungi and Humans

☑ **Reading Check**

4. **Explain** What may the disappearance of lichen from an area signal?

_____

_____

_____

● After You Read

Mini Glossary

hyphae (HI fee): the body of a fungus, made up of many-celled, threadlike tubes

lichen (LI kun): an organism formed when a fungus and a green alga or a cyanobacterium live together

mycorrhizae (mi kuh RI zee): web formed when fungi wrap around the roots of plants

sporangia (spuh RAN jee uh): reproductive structures of fungi; they grow from a zygospore and produce spores

1. Review the terms and their definitions in the Mini Glossary. Write a sentence that identifies the structures of fungi.

_____

_____

_____

2. In the diagram below, identify the three types of fungi. Give examples of each type.

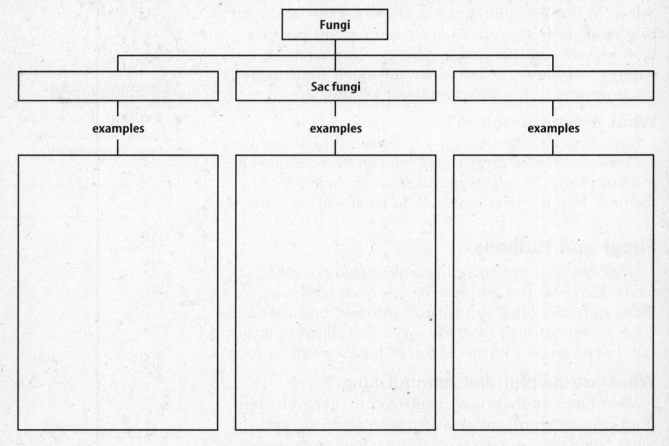

Fungi

| | Sac fungi | |

examples   examples   examples

End of Section

Science Online Visit **in6.msscience.com** to access your textbook, interactive games, and projects to help you learn more about fungi.

Plants

section ❶ An Overview of Plants

> **Standard—6.4.3:** Describe … body plans and internal structures animals and plants have that contribute to their being able to … food ….
> Also covers: 6.4.1, 6.4.5, 6.4.6, 6.4.8, 6.4.10

● Before You Read

What are your favorite plants? Why are they your favorites?

_____

_____

_____

What You'll Learn

- the characteristics common to all plants
- the adaptations that make it possible for plants to live on land
- how vascular and nonvascular plants are similar and different

● Read to Learn

Study Coach

Identify Answers Read each question heading aloud. When you have finished reading the section, read the question heading again. Answer the question based on what you have just read.

What is a plant?

Plants include trees, flowers, vegetables, and fruits. More than 260,000 plant species have been identified. Scientists expect more species will be found, mostly in tropical rain forests. Plants are important sources of food for humans. Most life on Earth would not be possible without plants.

All plants are made of cells and need water to live. Many have roots that hold them in the ground or onto an object such as a rock. Plants come in many sizes and live in almost every environment on Earth. Some grow in cold, icy regions. Others grow in hot, dry deserts.

What are the parts of a plant cell?

Every plant cell has a cell wall, a cell membrane, a nucleus, and other cell structures. A cell wall surrounds every plant cell. The cell wall gives the plant structure and provides protection. Animal cells do not have cell walls. ☑

Many plant cells have the green pigment, or coloring, called chlorophyll (KLOR uh fihl). Most green plants use chlorophyll to make food through a process called photosynthesis. Chlorophyll is found in cell structures called chloroplasts. The green parts of a plant usually have cells that contain many chloroplasts.

✔ Reading Check

1. **Explain** What surrounds every plant cell?

_____

_____

_____

Central Vacuole Most of the space inside a plant cell is taken up by a large structure called the central vacuole. The central vacuole controls the water content of the cell. Many other substances also are stored in the central vacuole, including the pigments that make some flowers red, blue, or purple.

Origin and Evolution of Plants

The first land plants probably could survive only in damp areas. Their ancestors may have been green algae that lived in the sea. Green algae are one-celled or many-celled organisms that use photosynthesis to make food. Because plants and green algae have the same type of chlorophyll, they may have come from the same ancestor.

Plants do not have bones or other hard parts that can become fossils. Plants usually decay instead. But there is some fossil evidence of plants. The oldest fossil plants are about 420 million years old. Scientists hypothesize that some of these early plants evolved into the plants that live today.

Plants that have cones, such as pine trees, probably evolved from plants that lived about 350 million years ago. Plants that have flowers most likely did not exist until about 120 million years ago. Scientists do not know the exact beginning of flowering plants.

Life on Land

Life on land has some advantages for plants. One advantage is that more sunlight and carbon dioxide are available on land than in water. Plants need sunlight and carbon dioxide for photosynthesis. During photosynthesis, plants give off oxygen. Over millions of years, as more plants grew on land, more oxygen was added to Earth's atmosphere. Because of this increase in oxygen, Earth's atmosphere became an environment in which land animals could live.

Adaptations to Land

Algae live in water or in very moist environments. Like green plants, algae make their own food through photosynthesis. To stay alive, algae need nutrients that are dissolved in the water that surrounds them. The water and dissolved nutrients enter and leave through the algae's cell membranes and cell walls. If the water dries up, the algae will die. Land plants have adaptations that allow them to conserve water.

💡 **Think it Over**

2. Conclude What do plants and green algae have in common?

_____

_____

_____

💡 **Think it Over**

3. Conclude How would a drought affect green algae?

_____

_____

_____

How are land plants supported and protected?

Plants cannot live without water. Plants that live on land have adaptations that help them conserve water. The stems, leaves, and flowers of many land plants are covered with a **cuticle** (KYEW tih kul). The cuticle is a waxy, protective layer that slows the loss of water. The cuticle is a structure that helps plants survive on land. ☑

Land plants also have to be able to support themselves. The cell walls that surround all plant cells contain **cellulose** (SEL yuh lohs). Cellulose is a chemical compound that plants can make out of sugar. Long chains of cellulose molecules form fibers in plant cell walls. These fibers give the plant structure and support.

The cell walls of some plants contain other substances besides cellulose. These substances help make the plant even stronger. Trees, such as oaks and pines, could not grow without very strong cell walls. Wood from trees can be used for building because of strong cell walls.

Life on land means that each plant cell is not surrounded by water. Land plants have tubelike structures that deliver water, nutrients, and food to all plant cells. These structures also help provide support for the plant.

How do plants reproduce on land?

Land plants reproduce by forming spores or seeds. These structures can survive dryness, cold, and other harsh conditions. They grow into new plants when the environmental conditions are right.

Classification of Plants

Plants can be classified into two major groups, vascular (VAS kyuh lur) and nonvascular plants. **Vascular plants** have tubelike structures that carry water, nutrients, and other substances to all the cells of the plant. **Nonvascular plants** do not have these tubelike structures. ☑

Scientists give each plant species its own two-word name. For example, the scientific name for a pecan tree is *Carya illinoiensis* and the name for a white oak is *Quercus alba*. In the eighteenth century a Swedish scientist, Carolus Linnaeus, created this system for naming plants.

✔ **Reading Check**

4. Identify the part of the plant that slows the loss of water.

_____

_____

_____

FOLDABLES™

A **Define** Make a four-tab book Foldable, as shown below. List each vocabulary word on the tabs. Inside, write a complete sentence definition of the word.

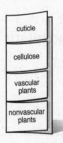

cuticle

cellulose

vascular plants

nonvascular plants

✔ **Reading Check**

5. Recall the two major groups of plants.

_____

_____

_____

● After You Read

Mini Glossary

cellulose: a chemical compound that forms the walls of plants; plants make it out of sugar

cuticle: a waxy, protective layer on the surface of the plant

nonvascular plants: plants without tubelike structures; move water and other substances through the plant in other ways

vascular plants: plants that have tubelike structures to carry water, nutrients, and other substances to the cells of the plant

1. Review the terms and their definitions in the Mini Glossary. Write a sentence that explains the difference between vascular and nonvascular plants.

_____

_____

_____

2. In the boxes below, describe four adaptations in plants that allow them to live on land. One adaptation is supplied for you.

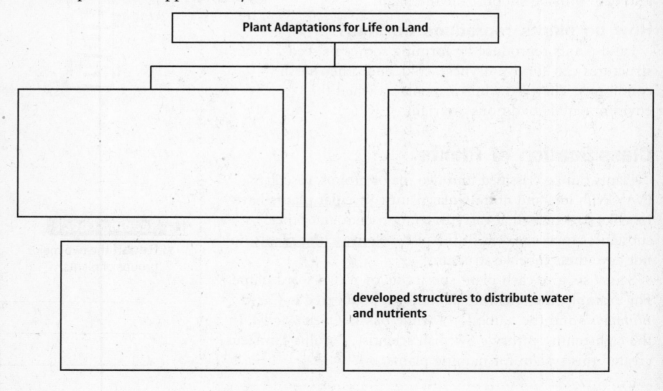

Plant Adaptations for Life on Land

developed structures to distribute water and nutrients

Science Online Visit **in6.msscience.com** to access your textbook, interactive games, and projects to help you learn more about plants.

 **Plants**

section ② Seedless Plants

Standard—**6.4.3:** Describe some of the great variety ... plants have that contribute to their being able to make or find food and reproduce.

● Before You Read

Ferns are a type of seedless plant that people grow as house plants. What do you think you would need to do to keep a fern alive indoors?

_____

_____

_____

_____

What You'll Learn

■ the differences between seedless nonvascular plants and seedless vascular plants
■ the importance of some nonvascular and vascular plants

● Read to Learn

Seedless Nonvascular Plants

Nonvascular plants are small and not always easy to notice. They include mosses, which you may have seen as green clumps on moist rocks or stream banks. Some other nonvascular plants are called hornworts and liverworts.

What are characteristics of seedless nonvascular plants?

Nonvascular plants do not grow from seeds. Instead, they reproduce by forming spores. They also do not have all of the parts that plants that grow from seed have. Nonvascular plants are usually only a few cells thick. They are not very tall, usually about 2 cm to 5 cm high. Nonvascular plants have structures that look like stems and leaves. Nonvascular plants do not have roots. Instead, they have **rhizoids** (RI zoydz). Rhizoids are threadlike structures that help to anchor the plants where they grow. Most nonvascular plants grow in damp places. They absorb water through their cell membranes and cell walls. ☑

Study Coach

Summarize As you read, make an outline to summarize the information in the section. Use the main headings in the section as the main headings in the outline. Complete the outline with the information under each heading in the section.

✔ Reading Check

1. Identify How do rhizoids help a plant?

_____

_____

_____

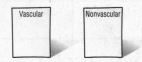
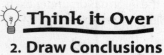
Mosses Most nonvascular plants are mosses. Mosses have green, leaflike growths arranged around a stalk. They also have rhizoids that anchor them to the ground. Moss rhizoids are made up of many cells. Mosses often grow on tree trunks, rocks, or the ground. Although most mosses live in damp places, some can live in deserts. Like all nonvascular plants, mosses reproduce by forming spores. In many moss species, a stalk grows up from the plant when it is ready to reproduce. Spores form in a cap at the top of the stalk.

Liverworts Liverworts got their name because people who lived during the ninth century used them to treat diseases of the liver. Liverworts have flattened, leaflike bodies. They usually have one-celled rhizoids.

Hornworts Hornworts have flattened, leaflike bodies like liverworts. Hornworts are usually less than 2.5 cm in diameter. Hornworts have one chloroplast in each of their cells. They get their name from the structures that produce spores, which look like tiny cattle horns.

How are nonvascular plants important?

Nonvascular plants need damp conditions to grow and reproduce. However, many species can withstand long, dry periods. Nonvascular plants can grow in thin soil and in soils where other plants cannot grow.

The spores of mosses, liverworts, and hornworts are carried by the wind. When a spore lands on the ground, it will grow into a new plant only if there is enough water and if other growing conditions are right.

Mosses, such as those pictured below, often are the first plants to grow in a new or disturbed environment, such as after a forest fire. Organisms that are the first to grow in new or disturbed areas are called **pioneer species**. As pioneer plant species die, they decay. As more and more plants grow and die, the decayed matter builds up. The decaying material and slow breakdown of rocks build soil. After enough soil is made, other organisms can move into the area.

Aaron Haupt

Seedless Vascular Plants

Both ferns and mosses reproduce by spores instead of seeds. But ferns are different from mosses because ferns have vascular tissues. Their long, tubelike cells carry water, minerals, and food to cells throughout the plant. Vascular plants can grow larger and thicker than nonvascular plants because the vascular tissue carries water and nutrients to all plant cells. ☑

What are the types of seedless vascular plants?

Seedless vascular plants include ferns, ground pines, spike mosses, and horsetails. Many species of seedless vascular plants are known only from fossils because they are now extinct. These plants covered much of Earth 360 million to 286 million years ago.

What are ferns?

Ferns are the largest group of seedless vascular plants. Ferns have stems, leaves, and roots. Fern leaves are called fronds as shown in the figure to the right. Spores form in structures found on the underside of the fronds. Although thousands of species of ferns are found on Earth today, many more species existed long

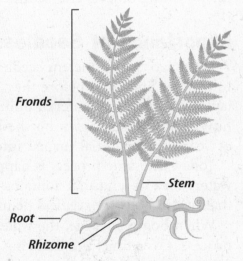

Fronds

Stem

Root

Rhizome

ago. Scientists have used clues from rock layers to learn that 360 million years ago much of Earth was covered with steamy swamps. The tallest plants were species of ferns that grew as tall as 25 m. The tallest ferns today are 3 m to 5 m tall and grow in tropical areas.

What are club mosses?

Ground pines and spike mosses are groups of plants that often are called club mosses. Club mosses are more closely related to ferns than to mosses. Club mosses have needle-like leaves. Their spores form at the end of the stems in structures that look like tiny pinecones. Ground pines grow in cold and hot areas. Ground pines are endangered in some places. They have been over-collected to make decorations such as wreaths.

☑ **Reading Check**

3. **Explain** How is having vascular tissue an advantage for plants?

_____

_____

_____

Picture This

4. **Identify** Circle the name of the structure where spores are found.

Spike mosses look a lot like ground pines. One species of spike moss, the resurrection plant, lives in desert areas. When there is not enough water, the plant curls up and looks dead. When water becomes available, the resurrection plant unfolds its green leaves and begins making food again. The plant can curl up again whenever conditions make it necessary.

How are horsetails different from other vascular plants?

Horsetails have a stem structure that is different from other vascular plants. The stem has a hollow center surrounded by a ring of vascular tissue. The stem also has joints. Leaves grow out around the stem at each joint. Horsetail spores form in conelike structures at the tips of some stems. The stems of horsetails contain silica, a gritty substance found in sand. In the past, horsetails were used for polishing objects and scouring cooking utensils. ☑

Importance of Seedless Plants

Long ago, when ancient seedless plants died, they sank into water and mud before they decayed. Over time, many layers of this plant material built up. Top layers became heavy and pressed down on the layers below. Over millions of years, this material turned into coal.

Today, the same process is happening in bogs. A bog is a watery area of land that contains decaying plants. Most plants that live in bogs are seedless plants like mosses and ferns.

When bog plants die, the watery soil slows the decaying process. Over time, the decaying plants are pressed into a substance called peat. Peat is mined from bogs to use as a low-cost fuel in places such as Ireland and Russia. Scientists hypothesize that over time, if the peat remains in the bog, it will become coal.

How are seedless vascular plants used?

Peat is used to enrich garden soil. Many people keep ferns as houseplants. Ferns also are sold as landscape plants for shady outdoor areas. Ferns sometimes are woven into baskets.

The rhizomes and fronds of some ferns can be eaten. The dried stems of one kind of horsetail can be ground into flour. Some seedless plants have been used as medicines for hundreds of years. For example, ferns have been used to treat bee stings, burns, and fevers. ☑

✔ Reading Check

5. Explain How do horsetails differ from other vascular plants?

_____

_____

_____

✔ Reading Check

6. Identify two ways seedless plants are used.

_____

_____

_____

● After You Read

Mini Glossary

pioneer species: organisms that are the first to grow in new or disturbed areas

rhizoid: threadlike structures that anchor nonvascular plants

1. Review the terms and their definitions in the Mini Glossary. Write a sentence to explain the importance of pioneer species to the environment.

_____

_____

2. Complete the Venn diagram below to help you compare nonvascular and vascular seedless plants. Include phrases that describe how the plant cells get nutrients and how the plants reproduce.

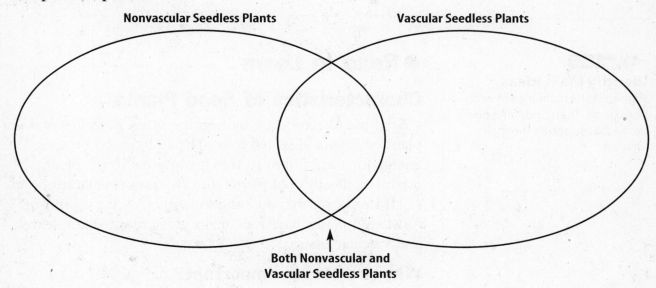

Nonvascular Seedless Plants   **Vascular Seedless Plants**

Both Nonvascular and Vascular Seedless Plants

3. How did summarizing the information in this section help you learn about nonvascular and vascular seedless plants?

_____

_____

 **Science Online** Visit **in6.msscience.com** to access your textbook, interactive games, and projects to help you learn more about seedless plants.

End of Section

section ③ Seed Plants

> **Standard—6.4.3:** Describe ... body plans and internal structures ... plants have that contribute to their being able to make or find food and reproduce.
> **Also covers:** 6.4.1, 6.4.13

What You'll Learn

- the characteristics of seed plants
- how roots, stems, and leaves function
- the characteristics of gymnosperms and angiosperms
- how monocots and dicots are different

Study Coach

Identify Main Ideas

Highlight the main idea in each paragraph. Then underline one detail that supports the main idea.

FOLDABLES™

C Classify Make a three-tab Foldable to write notes about the importance of plant leaves, stems, and roots.

● Before You Read

What are your favorite fruits? Where do these fruits come from?

_____

_____

_____

● Read to Learn

Characteristics of Seed Plants

Seed plants reproduce by forming seeds. A seed contains a plant embryo and stored food. The stored food provides energy for the embryo so that it can grow into a plant. Scientists classify seed plants into two groups: gymnosperms (JIHM nuh spurmz) and angiosperms (AN jee uh spurmz). Most seed plants have four main parts: roots, stems, leaves, and vascular tissue.

Why are leaves important?

The leaves of seed plants are the organs where food is made. The food-making process is called photosynthesis. Leaves come in many shapes, sizes, and colors.

What are the cell layers of a leaf?

A leaf has several layers of cells. A thin layer of cells called the epidermis covers and protects the top and bottom of the leaf. The epidermis of some leaves is covered with a waxy cuticle. Most leaves have small openings in the epidermis called **stomata** (STOH muh tuh) (singular, *stoma*). The stomata allow carbon dioxide, water, and oxygen to enter and exit the leaf. **Guard cells** located around each stoma open and close the stoma.

The palisade layer of a leaf is located just below the upper epidermis. This layer has long, narrow cells that contain chloroplasts. Plants make most of their food in the palisade cells.

The spongy layer is found between the palisade layer and the lower epidermis. The spongy layer is made of loosely arranged cells separated by air spaces. The veins of a leaf are made of vascular tissue and are located in the spongy layer. All the parts of the leaf can be seen in the figure below.

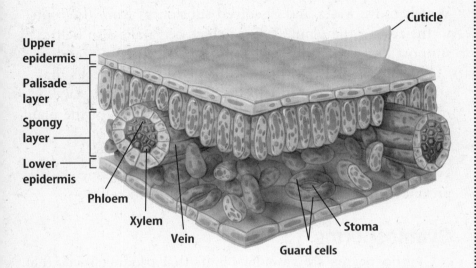

Upper epidermis

Palisade layer

Spongy layer

Lower epidermis

Cuticle

Phloem

Xylem

Vein

Guard cells

Stoma

Picture This

1. **Identify** Color in blue the plant layer that contains the chloroplasts. Color in red the plant layer that protects the leaf. Finally, underline the name of the part of the leaf that allows carbon dioxide, water, and oxygen to enter and exit the leaf.

What is the purpose of a plant's stem?

Plant stems are usually found above the ground. They support the branches, leaves, and reproductive structures of the plant. Materials move between the leaves and roots through vascular tissues in the stem. The stems of some plants also store food and water.

Plant stems can be woody or herbaceous (hur BAY shus). Herbaceous stems are soft and green, like those of a tulip. Woody stems are hard and rigid, like those of trees and shrubs. The trunk of a tree is a stem.

What do plant roots do?

The root system of most plants is the largest part of the plant. Roots contain vascular tissue. Water and dissolved substances move from the soil into the roots, and on up through the stems to the leaves. Roots also anchor plants and prevent them from being blown or washed away. Roots support the parts of the plant that are above ground—the stem, branches, and leaves. ☑

☑ Reading Check

2. **Identify** two things roots do for a plant.

_____

_____

_____

Roots can store food and water. They can take in oxygen that the plant needs for the process of respiration. For plants that grow in water, part or all of a plant's roots may grow above ground. Water does not have as much oxygen as air. The roots take in more oxygen from the air.

What are vascular tissues made of?

The vascular system in a seed plant contains three kinds of tissue—xylem, phloem, and cambium. <u>Xylem</u> (ZI lum) tissue is made of hollow, tubelike cells that are stacked one on top of the other to form a structure called a vessel. Vessels move water and dissolved substances from the roots to the rest of the plant. Xylem's thick cell walls also help support the plant.

<u>Phloem</u> (FLOH em) tissue is made of tubelike cells that are stacked to form structures called tubes. Phloem tubes move food from where it is made to other parts of the plant where the food is used or stored. ☑

Some plants have a layer of cambium tissue between xylem and phloem. <u>Cambium</u> (KAM bee um) tissue produces most of the new xylem and phloem cells.

Gymnosperms

<u>Gymnosperms</u> are vascular plants that produce seeds that are not protected by a fruit. Gymnosperms do not have flowers. The leaves of gymnosperms are usually shaped like needles or scales. Many gymnosperms are called evergreens because some green leaves always stay on their branches.

The gymnosperms are divided into four divisions. These four divisions are conifers, cycads, ginkgoes, and gnetophytes (NE tuh fites). The conifers are the most familiar gymnosperm division. Pines, firs, spruces, redwoods, and junipers are conifers. Conifers produce two types of cones—male and female. Seeds develop only on the female cone.

Angiosperms

An <u>angiosperm</u> is a vascular plant that forms flowers and produces one or more seeds that are protected inside a fruit. Peaches, apples, and tulips are examples of angiosperms. Angiosperms are common in all parts of the world. More than half of all known plant species are angiosperms.

Indiana Academic Standard Check

6.4.3: Describe some of the great variety of body plans and internal structures animals and plants have that contribute to their being able to make or find food and reproduce.

✔ **3. Describe** What does phloem tissue do?

_____

_____

_____

💡 **Think it Over**

4. Compare What is the difference between gymnosperms and angiosperms?

_____

_____

_____

What are the flowers of angiosperms like?

The flowers of angiosperms come in different shapes, sizes, and colors. Some parts of a flower grow into a fruit. Most fruits have seeds inside, like an apple. Some fruits have seeds on the surface, like a strawberry. Angiosperms are divided into two groups—monocots and dicots.

How do monocots and dicots differ?

A cotyledon (kah tul EE dun) is the part of a seed that stores food for the new plant. **Monocots** are angiosperms that have one cotyledon inside their seeds. **Dicots** are angiosperms that have two cotyledons inside their seeds.

Many foods come from monocots, including corn, rice, and wheat. Bananas and pineapples also are monocots. Familiar foods such as peanuts, peas, and oranges come from dicots. Most shade trees, such as oaks and maples, are dicots.

What is the life cycle of an angiosperm?

All organisms have life cycles—a beginning and an end. The angiosperm's life cycle begins with the seed and ends when the mature plant flowers and/or produces seed. Some angiosperms grow from seeds to maturity in less than a month. Some plants take as long as 100 years to grow from seed to maturity. Plants that complete their life cycles in one year are called annuals. Annuals must be grown from new seeds each year.

Plants that complete their life cycles in two years are called biennials (bi EH nee ulz). Biennials produce flowers and seeds only during the second year of growth. Angiosperms with life cycles that take longer than two years are called perennials. Most trees and shrubs are perennials.

Importance of Seed Plants

Gymnosperms are used for many purposes. Conifers are the most commonly used gymnosperm. Most of the wood used in building comes from conifers. Resin used to make chemicals found in soap, paint, and varnish also comes from conifers. ☑

Angiosperms are widely used by humans. Many of the foods you eat come from seed plants. Angiosperms are the source of many of the fibers used in making clothes. Paper is made from wood pulp that comes from trees. Desks and chairs are made from wood.

FOLDABLES

D **Compare** Make notes listing the characteristics of monocots and dicots in a two-tab Foldable. Include ways in which humans use each.

| Monocots | Dicots |

Reading Check

5. **Explain** Why are conifers important to the economy?

_____

_____

_____

● After You Read

Mini Glossary

angiosperm: vascular plant that flowers and produces one or more seeds inside a fruit

cambium: plant tissue that produces most of the new xylem and phloem cells

dicot: angiosperm that has two cotyledons inside its seeds

guard cells: cells that surround a stoma and open and close it

gymnosperm: vascular plant that produces seeds that are not protected by fruit

monocot: angiosperm that has one cotyledon inside its seeds

phloem: plant tissue made up of tubelike cells that are stacked to form tubes; tubes move food from where it is made to parts of the plant where it is used

stomata: small openings in the epidermis of the leaf

xylem: plant tissue made up of hollow, tubelike cells that are stacked one on top of the other to form vessels; vessels transport water and dissolved substances from the roots to all other parts of the plant

1. Review the terms and their definitions in the Mini Glossary. Write two sentences that explain what xylem and phloem do.

_____

_____

_____

2. Complete the chart below to list the four main parts of seed plants and describe what they do.

Parts of Seed Plants	What They Do

End of Section

 **Science**●nline Visit **in6.msscience.com** to access your textbook, interactive games, and projects to help you learn more about seed plants.

Invertebrate Animals

section ❶ What is an animal?

Standard—6.4.3: Describe some of the great variety of body plans and internal structures animals and plants have that contribute to their ....
Also covers: 6.4.1

● Before You Read

List the names of five animals on the lines below. Then write one thing that these animals have in common.

_____

_____

_____

● Read to Learn

Animal Characteristics

If you asked ten people what all animals have in common, you would get many different answers. Animals come in many different shapes and sizes. All animals, however, have five common characteristics.

1. All animals are many-celled organisms that are made of different kinds of cells.
2. Most animal cells have a nucleus and organelles. The nucleus and many of the organelles are surrounded by a membrane. A cell that contains a nucleus and organelles surrounded by membranes is called a eukaryotic (yew ker ee AH tihk) cell.
3. Animals cannot make their own food.
4. Animals digest their food.
5. Most animals can move from place to place.

What is symmetry?

As you study different groups of animals, you will look at their symmetry (SIH muh tree). **Symmetry** refers to the way parts of an object are arranged. If the parts are arranged in a way that allows the object to be divided into similar halves, it is symmetrical.

What You'll Learn

- the characteristics of animals
- the differences between vertebrates and invertebrates

Study Coach

Quiz Yourself As you read the section, write a question for each paragraph. Answer the question with information from the paragraph. Use the questions and answers to study the section.

💡 Think it Over

1. **Analyze** Name one reason animals need to move from place to place.

_____

_____

_____

What kind of symmetry do most animals have?

Most animals have either radial symmetry or bilateral symmetry. An animal with body parts arranged in a circle around a central point has radial symmetry. As you can see in the figure below, a sea anemone has radial symmetry. An animal with radial symmetry can find food and gather information from all directions. Other animals that have radial symmetry are jellyfish and sea urchins. ☑

An animal with bilateral symmetry has parts that are nearly mirror images of each other. You can draw a line down the center of its body to divide it into two similar parts. The figure below shows that a lobster has bilateral symmetry. A human also has bilateral symmetry.

☑ **Reading Check**

2. Explain What two forms of symmetry do most animals have?

_____

_____

_____

Sea anemones have radial symmetry.

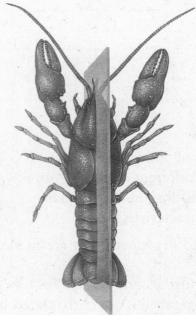

Lobsters have bilateral symmetry.

Many sponges are asymmetrical.

Picture This

3. Classify Draw a simple human figure beside the type of symmetry that humans have.

What is an asymmetrical animal like?

An animal with an uneven shape is called asymmetrical (AY suh meh trih kul). Its body cannot be divided into halves that are similar. Look at the sponge in the figure above. Notice that you cannot draw a line down the center of its body to divide it into two halves that are similar. As you learn more about invertebrates, think about their body symmetry. Notice how body symmetry affects the way they gather food and do other things.

Animal Classification

Animals have many characteristics in common. But when you think about the variety of animals you can name, you know that there are many different kinds of animals. Some animals have legs, others have wings. Some live on land, others live in water. Scientists use a classification system to place all animals into related groups.

Scientists separate animals into two groups—vertebrates (VUR tuh bruts) and invertebrates (ihn VUR tuh bruts). These two groups are shown in the figure below. Vertebrates are animals that have a backbone. **Invertebrates** are animals that do not have a backbone. About 97 percent of all animals are invertebrates.

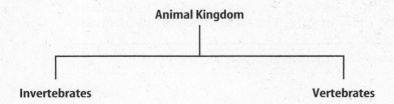

Scientists further classify the invertebrates into smaller groups, as shown in the figure below. The animals in each group share similar characteristics. These characteristics show that the animals within the group may have had a common ancestor.

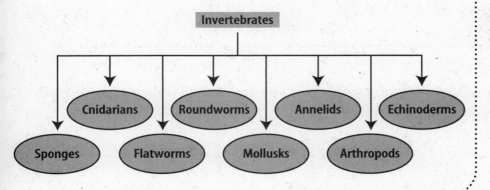

Applying Math

4. **Create a Circle Graph** In the circle below, draw a circle graph showing the percent of invertebrates and the percent of vertebrates.

Picture This

5. **Identify** Circle any words in the diagram that you do not know. When you have finished reading this chapter, review the words you circled and state a characteristic of each one.

● After You Read

Mini Glossary

invertebrates (ihn VUR tuh bruts): animals that do not have a backbone

symmetry (SIH muh tree): the way parts of an object are arranged

1. Review the terms and their definitions in the Mini Glossary. Write a sentence that explains the difference between an animal that has symmetry and one that is asymmetrical.

   _____

   _____

   _____

2. Fill in the table below to describe the common characteristics of all animals.

Common Characteristics of All Animals
1.
2.
3.
4.
5.

3. How did writing and answering quiz questions help you remember what you have read about animal characteristics and classification?

   _____

   _____

   _____

End of Section

 Visit **in6.msscience.com** to access your textbook, interactive games, and projects to help you learn more about the characteristics of animals.

Invertebrate Animals

section ➋ Sponges, Cnidarians, Flatworms, and Roundworms

 Standard—6.4.4: Recognize and describe that a species comprises all organisms that can mate with one another to produce fertile offspring.
Also covers: 6.4.3, 6.4.9

● Before You Read

On the lines below, list a difference between the way plants and animals get food.

_____

_____

● Read to Learn

Sponges

Sponges are classified as animals because they cannot make their own food. A sponge's body is made of two layers of cells. Adult sponges remain attached to one place for their lifetime. There are about 15,000 species of sponges.

How does a sponge eat?

All sponges are filter feeders. Sponges filter tiny food particles from the water that flows through their bodies. The inner part of a sponge's body is lined with collar cells. Thin, whiplike structures, called flagella (flah JEH luh), are attached to the collar cells. The whiplike movements of the flagella keep water moving through the sponge. Other cells digest the food, carry nutrients to all parts of the sponge, and remove wastes.

How does a sponge protect itself?

Many sponges have soft bodies that are supported by sharp, glass-like structures called spicules (SPIHK yewlz). Other sponges contain a substance called spongin, which is like foam rubber. Spongin makes sponges soft and stretchable. Some sponges have both spicules and spongin to protect their soft bodies.

What You'll Learn

- the structures of sponges and cnidarians
- how sponges and cnidarians get food and reproduce
- about flatworms and roundworms

Study Coach

Sticky-Note Discussions
As you read the section, use sticky-note paper to mark paragraphs you find interesting. Share the interesting information with a partner.

FOLDABLES™

A Explain Make a four-tab book Foldable, as shown below. Take notes on what you read about each classification of animal.

How do sponges reproduce?

Sponges can reproduce asexually and sexually. A sponge reproduces asexually when a bud on the side of the parent sponge develops into a small sponge. The small sponge breaks off, floats away, and attaches itself to a new surface. New sponges also can grow from pieces of a sponge.

Most sponges that reproduce sexually are hermaphrodites (hur MA fruh dites). This means they produce both eggs and sperm. The figure below shows sexual reproduction in sponges. Sponges release sperm into the water. The sperm float until they are drawn into another sponge. The sperm fertilizes an egg. A larva develops in the sponge. The larva leaves the sponge and settles to the bottom. It attaches to the surface on which it lands and grows into a new sponge.

Picture This

1. **Identify** Circle the names of two structures needed for sexual reproduction.

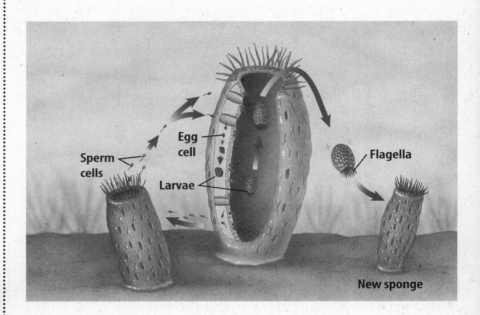

Sperm cells

Egg cell

Larvae

Flagella

New sponge

Indiana Academic Standard Check

6.4.9: Recognize and explain that two types of organisms may interact in a competitive or cooperative relationship, such as producer/consumer, predator/prey, or parasite/host.

✔ **2. Explain** Why does a cnidarian use stinging cells?

_____

_____

Cnidarians

Jellyfish, sea anemones, hydra, and corals are cnidarians. **Cnidarians** (nih DAR ee unz) are hollowed-bodied animals with two cell layers that are organized into tissues. Cnidarians have tentacles surrounding their mouths. The tentacles shoot out harpoon-like stinging cells to capture prey. Cnidarians have radial symmetry, so they can locate food that floats by from any direction. The inner cell layer digests the food. Nerve cells work together as a nerve net throughout the whole body. ☑

What kinds of body forms do cnidarians have?

Cnidarians have two different body forms. The vase-shaped body form is called a **polyp** (PAH lup). Sea anemones and hydras are polyps. Polyps usually remain attached to a surface. A jellyfish has a free-swimming, bell-shaped body that is called a **medusa** (mih DEW suh). Jellyfish are not strong swimmers. Instead they drift with the ocean currents. Some cnidarians go through both a polyp stage and a medusa stage during their life cycles. ☑

How do cnidarians reproduce?

Cnidarians reproduce both sexually and asexually. The polyp form of a cnidarian reproduces asexually by budding. The bud falls off the parent and develops into a new polyp. Some polyps also can reproduce sexually by releasing eggs or sperm into the water. Eggs that are fertilized by the sperm develop into new polyps.

The medusa form of a cnidarian has a two-stage life cycle, as shown in the figure below. A medusa reproduces sexually to produce polyps. Then each polyp reproduces asexually to form new medusae.

✔ **Reading Check**

3. **Identify** the two body forms of cnidarians.

_____

_____

Picture This

4. **Apply** Draw a circle around the three pictures of the medusae in the diagram.

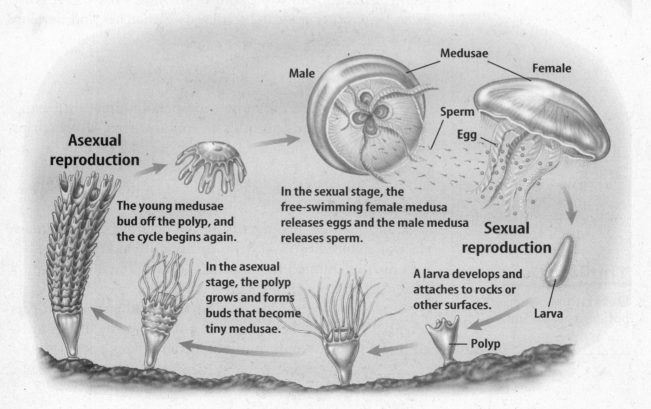

Asexual reproduction

The young medusae bud off the polyp, and the cycle begins again.

In the asexual stage, the polyp grows and forms buds that become tiny medusae.

Male

Medusae

Female

Sperm

Egg

In the sexual stage, the free-swimming female medusa releases eggs and the male medusa releases sperm.

Sexual reproduction

A larva develops and attaches to rocks or other surfaces.

Larva

Polyp

Flatworms

Unlike sponges and cnidarians, flatworms search for food. Flatworms are invertebrates with long, flattened bodies and bilateral symmetry. A flatworm's body is soft and has three layers of tissue organized into organs and organ systems. Some kinds of flatworms can move around and search for food. These flatworms have a digestive system with one opening. Most flatworms are parasites that live in or on their hosts. A parasite gets its food and shelter from its host.

What are tapeworms?

Tapeworms are flatworms that live in the intestines of their hosts. A tapeworm does not have a digestive system. It gets its nutrients from digested food in the host's intestine. A tapeworm's head has hooks and suckers that attach to the host's intestine. A human can be a host for a tapeworm. ☑

How do tapeworms reproduce?

The body of a tapeworm is made up of segments. A tapeworm grows by adding segments directly behind its head. Each body section has both male and female reproductive organs. Eggs and sperm are released inside the segment. After it is filled with fertilized eggs, the segment breaks off. The segment passes with wastes out of the host's body. If it is eaten by another host, the fertilized egg hatches and develops into a tapeworm.

Roundworms

Roundworms are the most widespread animal on Earth. There are thousands of kinds of roundworms. Heartworms, which can infect the hearts of dogs, are one kind of roundworm.

A roundworm's body is a tube inside a tube. Between the two tubes is a cavity full of fluid. The fluid-filled cavity separates the digestive tract from the body wall. The digestive tract of a roundworm has two openings. Food enters the roundworm through the mouth, is digested in a digestive tract, and wastes exit through the anus.

Some roundworms are decomposers. Other roundworms are predators. The heartworm is a roundworm that is an animal parasite. Some roundworms are plant parasites.

☑ Reading Check

5. **Explain** how a tapeworm attaches to the host's intestine.

_____

_____

_____

💡 Think it Over

6. **Determine** What is the host for a heartworm?

_____

● After You Read

Mini Glossary

cnidarian (nih DAR ee un): a hollow-bodied animal with tentacles for catching food and two cell layers that are organized into tissues

medusa (mih DEW suh): a free-swimming, bell-shaped body of a cnidarian

polyp (PAH lup): a vase-shaped body of a cnidarian

1. Review the terms and their definitions in the Mini Glossary. Choose the term that names an invertebrate. Write a sentence describing the animal.

_____

_____

_____

2. Complete the Venn diagram below to help you compare flatworms and roundworms.

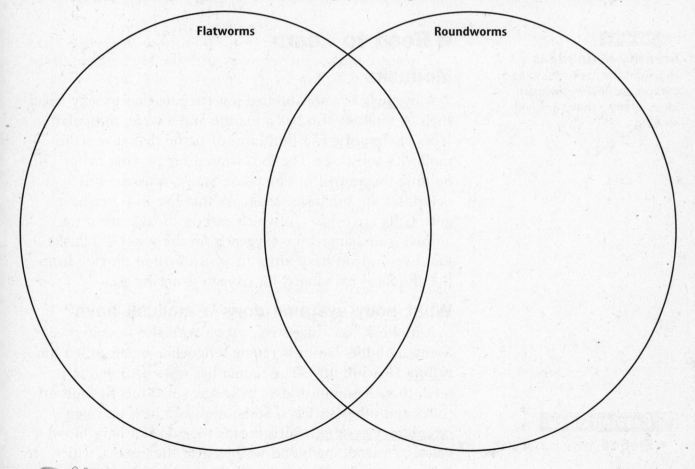

Flatworms   Roundworms

Science Online Visit **in6.msscience.com** to access your textbook, interactive games, and projects to help you learn more about sponges, cnidarians, flatworms, and roundworms.

End of Section

section ❸ Mollusks and Segmented Worms

 Standard—6.4.3: Describe some of the great variety of body plans and internal structures animals and plants have that contribute to their being able ....
Also covers: 6.4.1, 6.4.9

What You'll Learn

- the characteristics of mollusks
- differences between an open and a closed circulatory system
- the characteristics of segmented worms
- the digestive process of an earthworm

● Before You Read

On the lines below, describe some characteristics of an earthworm.

_____

_____

_____

◀ **Mark the Text**

Identify Main Ideas
Highlight the main idea in each paragraph. Review the main ideas after you have finished reading.

● Read to Learn

Mollusks

A **mollusk** is a soft-bodied invertebrate that usually has a shell. A mollusk also has a mantle and a large, muscular foot. The **mantle** is a thin layer of tissue that covers the mollusk's soft body. The foot is used for moving or for holding the animal in one place. Snails, mussels, and octopuses are mollusks. Mollusks that live in water have gills. **Gills** are organs in which carbon dioxide from the animal is exchanged for oxygen from the water. Mollusks that live on land have lungs in which carbon dioxide from the animal is exchanged for oxygen from the air.

What body systems does a mollusk have?

A mollusk has a digestive system with two openings. Many mollusks have a scratchy tonguelike organ called the **radula** (RA juh luh). The radula has rows of tiny, sharp teeth that the mollusk uses to scrape small bits of food off rocks and other surfaces. Some mollusks have an **open circulatory system**, which means they do not have blood vessels. Instead, the blood washes over the organs, which are grouped together in a fluid-filled cavity inside the animal's body. ☑

☑ **Reading Check**

1. Define What is a radula?

_____

_____

Types of Mollusks

Scientists use three characteristics to classify a mollusk.

1. Does the mollusk have a shell?
2. If the mollusk has a shell, what kind of shell is it?
3. What type of foot does the mollusk have?

What are gastropods?

Gastropods are the largest group of mollusks. Most gastropods have one shell. Snails and conchs are examples of single-shelled gastropods. A slug is a gastropod that has no shell. Some gastropods live in water and others live on land. A gastropod uses its large, muscular foot to move about. Gastropods secrete mucus, which helps them glide across surfaces.

What are bivalves?

Bivalves are mollusks with two shell halves joined by a hinge. Scallops and clams are bivalves. Large, powerful muscles open and close the shell halves. Bivalves are water animals. A bivalve filters food from water that enters into and is filtered through the gills.

What are cephalopods?

Squid and octopuses are cephalopods (SE fah lah pawdz). Most cephalopods have a stiff plate inside their bodies instead of a shell on the outside. They have a well-developed head and a "foot" that is made up of tentacles with suckers. The mouth is at the base of the tentacles. A cephalopod has a **closed circulatory system** in which blood is carried through blood vessels.

Cephalopods can move quickly through the water. The figure below compares the movement of a squid as it releases water to the movement of a balloon as it releases air.

FOLDABLES

B **Describe** Make a six-tab book Foldable, as shown below. Write the main ideas as you read about each type of mollusk or segmented worm.

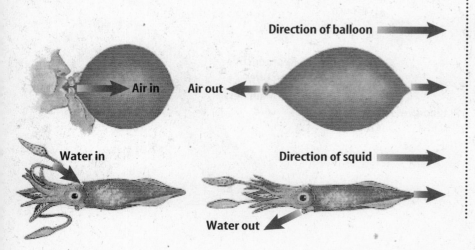

Direction of balloon

Air in   Air out

Water in   Direction of squid

Water out

Picture This

2. **Explain** Use the figure to explain to a partner how a squid moves.

How does a cephalopod move?

A muscular envelope, called the mantle, surrounds a cephalopod's internal organs. Water enters the space between the mantle and the body organs. When the mantle closes, water is squeezed through a funnel-like structure called a siphon. This squeezing creates a force that causes the animal to move in the opposite direction of the stream of water.

Segmented Worms

Earthworms, leeches, and marine worms are segmented worms. Segmented worms are also called annelids (A nul idz). A segmented worm's body is made up of repeating rings that make the worm flexible. Each ring or segment has nerve cells, blood vessels, part of the digestive tract, and the coelom (SEE lum). The coelom is a body cavity that separates the internal organs from the inside of the body wall. A segmented worm has a closed circulatory system and a complete digestive system with two body openings. ✔

How does an earthworm move and eat?

An earthworm has more than 100 rings or segments. Each segment has bristles, or setae (SEE tee), on the outside. Setae are used to grip the soil while two sets of muscles move them through the soil. As the earthworm moves, it takes soil into its mouth. The earthworm gets its food from the soil. The soil moves from the mouth, to the crop, to the gizzard. In the gizzard, the food and the soil are ground. In the intestine, the food is broken down and absorbed by the blood. Waste materials and undigested soil leave the earthworm through the anus. All of these structures are shown in the figure below.

✔ Reading Check

3. **Describe** What separates the internal organs of an earthworm from the body wall?

_____

_____

Picture This

4. **Identify** Circle the parts of an earthworm that are also found in humans.

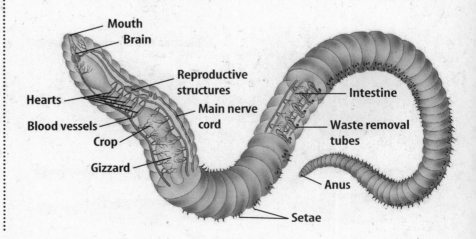

Mouth
Brain
Reproductive structures
Hearts
Blood vessels
Main nerve cord
Crop
Gizzard
Intestine
Waste removal tubes
Anus
Setae

How does an earthworm breathe?

An earthworm does not have lungs or gills. An earthworm breathes through its mucous-covered skin. Carbon dioxide moves out of the body and oxygen moves into the body through the skin. If the mucus covering the skin is removed, the earthworm may die of suffocation. ☑

How does a leech get its food?

Leeches can be found in freshwater, salt or marine water, and on land. A leech is a segmented worm with a flat body. It has suckers on both ends that it uses to attach itself to an animal to remove blood.

A leech can store large amounts of blood that it slowly releases into its digestive system when it needs food. Some leeches can store as much as ten times their own weight in blood, and the blood can be stored for months. Although leeches like a diet of blood, most can eat small water animals.

What are the characteristics of a marine worm?

There are more than 8,000 kinds of marine worms. Marine worms are the most varied group of annelids. The word **polychaete** means "many bristles." A marine worm has bristles, or setae, along the sides of its body. Because of these bristles, marine worms are sometimes called bristle worms. Marine worms can use these setae to walk, swim, or dig. ☑

Some marine worms are filter feeders. They either dig down into the mud or build hollow tubes. Then they use their bristles to filter food from the water. Others eat plants or decaying materials. Some marine worms are predators and some are parasites. The many ways that marine worms get food explains why they are so varied.

☑ Reading Check

5. Explain how an earthworm breathes.

_____

_____

_____

☑ Reading Check

6. Apply How do marine worms use setae?

_____

_____

_____

● After You Read

Mini Glossary

closed circulatory system: a circulatory system in which blood is carried through blood vessels

gill: an organ in which carbon dioxide from an animal is exchanged for oxygen from the water

mantle: a thin layer of tissue that covers a mollusk's soft body

mollusk: a soft-bodied invertebrate that has a mantle and a large muscular foot; usually has a shell

open circulatory system: a circulatory system without blood vessels in which blood washes over the organs

radula (RA juh luh): a tonguelike organ in mollusks

1. Review the terms and their definitions in the Mini Glossary. Write two sentences that explain the difference between an open circulatory system and a closed circulatory system.

   _____

   _____

   _____

2. Fill in the table below to identify the main characteristics of mollusks and segmented worms.

	Main Characteristics
Mollusks	1. 2. 3. 4. 5. 6.
Segmented Worms	1. 2. 3. 4.

End of Section

Visit **in6.msscience.com** to access your textbook, interactive games, and projects to help you learn more about mollusks and segmented worms.

section ❹ Arthropods and Echinoderms

> **Standard—6.4.3:** Describe some of the great variety of body plans and internal structures animals and plants have that contribute to their being able . . . .
> **Also covers: 6.4.9**

● Before You Read

On the lines below, list three kinds of insects. Next to the name of each insect, write a short description of the insect.

_____

_____

_____

● Read to Learn

Arthropods

An **arthropod** (AR thruh pahd) is an invertebrate animal with jointed appendages (uh PEN dih juz). **Appendages** are structures such as claws, legs, or antennae that grow from the body. Arthropods have bilateral symmetry and segmented bodies.

How does an arthropod protect itself?

Arthropods have hard body coverings called **exoskeletons.** The exoskeleton protects and supports the animal's body and reduces water loss. As the animal grows, the old exoskeleton must be shed because it does not grow with the animal. The process of shedding the exoskeleton is called molting.

What are the characteristics of insects?

Insects make up the largest group of arthropods. Scientists have classified more than 700,000 species of insects. Insects have three body regions—head, thorax, and abdomen. Insects have an open circulatory system. Many insects, such as butterflies, completely change their body form as they grow. This change in body form is called **metamorphosis** (met uh MOR fuh sus).

What You'll Learn

- the features used to classify arthropods
- the structure and function of the exoskeleton
- the features of echinoderms

Study Coach

Summarize As you read this section, stop after every paragraph and summarize what you have just read in your own words.

FOLDABLES

❸ **Compare** Make a two-tab book Foldable, as shown below. Write statements or phrases about Arthropods and Echinoderms as you read. Use the statements to compare these animals.

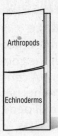

Arthropods

Echinoderms

What are two kinds of metamorphosis?

There are two kinds of insect metamorphosis—complete and incomplete. Complete metamorphosis is shown on the left in the figure below. It has four stages—egg, larva, pupa (PYEW puh), and adult. Notice that each stage is different from the others. The three stages of incomplete metamorphosis—egg, nymph, and adult—are shown on the right in the figure below. A nymph looks like a small adult.

Complete Metamorphosis

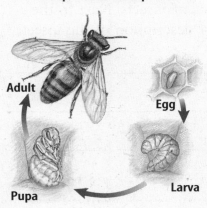

Adult

Egg

Pupa

Larva

Incomplete Metamorphosis

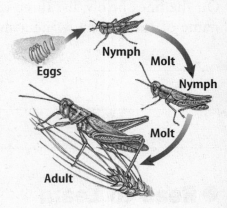

Eggs

Nymph

Molt

Nymph

Molt

Adult

Picture This

1. **Identify** Circle the names of the stages that are the same for complete and incomplete metamorphosis.

What is an arachnid?

Arachnids (uh RAK nudz) are arthropods that have only two body regions—a cephalothorax (sef uh luh THOR aks) and an abdomen. The cephalothorax is a body region made up of a head and a thorax. An arachnid has four pairs of legs attached to its cephalothorax. Spiders, ticks, mites, and scorpions are arachnids.

How do spiders catch their food?

Spiders are predators that use a pair of appendages near their mouths to inject venom, or poison, into their prey. The venom makes the prey unable to move. After the prey has been injected with venom, spiders inject another substance that turns the prey's body into a liquid, which spiders drink. Some spiders weave webs to trap their prey. Other spiders chase and catch their prey.

What are centipedes and millipedes?

Centipedes and millipedes are long, thin segmented animals. Centipedes have one pair of jointed legs attached to each segment. They are predators that use poison to catch prey. Millipedes have two pairs of jointed legs attached to each segment. They eat plants.

Applying Math

2. **Calculate** Complete the following sentence by filling in the correct numbers. A centipede with 30 segments has _____ legs. A millipede with 30 segments has _____ legs.

What are the characteristics of crustaceans?

Crustaceans include some of the largest arthropods, such as crabs and lobsters. Most crustaceans are small marine animals called zooplankton. Zooplankton are tiny free-floating animals that serve as food for other marine animals.

Most crustaceans have two pairs of antennae attached to the head, three types of chewing appendages, and five pairs of legs. Many crustaceans that live in water also have appendages called swimmerets on the abdomen. Swimmerets help exchange carbon dioxide from the animal for oxygen in the water. ☑

Echinoderms

Echinoderms (ih KI nuh durmz) are animals that have radial symmetry. Sea stars and sand dollars are echinoderms. Echinoderms have spines of different lengths that cover the outside of their bodies. Most echinoderms have an internal skeleton made up of bonelike plates that supports and protects the animal. Echinoderms have a simple nervous system, but no head or brain. Some echinoderms are predators, some are filter feeders, and some feed on decaying matter.

What is a water-vascular system?

An echinoderm has a water-vascular system, which is a network of water-filled canals and thousands of tube feet. The tube feet work like suction cups to help the animal move and capture prey. The figure below shows the parts of a sea star. A sea star eats by pushing its stomach out of its mouth and into the opened shell of its prey. After the prey's body is digested, the sea star pulls in its stomach. Like some other invertebrates, sea stars can regrow lost or damaged parts.

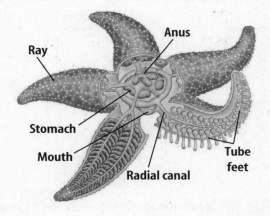

Ray
Anus
Stomach
Mouth
Radial canal
Tube feet

✔ **Reading Check**

3. **Determine** What is the purpose of swimmerets?

_____

_____

_____

Picture This

4. **Explain** Use the diagram to explain to a partner how the sea star eats.

● After You Read

Mini Glossary

appendage (uh PEN dihj): a structure such as a claw, leg, or antennae that grows from the body

arthropod (AR thruh pahd): an invertebrate animal with jointed appendages and an exoskeleton

exoskeleton: a hard body covering that protects and supports the body and reduces water loss

metamorphosis (met uh MOR fuh sus): a change in body form

1. Review the terms and their definitions in the Mini Glossary. Write a sentence that describes how an arthropod might use an appendage.

_____

_____

_____

2. Complete the concept map below about arthropod classification.

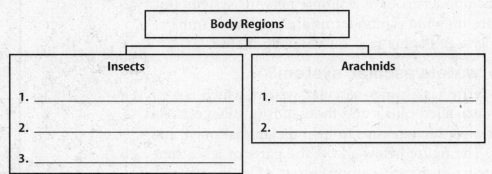

3. Complete the flowcharts to compare complete and incomplete metamorphosis.

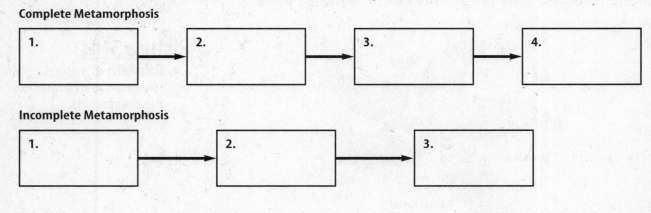

End of Section

Science Online Visit **in6.msscience.com** to access your textbook, interactive games, and projects to help you learn more about arthropods and echinoderms.

Vertebrate Animals

section ❶ Chordate Animals

Standard—**6.4.3:** Describe some of the great variety of body plans and internal structures animals and plants have that contribute to their being able .... Also covers: 6.4.9

● Before You Read

List three animals on the lines below. Then write one thing that all these animals have in common with humans.

_____

_____

_____

What You'll Learn
- the characteristics of chordates
- the characteristics of all vertebrates
- the difference between ectotherms and endotherms
- the three classes of fish

● Read to Learn

What is a chordate?

<u>Chordates</u> (KOR dayts) are animals that have the following three characteristics—a notochord (NOH tuh cord), a nerve cord, and pharyngeal (fur RIN jee uhl) pouches at some time during their development.

The notochord is a flexible rod that runs the length of the developing organism. The nerve cord is made of nerve tissue. In most chordates, one end of the nerve cord develops into the organism's brain.

Pharyngeal pouches are slitlike openings between the inside of the body and the outside of the body. They are present only in the early stages of the organism's development. In some chordates, like the lancelet in the figure below, the pharyngeal pouches develop into gill slits.

Study Coach

Create a Quiz Write a question about the main idea under each heading. Exchange quizzes with another student. Together discuss the answers to the quiz questions.

FOLDABLES

Ⓐ Define Use a quarter sheet of notebook paper, as shown below, to define the key words in this section—chordate, ectotherm, endotherm, and cartilage.

Chordate
Ectotherm
Endotherm
Cartilage

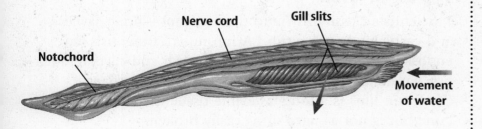

Notochord **Nerve cord** **Gill slits**

Movement of water

What are the characteristics of vertebrates?

Chordates are classified into several smaller groups. The largest group of chordates is made up of the vertebrates, which include humans. All vertebrates have an internal system of bones called an endoskeleton. The endoskeleton supports and protects the body's internal organs. For example, the skull is the part of the endoskeleton that surrounds and protects the brain.

How do vertebrates control body temperature?

Vertebrates are either ectotherms or endotherms. __Ectotherms__ (EK tuh thurmz) are cold-blooded animals. Their body temperature changes as the temperature of their surroundings changes. Fish are ectotherms.

__Endotherms__ (EN duh thurmz) are warm-blooded animals. Their body temperature does not change with the surrounding temperature. Humans are endotherms. Your body temperature is usually about 37°C.

Fish

Fish are the largest group of vertebrates. All fish are ectotherms and live in water. Some species of fish are adapted to live in freshwater and other species are adapted to live in salt water.

Fish have gills. Gills are fleshy filaments where carbon dioxide and oxygen are exchanged. Water that contains oxygen passes over the gills. When blood is pumped into the gills, the oxygen in the water moves into the blood. At the same time, carbon dioxide moves out of the blood in the gills and into the water. ☑

Most fish have pairs of fanlike fins. Fish use fins to steer, balance, and move. The motion of the tail fin pushes the fish through the water.

Most fish have scales. Scales are thin structures made of a bony material that overlap to cover the skin.

Types of Fish

Scientists classify fish into three groups—bony, jawless, and cartilaginous (kar tuh LA juh nuhs). Bony fish have endoskeletons made of bone. Jawless fish and cartilaginous fish have endoskeletons made of cartilage. __Cartilage__ (KAR tuh lihj) is a tough, flexible tissue that is similar to bone but is not as hard or as easily broken.

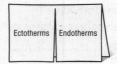

What are the characteristics of bony fish?

About 95 percent of all fish species are bony fish. Goldfish, trout, and marlins are examples. The body structure of a bony fish is shown in the figure below. Bony fish swim easily in water because their scales are covered with slimy mucus.

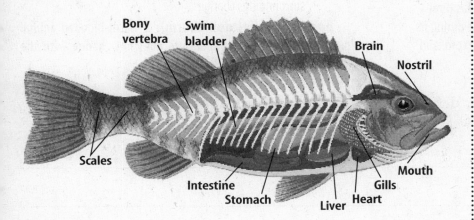

Most bony fish have a swim bladder. A swim bladder is an air sac that helps control the depth at which the fish swims. Gases move between the swim bladder and the fish's blood. When gases move into the swim bladder, the fish rises in the water. When gases leave the swim bladder, the fish sinks lower in the water.

How do bony fish reproduce?

Most bony fish reproduce using external fertilization (fur tuh luh ZAY shun). External fertilization takes place when egg and sperm cells join outside the female's body. First, a female releases large numbers of eggs into the water. Then, a male swims over the eggs, releasing sperm into the water. Many eggs are fertilized by the sperm. ☑

What are jawless and cartilaginous fish?

Jawless fish have long, tubelike bodies with no scales. They have round, muscular mouths with no jaw. Their mouths have sharp toothlike structures. Their endoskeleton is made of cartilage. Lampreys are jawless fish that attach to another fish with their strong mouths. Lampreys feed by removing blood and other body fluids from the host fish.

Cartilaginous fish also have endoskeletons made of cartilage. They have movable jaws that usually have well-developed teeth. Their bodies are covered with sandpaperlike scales. Sharks, skates, and rays are cartilaginous fish. Most cartilaginous fish are predators.

Picture This

2. Highlight In the drawing of a bony fish, color the skeleton of the fish and label it *Skeleton*.

☑ **Reading Check**

3. Determine How does external fertilization take place?

_____

_____

_____

● After You Read

Mini Glossary

cartilage (KAR tuh lihj): a tough, flexible tissue that is similar to bone, but not as hard or as easily broken

chordate (KOR dayt): an animal that has three characteristics present at some time during its development—a notochord, nerve cord, and pharyngeal pouches

ectotherm (EK tuh thurm): a cold-blooded animal whose body temperature changes as the temperature of its surroundings changes

endotherm (EN duh thurm): a warm-blooded animal whose body temperature does not change with the temperature of its surroundings

1. Review the terms and their definitions in the Mini Glossary. Write a sentence that explains the difference between an ectotherm and an endotherm.

_____

_____

_____

2. Complete the concept map below to show the three classes of fish.

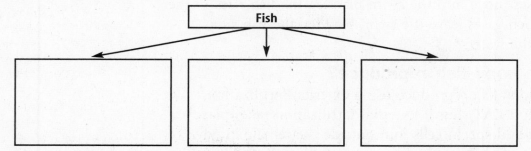

3. How does working with a partner to ask and answer quiz questions prepare you for a test that covers the material you have read?

_____

_____

_____

End of Section

Science○**nline** Visit **in6.msscience.com** to access your textbook, interactive games, and projects to help you learn more about chordate animals.

230 Vertebrate Animals

chapter 15 Vertebrate Animals

section 2 Amphibians and Reptiles

> **Standard—6.4.3:** Describe some of the great variety of body plans and internal structures animals and plants have that contribute to their being able ....
> **Also covers: 6.4.9**

● Before You Read

On the lines below, write four characteristics of frogs and lizards.

_____

_____

_____

● Read to Learn

Amphibians

Amphibians (am FIH bee unz) are animals that spend part of their lives in water and part on land. They have many adaptations that allow for life both on land and in the water. Amphibians include frogs, toads, salamanders, and newts.

How do amphibians adjust when the temperature changes?

Amphibians are ectotherms. Their body temperature changes along with changes in the temperature of their environment. In cold weather, amphibians become inactive. They bury themselves in mud or leaves until the temperature warms. This time of inactivity during cold weather is called **hibernation**. Amphibians that live in hot, dry climates become inactive and hide in the ground when the temperature becomes too hot. This time of inactivity during hot temperatures is called **estivation** (es tuh VAY shun).

What is the body structure of amphibians?

Amphibians are vertebrates with a strong endoskeleton made of bones. The skeleton helps support their body while on land. Adult frogs and toads have strong hind legs that they use for swimming and jumping.

Think it Over

1. **Describe** two characteristics that allow amphibians to live on land.

_____

_____

_____

Picture This

2. **Compare** Circle the stage of metamorphosis in which frogs are most like fish.

How do amphibians live on land?

Adult amphibians use lungs instead of gills to exchange oxygen and carbon dioxide. Lungs are an important adaptation for living on land. Amphibians have three-chambered hearts, in which blood carrying oxygen mixes with blood carrying carbon dioxide. This mixing makes less oxygen available to the amphibian. Adult amphibians also exchange oxygen and carbon dioxide through their moist skin, which increases their oxygen supply. Amphibians can live on land, but they must stay moist for the exchange of oxygen and carbon dioxide to occur.

Amphibian hearing and vision also are adapted to life on land. Amphibians have tympanums (TIHM puh nuhmz), or eardrums, that vibrate in response to sound waves. Large eyes help some amphibians catch their prey. Land environments provide many insects as food for adult amphibians. They have long, sticky tongues used to capture the insects.

How do amphibians develop?

Most amphibians go through a series of body changes called metamorphosis (me tuh MOR fuh sus). Eggs are most often laid in water and hatch into larvae. Young larval forms of amphibians live in water. They have no legs and breathe through gills. Over time, they develop the body structures needed for life on land, including legs and lungs. The rate of metamorphosis depends on the species, the water temperature, and the amount of available food. The figure below shows the stages of development for one amphibian—the frog.

Stage 2: Fertilized frog eggs are hatched into tadpoles. Tadpoles live in water. They use their gills for gas exchange.

Stage 4: The adult frog can live and move about on land.

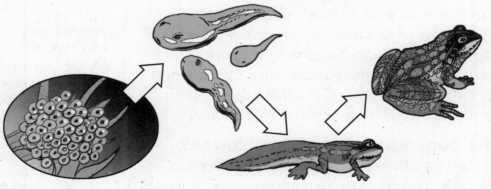

Stage 1: Frog eggs are laid and fertilized.

Stage 3: Tadpoles begin to grow into adults. They develop legs and lungs.

How do amphibians reproduce?

Most amphibians have external fertilization and require water for reproduction. Most female amphibians lay eggs in a pond or lake. However, some amphibians reproduce away from large bodies of water. For example, some tree frogs that live in the rain forest lay eggs in rainwater that collects in leaves.

Reptiles

Snakes, lizards, turtles, and crocodiles are reptiles. Reptiles are vertebrates and ectotherms. Most reptiles live their entire lives on land and do not depend on water for reproduction.

What are some types of reptiles?

Turtles have bodies covered with a hard shell. Most turtles can bring their heads and legs into the shell for protection. Alligators and crocodiles are large reptiles that live in or near water. Alligators and crocodiles are predators that live in warmer climates.

Lizards and snakes make up the largest group of reptiles. These reptiles have a highly developed sense of smell. An organ in the roof of the mouth senses molecules collected by the tongue. The constant in-and-out motion of the tongue allows a snake or lizard to smell its surroundings. Lizards have movable eyelids and external ears. Most lizards have legs with clawed toes on each foot. Snakes move without legs. They don't have eyelids or ears. Snakes feel vibrations in the ground instead of hearing sounds. ☑

What are some reptile adaptations?

A thick, dry waterproof skin is an adaptation that allows reptiles to live on land. Reptile skin is covered with scales to reduce water loss and help prevent injury. Reptiles breathe with lungs. Reptiles that live in water, like sea turtles, must come to the surface to breathe.

Two adaptations allow reptiles to reproduce on land—internal fertilization and laying shell-covered eggs. Sperm are deposited directly into the female's body. Female reptiles lay fertilized eggs that are covered by tough shells. These eggs are called amniotic (am nee AH tihk) eggs. An **amniotic egg** supplies the embryo with everything it needs to develop. A leathery shell protects the embryo and yolk. The yolk gives the embryo a food supply. When it hatches, a reptile is fully developed. ☑

> **Reading Check**
>
> 3. **Identify** the largest group of reptiles.
>
> _____
>
> _____
>
> _____

> **Reading Check**
>
> 4. **Determine** What is the purpose of the yolk in the amniotic egg?
>
> _____
>
> _____
>
> _____

● After You Read

Mini Glossary

amniotic egg: the environment for the development of a reptile embryo

estivation (es tuh VAY shun): a time of inactivity during hot temperatures

hibernation: a time of inactivity during cold weather

1. Review the terms and their definitions in the Mini Glossary. Choose one term that describes an adaptation of an amphibian to its environment. Explain this adaptation in one or two sentences.

_____

_____

_____

2. Complete the concept web below to show the adaptations of reptiles for life on land.

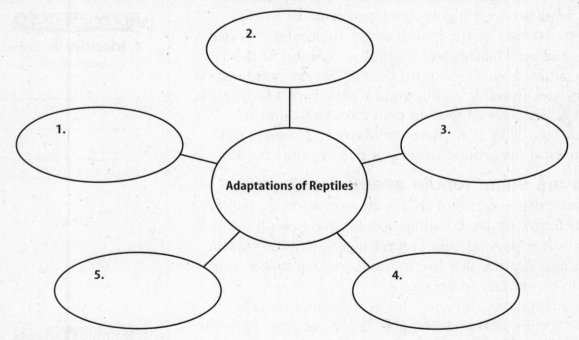

Science Online Visit **in6.msscience.com** to access your textbook, interactive games, and projects to help you learn more about amphibians and reptiles.

Vertebrate Animals

section ❸ Birds

> **Standard—6.4.3:** Describe some of the great variety of body plans and internal structures animals and plants have that contribute to their being able ....
> **Also covers:** 6.4.13

● Before You Read

Think of the wide variety of birds. On the lines below, list three things all birds have in common.

_____

_____

_____

What You'll Learn
- the characteristics of birds
- the adaptations birds have for flight
- the function of feathers

● Read to Learn

Characteristics of Birds

Birds are vertebrates that have two wings, two legs, and a bill or beak. Birds are covered mostly with feathers. They lay eggs with hard shells and sit on their eggs to keep them warm until they hatch. All birds are endotherms. There are more than 8,600 species of birds. Different species have different adaptations. For example, ostriches have strong legs for running. Penguins can't fly, but they are excellent swimmers. Wrens have feet that allow them to perch on branches.

Adaptations for Flight

The bodies of most birds are designed for flight. They are streamlined and have light, strong skeletons. The inside of a bird's bones is almost hollow. Special structures make the bones strong, but lightweight. A bird's tail is designed to provide the stiffness, strength, and stability needed for flight. Birds use their tail to steer.

Birds need a lot of energy and oxygen to fly. They eat high-energy foods like nectar, insects, and meat. They have a large, efficient heart. A bird's lungs connect to air sacs that provide a constant supply of oxygen to the blood and make the bird more lightweight.

Study Coach

Summarize the Main Ideas Read the section. Recall and write down the main ideas. Go back and check the main ideas to make sure they are accurate.

💡 Think it Over

1. **Infer** What features do airplanes have that are similar to birds?

_____

_____

_____

How do birds fly?

Birds beat their wings up and down as well as forward and backward. As wind passes above and below the wing, it creates lift. Lift is what allows birds to stay in flight.

Functions of Feathers

Birds are the only animals with feathers. They have two main types of feathers—contour feathers and down feathers. **Contour feathers** are strong and lightweight. They give adult birds their streamlined shape and coloring. Contour feathers have parallel strands, called barbs, that extend from the main shaft. Outer contour feathers on the wings and tail help a bird move, steer, and keep from spinning out of control. Feather color and patterns help attract mates. The color patterns also protect birds from predators by helping the birds blend into their surroundings.

Have you ever noticed that the hair on your arm stands up on a cold day? This response is one way your body works to trap and keep warm air close to your skin. Birds have **down feathers,** such as the one below, that trap and keep warm air next to their bodies. In adult birds, down feathers provide a layer of insulation under the contour feathers. Down feathers cover the bodies of some young birds.

Buddy Mays/CORBIS

How do birds care for their feathers?

Feathers need to be cared for to keep birds dry, warm, and able to fly. Birds preen, or use their bills, to clean and rearrange their feathers. During preening, birds also spread oil over their bodies and feathers. This oil comes from a gland found on the bird's back near its tail. The oil keeps the bird's skin soft and keeps feathers and scales from becoming brittle. ☑

✔ Reading Check

2. Identify What term is used to describe birds cleaning and rearranging their feathers?

_____

_____

_____

After You Read

Mini Glossary

contour feathers: strong, lightweight feathers that give adult birds their stream-lined shape and coloring

down feathers: feathers that trap and keep warm air next to birds' bodies

1. Review the terms and their definitions in the Mini Glossary. Write two sentences that compare and contrast contour feathers and down feathers.

   _____

   _____

   _____

2. Complete the concept web below. List any six adaptations birds have for flight.

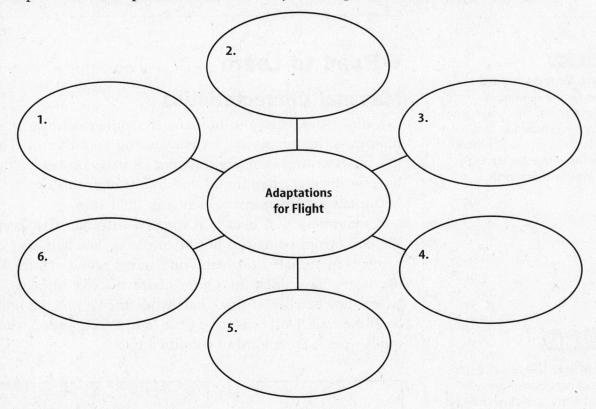

Science Online Visit **in6.msscience.com** to access your textbook, interactive games, and projects to help you learn more about birds.

End of Section

Vertebrate Animals

section ❹ Mammals

 Standard—6.4.3: Describe some of the great variety of body plans and internal structures animals and plants have that contribute to their being able ....

What You'll Learn

- the characteristics of mammals
- how mammals are adapted to different environments
- the differences among monotremes, marsupials, and placentals

Mark the Text

Define Words Skim the section before reading it. Highlight words that you do not know. As you read the section, underline the portion of the text that helps you understand the meaning of these words.

FOLDABLES™

❸ **Define** Use two quarter-sheets of notebook paper, as shown below, to define the key words in this section—herbivore, carnivore, omnivore, monotreme, marsupial, and placental.

Herbivore	Monotreme
Carnivore	Marsupial
Omnivore	Placental

◉ Before You Read

Make a list of five mammals. Describe one feature that they have in common.

_____

_____

_____

◉ Read to Learn

Mammal Characteristics

Moles, dogs, bats, and humans are some examples of mammals. Mammals are vertebrates and endotherms. They live in water and in many different climates on land. They burrow through the ground and fly through the air. Mammals have mammary glands in their skin.

A mammal's skin usually is covered with hair that keeps the body from being too hot or too cold. The hair also protects mammals from wind and water. Some mammals, like bears, have thick fur. Other mammals, like humans, have a few patches of thick hair while the rest of the body has little hair. Dolphins have little hair. Porcupines have quills, which are a kind of modified hair.

238 Vertebrate Animals

Why do mammals have mammary glands?

In females, the mammary glands produce and release milk for the young. For the first few weeks or months of life, the milk provides all the nutrients the young mammal needs.

What kinds of teeth do mammals have?

Plant-eating animals are called <u>herbivores</u>. Animals that eat meat are called <u>carnivores</u>. Animals that eat plants and meat are called <u>omnivores</u>.

Mammals have teeth that are specialized for the type of food they eat. The four types of teeth are incisors, canines, premolars, and molars. As you can see in the figure below, you usually can tell from the kind of teeth a mammal has whether it eats plants, meat, or both.

Mountain lions are carnivores. They have sharp canines that are used to rip and tear flesh.

Humans are omnivores. They have incisors that cut vegetables, premolars that are sharp enough to chew meat, and molars that grind food.

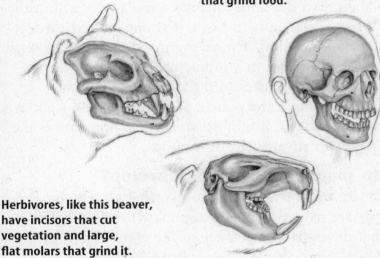

Herbivores, like this beaver, have incisors that cut vegetation and large, flat molars that grind it.

What body systems do mammals have?

Mammals have well-developed lungs. Mammal lungs are made of millions of small sacs called alveoli. Alveoli allow the exchange of carbon dioxide and oxygen during breathing. Mammals also have a complex nervous system that lets them learn and remember more than many other animals. Mammals have larger brains than other animals of similar size.

All mammals have internal fertilization. After an egg is fertilized, the developing mammal is called an embryo. Most mammal embryos develop inside the female in an organ called the uterus. ✓

Picture This

1. **Identify** Circle the teeth that carnivores use to rip and tear flesh. Highlight the teeth that omnivores and herbivores use to cut vegetables.

✔ **Reading Check**

2. **Apply** What kind of fertilization do all mammals have in common?

_____

_____

_____

Mammal Types

Mammals are divided into three groups based on where their embryos develop. The three groups of mammals are monotremes, marsupials, and placentals.

How do monotreme embryos develop?

Unlike other mammals, **monotremes** lay eggs with tough, leathery shells instead of having live births. This small group of mammals includes duck-billed platypuses and spiny anteaters. The female monotreme sits on the eggs for about ten days before they hatch. Monotremes also differ from other mammals because their mammary glands do not have nipples. The milk seeps through the skin onto their fur. The young monotremes lick the milk off the fur. Monotremes live in New Guinea and Australia. ✔

How do young marsupials develop?

Most **marsupials** carry their young in a pouch. A marsupial embryo develops for only a few weeks within the uterus. When a marsupial is born, it is not fully formed. It has no hair and is blind. The young marsupial uses its sense of smell to find its way to a nipple usually within the mother's pouch. It attaches to the nipple to feed and finishes developing in the pouch. Most marsupials, such as kangaroos and koalas, live in Australia. The opossum is the only marsupial native to North America.

How do placental embryos develop?

Most mammals belong to a group called placentals. **Placentals** are named for the placenta, which is a saclike organ that develops from tissues of the embryo and uterus. An umbilical cord connects the embryo to the placenta. A human embryo is shown in the figure below.

Human Embryo at Two Months

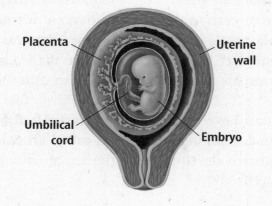

Placenta · Uterine wall · Umbilical cord · Embryo

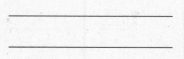

Reading Check

3. **Compare** the mammary glands of monotremes to other mammals.

_____

_____

_____

Picture This

4. **Determine** What connects the embryo to the placenta?

_____

_____

_____

How does the embryo obtain food and oxygen?

In the placenta, food, oxygen, and wastes are exchanged between the mother's blood and the embryo's blood, but their bloods do not mix. The umbilical cord connects the embryo to the placenta. Food and oxygen are absorbed from the mother's blood. Blood vessels in the umbilical cord carry food and oxygen to the developing young. The blood vessels also take away wastes. In the placenta, the mother's blood absorbs wastes from the developing young.

The time of development from fertilization to birth is called the gestation period. Gestation periods vary widely, from about 21 days in rats to about 616 days in elephants. Human gestation lasts about 280 days. ☑

Mammals Today

There are more than 4,000 species of mammals on Earth today. Mammals can be found on every continent, from cold arctic regions to hot deserts. Each kind of mammal has adaptations that enable it to live successfully within its environment.

What roles do mammals have?

Mammals, like all other groups of animals, have an important role in maintaining a balance in the environment. Large carnivores, such as wolves, prey on herbivores, such as deer. This helps prevent overcrowding and overgrazing. Bats and other small mammals help pollinate flowers. Other mammals spread seeds that stick to their fur.

What are some mammals in danger?

Some species of mammals are in danger of becoming extinct because their habitats are being destroyed. They are left without enough food, shelter, and space to survive because their habitats are damaged by pollution or developed for human needs. The grizzly bear of North America and Europe is a threatened species. A threatened species is one that is likely to become endangered in the near future. Grizzly bears were once found all over the western half of the United States. Today, they are found only in Alaska, Montana, Wyoming, Idaho, and Washington. Habitat loss due to human settlement has greatly reduced the grizzly bear population. If the grizzly bear population continues to decline and becomes endangered, the species will be in danger of becoming extinct. ☑

✔ Reading Check

5. **Define** What is the gestation period?

_____

_____

_____

✔ Reading Check

6. **Explain** Why has the grizzly bear population in the United States been greatly reduced?

_____

_____

_____

● After You Read

Mini Glossary

carnivore: an animal that eats meat
herbivore: a plant-eating animal
marsupial: a mammal that carries its young in a pouch where it continues to develop after birth

monotreme: a mammal that lays eggs with tough, leathery shells
omnivore: an animal that eats plants and meat
placental: a mammal whose embryos depend on the mother's placenta for food and oxygen

1. Review the terms and their definitions in the Mini Glossary. Write one or more sentences to explain how herbivores, carnivores, and omnivores are different.

_____

_____

_____

2. Complete the diagram below to identify the three types of mammals.

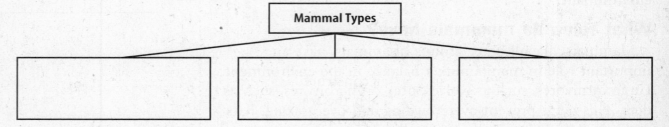

```
                    ┌──────────────────┐
                    │   Mammal Types   │
                    └──────────────────┘
        ┌──────────────────┬──────────────────┐
   ┌─────────┐        ┌─────────┐        ┌─────────┐
   │         │        │         │        │         │
   │         │        │         │        │         │
   └─────────┘        └─────────┘        └─────────┘
```

3. Complete the table below to list the common characteristics of mammals.

Common Characteristics of Mammals
1.
2.
3.
4.
5.
6.

chapter 16

The Human Body

section ❶ Body Systems

> **Standard—6.4.11:** Describe that human beings have body systems for obtaining and providing energy, defense, ... coordination of body functions.
> **Also covers:** 6.4.12, 6.7.1

● Before You Read

Why do you think communities often have blood drives? On the lines below write a slogan that urges people to donate blood.

_____

_____

_____

● Read to Learn

Structure and Movement

Have you ever seen a building under construction? First, a framework of steel or wood is built. Then the framework is covered by walls. The bones are the framework of your body. Bones are covered by skin and muscle.

What does the skeletal system do?

All the bones in your body make up your **skeletal system**. It gives your body its shape and support. The skeletal system also protects the internal organs. For example, your skull protects your brain.

Bones are made of living cells. The cells need nutrients and use energy. The calcium and phosphorus in bones make bones hard.

What do joints do?

Your bones can move. Joints make the movements possible. The place where two or more bones come together is called a joint. The shoulder joint is shown to the right. Muscles can move your bones by moving your joints.

What You'll Learn
- how the skeletal and muscular systems provide structure and allow movement
- the functions of the digestive, respiratory, and circulatory systems
- the differences between the nervous and endocrine system

Study Coach

Create a Quiz As you study the information in this section, create questions about the information you read. Be sure to answer the questions.

✔ **Reading Check**

1. **Explain** What do calcium and phosphorus do?

_____

_____

_____

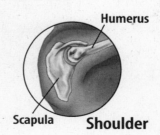

Humerus

Scapula   **Shoulder**

Picture This

3. Identify Add the word *shorter* beneath the correct labels to indicate what happens as the muscles work.

What purpose does the skin serve?

The skin is the largest human body organ. The skin has several purposes. Skin forms a protective covering for your body. It can protect your body from disease-causing organisms. The pigment, or coloring, in the skin protects it from damage by ultraviolet light. The pigment is called **melanin** (MEH luh nun). The skin is a sense organ. The skin has special nerve cells that help you sense heat or cold. They can help you feel a sharp object. The skin helps control your body temperature. Sweat is made by sweat glands in your skin. Sweat helps to cool down the body. ☑

The skin also helps provide vitamin D, a nutrient your body needs for good health. Vitamin D is formed when your skin receives ultraviolet light from the Sun. This vitamin helps the body absorb calcium from food in the digestive tract.

What does the muscular system do?

Muscles attach to bones and help them move. A **muscle** is an organ that can relax, contract, and provide force to move you and your body parts. Some muscles are voluntary muscles. You can choose to move them. Other muscles, such as your heart, are not controlled consciously. They are called involuntary muscles.

Voluntary muscles work in pairs. One muscle contracts, or gets shorter, while another muscle relaxes or returns to its original length, as shown in the figure below.

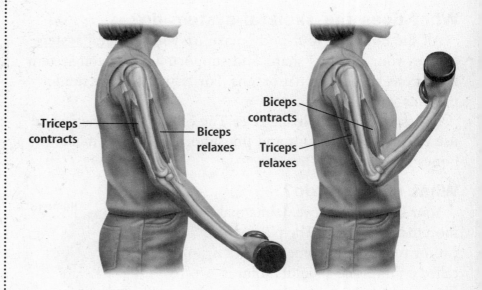

Triceps contracts — Biceps relaxes — Biceps contracts — Triceps relaxes

Digestion and Excretion

Your body gets the energy it needs through the food you eat. Food enters the body's digestive system through your mouth. As the food moves through the organs of the digestive system, it is broken down into smaller molecules. These molecules are absorbed from the digestive system and enter the blood. Then the food molecules move into the cells. Food that is undigested is eliminated from the digestive system.

What are the organs of the digestive system?

Food is moistened in the mouth by saliva. The teeth break the food down into smaller particles. Food enters the esophagus (ih SAH fuh gus) and moves to the stomach. Chemicals in the stomach break down the food, which then moves into the small intestine. Most of the food is absorbed in the small intestine. Food particles in the small intestine move from the digestive tract into the blood. The blood carries the food particles to the body's cells. The remaining food moves into the large intestine where water is absorbed. The undigested food is excreted from the body. ☑

✔ **Reading Check**

4. **Explain** What happens in the small intestine?

_____

_____

_____

Why are nutrients important?

Your body needs certain foods to stay healthy. <u>Nutrients</u> (NEW tree unts) are the substances in food that provide for cell development, growth, and repair. There are six kinds of nutrients—proteins, carbohydrates (kar boh HI drayts), lipids, vitamins, minerals, and water. Proteins, carbohydrates, lipids, and vitamins contain the element carbon. So they are called organic nutrients. Minerals and water do not contain carbon. So they are called inorganic nutrients.

The chart below shows why organic nutrients are important and what foods provide them.

Organic Nutrient	What It Does	Where It Is Found
Proteins	replace and repair cells; cell growth	meats, poultry, eggs, fish, beans, nuts
Carbohydrates	main energy source	sugar, honey, fruits, vegetables, grains, breads, cereals
Lipids (fats)	provide energy; help body absorb vitamins; cushion internal organs	meats, butter, oils
Vitamins	help growth; regulate body functions; prevent some diseases	fruits, vegetables, beans, cereals

Picture This

5. **Identify** Highlight the two nutrients that meat provides.

How do vitamins help the body?

Vitamins are nutrients that are needed in small amounts. Vitamins do many things. They regulate body functions and prevent some diseases. No single food supplies all the vitamins your body needs. There are two kinds of vitamins. Water-soluble vitamins dissolve easily in water. They are not stored in the body. Fat-soluble vitamins dissolve only in fat and can be stored by the body.

What are inorganic nutrients?

Minerals control many chemical reactions. Minerals, like vitamins, are needed in small amounts. Calcium and phosphorus are two minerals that the body uses in the largest amounts. These two minerals are important for making and keeping bones healthy. ☑

People cannot live for more than a few days without water. The body cannot use most of the other nutrients unless they are carried in water. Cells need water to carry out the chemical reactions that are needed to live.

What is the purpose of the urinary system?

The digestive system gets rid of some body wastes. However, wastes that are made by cells are removed by the blood through the urinary system. The main organs in the urinary system, as shown in the figure to the right, are the kidneys. The kidneys get rid of excess water, salts, and other wastes from the blood. The wastewater, called urine, passes through tubes called ureters (YOO ruh turz) into the bladder. The bladder holds the urine until it is ready to leave the body. Urine leaves the bladder through the body by the urethra (yoo REE thruh).

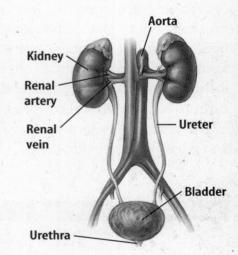

Aorta

Kidney

Renal artery

Renal vein

Ureter

Bladder

Urethra

What are the other organs of the excretory system?

Wastes are also removed in other ways. The respiratory system removes waste gases, such as carbon dioxide. Salt and other wastes are lost through the skin.

☑ Reading Check

6. **List** What are two minerals that the body needs to keep bones healthy?

_____

_____

_____

Picture This

7. **Explain** Draw arrows showing how urine moves from the kidneys to the bladder.

Respiration and Circulation

The cells in the body need oxygen, a gas that is found in the air. The body's cells make carbon dioxide. This is a waste gas that must be removed from the body.

What is the purpose of the respiratory system?

The <u>respiratory system</u> is made up of structures and organs that help move oxygen into the body and waste gases out of the body. When you breathe in, air enters through the mouth or nose and travels through a series of passageways. Bronchi (BRAHN ki) then carry air into your lungs. In the lungs, bronchi branch into smaller tubes called bronchioles (BRAHN kee ohlz). As you can see in the figure below, grapelike clusters of air sacs called <u>alveoli</u> (al VEE uh li) are at the end of each bronchiole. Tiny blood vessels called <u>capillaries</u> (KAP uh ler eez) surround each alveolus (singular of *alveoli*). Air moves through bronchioles and reaches the alveoli.

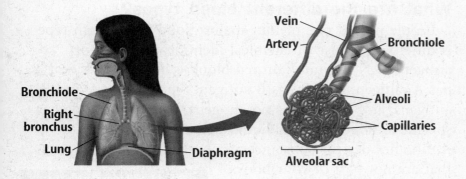

Vein
Artery
Bronchiole
Alveoli
Capillaries
Alveolar sac
Bronchiole
Right bronchus
Lung
Diaphragm

Oxygen leaves alveoli and enters capillaries. Blood carries the oxygen to every cell in the body. The body's waste gases, such as carbon dioxide, are carried to the lungs through the blood. The gases are removed when you exhale.

What does the circulatory system do?

The job of the circulatory system is to get nutrients and oxygen to the cells and to remove wastes. The circulatory system is made up of the heart, blood vessels, and blood.

The heart pumps blood to all the cells. Blood that is pumped out of the heart travels through blood vessles—arteries (AR tuh reez), capillaries, and then veins. Arteries carry blood away from the heart. Veins carry blood back to the heart. Capillaries connect arteries and veins. Because capillaries are very thin, nutrients can move easily from capillaries into the cells. Waste materials can leave body cells and enter the capillaries. ✔

Picture This

8. Identify Highlight the name of the blood vessels that surround the alveoli.

✔ Reading Check

9. Explain Which part of the circulatory system carries blood away from the heart?

_____

_____

Think it Over

10. **Analyze** What would happen if a blood clot did not form?

_____

_____

_____

Picture This

11. **Analyze** Circle the blood type that hospitals would like to have in large supply. Explain your choice on the lines below.

_____

_____

_____

Why is blood important?

Blood is important to your body's cells. They would die without blood because they could not get the oxygen and nutrients needed for life. Blood also removes wastes from the cells. Blood is made up of liquid and cells. Oxygen is carried by red blood cells. White blood cells fight infections and heal wounds.

When you cut yourself, special cell fragments called platelets (PLAYT luts) in the blood form a clot. This clot plugs the wounded blood vessels and acts like a bandage. Blood clots stop bleeding in minor wounds.

If a person loses a lot of blood because of a serious wound, he or she might need a blood transfusion. A person who receives a blood transfusion receives donated human blood. All humans have similar blood. However, blood must be classified or typed. A person has to receive the correct blood type, or the person may die.

What are the different blood types?

People inherit one of four major blood types. Each type is different because of chemical identification tags, or antigens (AN tih junz), on red blood cells. Type A blood has A antigen, type B has B antigen, type AB has A and B antigens, and type O has no antigens. Each blood type has specific antibodies in the liquid part of the blood. Antibodies destroy substances that are not part of your body. Because of antibodies, certain types of blood types cannot be mixed when receiving blood transfusions. The table to the right shows blood transfusion possibilities.

Blood Transfusion Possibilities		
Type	Can Receive	Can Donate To
A	O, A	A, AB
B	O, B	B, AB
AB	All	AB
O	O	All

Rh factor is another identification tag of red blood cells. If a person's red blood cells have an Rh factor, that person has Rh-positive (RH+) blood. If the factor is not there, the person has Rh-negative (Rh−) blood. An Rh− person cannot receive Rh+ blood in a blood transfusion.

How are extra tissue fluids collected?

Water and other dissolved substances become part of tissue fluid, which is found between cells. The fluid is collected and returned to the blood through the lymphatic (lihm FA tihk) system.

What is the purpose of the lymphatic system?

The lymphatic system has vessels like the circulatory system. But it does not have an organ like the heart to pump the fluid. The fluid moves because of the contraction of muscles in the walls of the lymph vessel and skeletal muscles. The lymphatic vessels also have cells called lymphocytes. These cells help defend the body against disease-causing organisms.

How does the body protect itself from disease?

The body has many ways to defend itself against disease-causing organisms. Disease-causing organisms cannot get through unbroken skin. Certain parts of the respiratory system trap disease organisms. The circulatory system has white blood cells that destroy invading disease-causing organisms. These are first-line defenses.

A second-line of defense, called specific immunity, attacks disease-causing organisms that get past the first-line defenses. In specific immunity, the body makes antibodies that can destroy disease-causing organisms. For example, when you get a cold, your body makes antibodies that attack that cold virus. This helps the body fight off the infection.

You also can develop antibodies to fight off diseases when you receive vaccinations. You received vaccinations against many diseases, such as mumps and polio, before you started school. Your body formed antibodies against these diseases after you received the vaccinations.

Control and Coordination

The nervous and endocrine systems help make all the body systems work together. They are the control systems of the body, and they coordinate your body functions.

What does the nervous system do?

The nervous system is made up of the brain, spinal cord, nerves, and nerve receptors. The neuron (NOO rahn), or nerve cell, is the basic unit of the nervous system. Neurons are made up of a cell body and branches called dendrites and axons (AK sahns). Messages travel from one neuron to another. Dendrites receive messages from other neurons and send them to the cell body. Axons carry messages away from the cell body. For example, a prick from a pin can move from a skin nerve receptor to a neuron, then from one neuron to the next until the message reaches the brain. The brain coordinates all the body's activities. ☑

FOLDABLES

A Explain Make a two-tab Foldable, as shown below. As you read, list the ways your body defends itself from disease. Organize your notes into first-line defenses and second-line defenses.

First-Line Defenses | Second-Line Defenses

✔ Reading Check

12. Identify What is the basic unit of the nervous system?

_____

What is a reflex?

When you touch something very hot and pull your hand away quickly, you are experiencing a reflex. A **reflex** is an involuntary, automatic response to a stimulus. You cannot control a reflex. Reflexes help protect your body by allowing your body to respond without having to think about what to do.

What is the purpose of the endocrine system?

The endocrine (EN duh krun) system is the other control system in the body. In the nervous system, messages travel quickly through nerves to and from all parts of your body. In the endocrine system, chemicals called hormones (HOR mohnz) carry messages throughout the body. Hormones are released by endocrine glands directly into the bloodstream. The hormones travel through the blood to reach certain tissues. ☑

Some endocrine glands are found in the brain. The pineal gland makes a hormone that regulates sleeping and waking. The pituitary (pih TEW uh ter ee) gland makes several hormones that regulate many body activities, such as growth and reproduction. The thyroid gland, shown in the figure below, secretes a hormone that controls the rate of chemical reactions in your body.

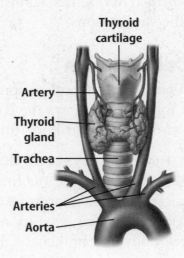

Some endocrine glands are found in the abdomen area. The pancreas is a gland that makes a hormone that controls the amount of sugar that is in the bloodstream. The adrenal glands make several hormones. They include hormones that help the body respond in times of stress.

☑ **Reading Check**

13. Identify What part of the endocrine system carries messages throughout the body?

_____

_____

Picture This

14. Conclude Examine the other structures around the thyroid gland. Where in the body is this gland located?

_____

_____

● After You Read

Mini Glossary

alveoli (al VEE uh li): grapelike clusters of air sacs at the end of the bronchiole

capillary (KAP uh ler ee): small blood vessel that connects arteries and veins

melanin (MEH luh nun): the pigment in the skin that protects it from damage by ultraviolet light

muscle: an organ that can relax, contract, and provide force to move a person and to move body parts

nutrient (NEW tree unt): the substance in food that provides for cell development, growth, and repair

reflex: an involuntary, automatic response to a stimulus

respiratory system: the structures and organs that help move oxygen into the body and waste gases out of the body

skeletal system: the bones in the body that provide the body's framework

1. Review the terms and their definitions in the Mini Glossary. Choose one of the terms and write a sentence that explains its purpose in the body.

_____

_____

2. In the chart below, explain the function of the body systems listed and identify the parts of the system.

Body Systems	Function of System	Parts of System
Skeletal system		
Digestive system		
Respiratory system		
Circulatory system		
Nervous system		

 Visit **in6.msscience.com** to access your textbook, interactive games, and projects to help you learn more about body systems.

End of Section

The Human Body

section ② Human Reproduction

 Standard—6.4.11: Describe that human beings have body systems for … defense, reproduction, and the coordination of body functions.
Also covers: 6.4.12, 6.7.1

What You'll Learn

- the organs of the male and female reproductive systems
- the stages in the menstrual cycle
- the stages of development before birth
- the life stages of humans

Study Coach

Summarize Read each section—"Male Reproductive System," "Female Reproductive System," and "Life Stages." After you finish reading write a sentence or two that summarizes the main idea of each section.

Picture This

1. **Identify** Draw arrows on the figure to indicate how semen moves through the male reproductive system.

● Before You Read

Think about a time you observed a baby. What kinds of skills did the baby have? What skills did the baby still need to learn?

_____

_____

_____

● Read to Learn

Male Reproductive System

The reproductive system, unlike other systems, is different in males and females. The male reproductive system, shown in the figure below, is made up of several organs and structures. The scrotum has two testes (TES teez) that make the male hormone testosterone and **sperm,** the male reproductive cells. Testosterone and sperm are made in sexually mature males.

After sperm are made in the testes, they travel through the sperm ducts. Fluid from the seminal vesicles, which are organs behind the bladder, is mixed with the sperm. This mixture is called **semen** (SEE mun). Semen leaves the body through the urethra. This is the same tube that carries urine from the body. However, a muscle in the bladder does not allow urine to enter the urethra when sperm leave the body.

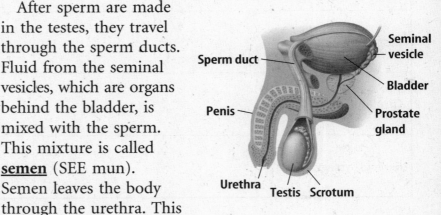

Female Reproductive System

The female's reproductive organs are inside a female's body. Ovaries are the female sex organs that produce eggs and the female sex hormones, estrogen (ES truh jun) and progesterone (proh JES tuh rohn). These hormones are produced when a female matures sexually. The hormones help prepare the female body for having a baby. ☑

Egg Production The female sex hormones control the development and release of eggs from the ovaries. About every 28 days, one of the ovaries releases an egg. This process is called **ovulation** (ahv yuh LAY shun). The ovaries usually take turns releasing eggs.

The released egg moves into the oviduct. The egg moves along the oviduct to the uterus, a muscular, pear-shaped organ. If the egg is fertilized by a sperm while it is in the oviduct, the egg can grow and develop in the uterus. The lower part of the uterus, as shown in the figure to the right, is the cervix. It connects the uterus to the vagina. The vagina is a muscular tube that is known as the birth canal. When a baby is being born, the baby moves from the uterus through the vagina to outside the mother's body.

Reading Check

2. **List** the two female sex hormones.

_____

_____

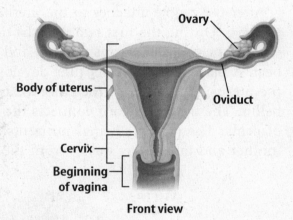

Ovary

Body of uterus

Oviduct

Cervix

Beginning of vagina

Front view

Picture This

3. **Identify** Draw arrows on the figure to indicate how an egg would move from an ovary to the uterus.

What is the menstrual cycle?

The **menstrual cycle** is the monthly cycle of changes to the female reproductive system. The average length of the menstrual cycle is 28 days. However, the cycle can range from 20 to 40 days.

The menstrual cycle is divided into three parts, or phases. The first phase is the menstrual flow, or menstruation (men STRAY shun). The flow is made of tissue cells from the thickened lining of the uterus and blood. This flow usually lasts from four to six days.

In phase two of the menstrual cycle, an egg develops in the ovary and the lining of the uterus thickens. Ovulation occurs about 14 days before the menstrual flow begins.

Phase three Phase three is the phase between ovulation and menstruation. The lining of the uterus continues to thicken. If the egg is fertilized, it can attach to the uterus wall and start to develop while hormones continue to be produced. If the egg is not fertilized, the hormone levels decrease. Decreased hormone levels cause the lining of the uterus to break down, and menstruation begins.

Life Stages

Humans begin to develop when an egg from the female is united with a sperm from the male. This is called fertilization. It usually happens in the oviduct. The nucleus of the egg and the nucleus of the sperm join together to make a fertilized cell called a zygote. As this cell moves through the oviduct, it divides many times. If the zygote attaches to the uterus, it will develop into a baby in about nine months. The time of development from fertilized egg to birth is called **pregnancy**.

How does the body develop before birth?

After the zygote attaches to the uterine wall, it is called an **embryo**. During the first two months of pregnancy, the embryo period, the organs develop and the heart begins to beat. A placenta (pluh SEN tuh) develops from tissues of the uterus and tissues of the embryo, as shown in the figure below. The umbilical cord connects the embryo to the placenta. The placenta brings nutrients and oxygen from the mother and takes away wastes from the embryo.

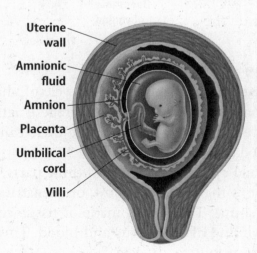

After two months, the embryo is called a **fetus**. It continues to grow and develop during the pregnancy. At nine months the fetus is usually in a head-down position in the uterus.

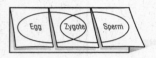
Picture This

4. **Identify** Circle the structure that connects the embryo to the placenta.

What happens during birth?

Birth begins with labor, when the muscles of the uterus contract. As the contractions become stronger and closer together, the opening to the uterus widens and the baby is pushed out through the vagina. Then the umbilical cord is clamped and cut. The placenta also is pushed out of the mother's body after the baby is born by the contractions in the uterus.

What are the stages after birth?

Humans go through four stages of development after birth. These stages are infancy, childhood, adolescence, and adulthood.

Infancy is the time from birth until 18 months of age. During this stage, the infant's nervous and muscular systems develop and the infant begins to interact with the world.

Childhood lasts from 18 months until around 12 years of age. The child learns many new skills during this time. The skills include control of the bladder, dressing and undressing, speaking, reading, writing, and reasoning. Children develop at different rates.

Adolescence starts around 12 to 13 years of age. During this time puberty occurs. This means that the person is maturing sexually. Puberty generally starts in girls between ages 9 and 13. It starts in boys between ages 13 and 16. During puberty, girls develop breasts and grow pubic and underarm hair. Boys develop a deeper voice, an increase in muscle size, and facial, pubic, and underarm hair.

The final stage of human development is adulthood. It starts at the end of adolescence and continues through the rest of a human's life. During this time the muscular and skeletal systems stop growing. The average human life span is about 75 years. Some people, however, live much longer. As body systems get older, they break down, and eventually the result is death. ✓

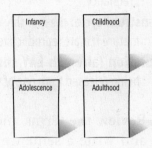

5. **Explain** What happens to body systems during adulthood?

_____

_____

_____

● After You Read

Mini Glossary

embryo: the zygote after it attaches to the wall of the uterus

fetus: the developing embryo after the first two months of pregnancy

menstrual cycle: the monthly cycle of changes in a sexually mature female reproductive system

ovulation (ahv yuh LAY shun): the process of an egg being released from one of the ovaries

pregnancy: the period of development from fertilized egg to birth

semen (SEE mun): the mixture of fluid from the seminal vesicles and sperm

sperm: the male reproductive cells

1. Review the terms and their definitions in the Mini Glossary. Choose two or three terms and write a sentence that shows how the body develops before birth.

   _____

   _____

2. In the sequence chart below, list the stages of development after birth and describe one development in each stage.

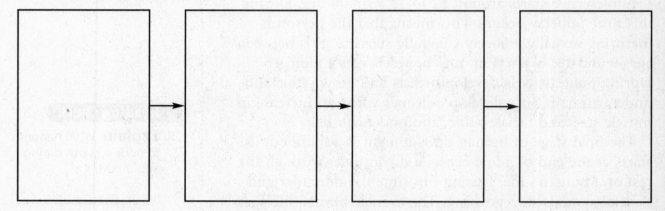

3. How did summarizing the main idea in each section help you understand the information about human reproduction?

   _____

   _____

End of Section

Science Online Visit **in6.msscience.com** to access your textbook, interactive games, and projects to help you learn more about human reproduction.

Matter and Its Changes

section ❶ Physical Properties and Changes

 Standard—6.3.20: Investigate that equal volumes of different substances usually have different masses as well as different densities.
Also covers: 6.2.7

● Before You Read

Describe an object in your classroom. What color is it? How is it shaped? What else can you say about the object?

_____

_____

● Read to Learn

Using Your Senses

Most people make observations when they walk into a new room. Observing involves seeing, hearing, tasting, touching, and smelling. You use your senses to observe the physical properties of materials. **Physical properties** are characteristics of materials that can be observed or measured without changing the material. You can observe the color or smell of a material without changing the material.

You use your senses to observe materials in the laboratory. Remember never to smell, taste, or touch any materials in the lab without instructions. It may be unsafe. The figure shows which senses you should and should not use in the laboratory.

 Watch

 Listen

 Do NOT touch

 Do NOT smell

 Do NOT taste

Picture This
1. **Conclude** Why do some symbols have a slash across them and some don't?

_____

_____

_____

_____

Physical Properties

There are many physical properties that can be observed easily. You can determine the color of an object by looking at it. You can also determine its shape. Other properties can be measured. You can measure the length or the mass of an object. Its volume or density also can be measured.

💡 Think it Over

2. **Apply** List two examples of matter.

_____

_____

💡 Think it Over

3. **Describe** something that you could do to wood to cause a physical change.

_____

_____

Picture This

4. **Identify** Which would you use to find the length of your textbook?

   a. measuring cup
   b. scale
   c. meterstick
   d. stopwatch

What is matter?

Imagine you are shopping for groceries. Everything in the grocery store is matter. **Matter** is anything that has mass and takes up space. The cans of vegetables and the potatoes and pineapples are all matter.

What can you observe about matter?

Suppose you need laundry soap. Laundry soap comes in bottles and boxes of different colors. Color is a physical property that is easy to observe. The bottles and boxes are also different shapes.

Most bottles are made of plastic. Plastic changes shape when it is molded into a bottle, but it is still plastic. The plastic went through a physical change. In a **physical change,** the physical properties of a substance change but the identity of the substance does not change. The laundry soap bottles are all made of plastic, regardless of the physical differences in color or shape.

What physical properties can be measured?

Some physical properties can be identified by measuring. Other physical properties can be identified by using your senses.

Length Length is one physical property that can be measured. A ruler, a meterstick, or a tape measure is used to find length. Objects can be classified by their lengths. Suppose you bought a cake mix. The directions might say to bake the cake in an 8-in-square cake pan. A 9 × 13 in cake pan has longer sides, but it is still a cake pan. The figure shows a beaker and a meterstick, which can be used to measure physical properties.

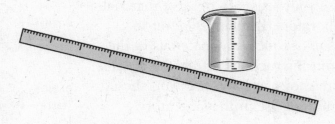

Mass Think about the laundry soap. A company may sell a small box and a large box of laundry soap. Both boxes contain laundry soap, but one will feel heavier than the other. This is because it has more mass. Mass is a physical property that describes the amount of matter in an object. Your senses can tell you which box has more mass.

Volume Volume measures the amount of space an object takes up. Liquids are usually measured by volume. The juice bottles on your grocery list are probably measured by volume.

Density Another measurable physical property is density. <u>Density</u> is the amount of mass a material has in a given volume. You notice density when you try to lift two things that have the same volume but different masses. You can find density by dividing the mass of an object by its volume.

$$\text{density} = \text{mass/volume, or } D = m/V$$

Suppose you want to find the density of a piece of nickel. It has a mass of 39.2 g and a volume of 4 cm^3. Multiply 39.2 by 4. The density of the piece of nickel is 9.8 g/cm^3.

Can two objects be the same size but have different masses?

Two balls that are the same size may not have the same mass. A bowling ball is more dense than a kickball. Think about the bags of groceries you bought at the store. They all have different densities. How is a bag that is filled with canned goods different from a bag that contains only paper napkins? The bags are the same size but the bag with canned goods has more mass. The bag with the canned goods is more dense than the one with the napkins. The table below lists the densities of some elements.

Material	Density (g/cm^3)	Material	Density (g/cm^3)
Air	0.001293	Lead	11.3
Aluminum	2.7	Magnesium	1.7
Carbon dioxide	0.001977	Mercury	13.6
Copper	8.9	Milk	1.03
Gold	19.3	Platinum	21.4
Hydrogen	0.00009	Uranium	18.7
Iron	7.8	Water	1.00

Does density of a material change?

The density of a material does not change as long as temperature and pressure stay the same. But if the temperature or pressure are changed, the density of the material will change.

Applying Math

5. **Calculate** Use a calculator to find the density of 15.6 grams of lead with a volume of 2 cm^3. The units will be g/cm^3.

_____

Picture This

6. **Identify** Which material in the table has the greatest density? What is its density? Which material has the least density? What is its density?

_____

_____

_____

_____

7. **Explain** Why did the identity of the water not change when it formed ice?

_____

_____

8. **Determine** What two things does the state of matter of a substance depend on?

_____

_____

FOLDABLES™

Ⓐ Compare Make the following Foldable to compare and contrast the characteristics of solids, liquids, and gases.

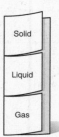

Change of State Water at room temperature has a density of 1.00 g/cm³. Water kept in the freezer at 0°C is in the form of ice. The density of ice is 0.9168 g/cm³. Has the identity of water changed? No, but the water has changed to a different state.

States of Matter

How does water change when it goes from 20°C to 0°C? It changes from a liquid to a solid. It changes state or form. The four **states of matter** are solid, liquid, gas, and plasma (PLAZ muh). A substance's state of matter depends on its temperature and pressure. The solid, liquid, and gas states are common. But the plasma state is unusual. The plasma state happens at very high temperatures. Plasma is found in fluorescent (floo RE sunt) lightbulbs, the atmosphere, and in lightning strikes. ☑

The state of matter of a material is another physical property. You could classify the items on your grocery list according to their states of matter.

How is energy related to states of matter?

Matter is made up of moving particles. The state of matter of a substance is determined by how much energy the particles have.

Solid The particles of a solid vibrate, or move back and forth, in a fixed place. They are packed close together and stay this way. This is why a solid has a definite shape and volume.

Liquid Particles in a liquid move much faster. They have enough energy to slide past one another. This is why a liquid takes the shape of its container.

Gas The particles of a gas move very quickly. They have enough energy to move freely away from other particles. The particles of a gas take up as much space as possible. They will spread out to fill any container.

Does temperature affect the movement of particles?

Particles of matter move faster at higher temperatures. What would happen if you added food coloring to a beaker of cold water and a beaker of hot water? The color would spread faster in the beaker of hot water.

Does matter change states?

Have you ever watched ice cubes melt? You watched matter change states. Water changed from a solid to a liquid. What happens when you put water in a freezer? It changes to a solid. The water itself does not change identity. Its state is all that changes.

What are melting and boiling points?

At what temperature will liquid water change to a gas? At what temperature will ice change into liquid water?

Melting Point <u>Melting point</u> is the temperature at which a solid becomes a liquid. Melting points are different for different substances. But the melting point of a pure substance never changes, no matter how much of the substance there is. This means that a small sliver of ice and a huge chunk of ice both will melt at 0°C. Lead always melts at 327.5°C. When a substance melts, it changes from a solid to a liquid. This is a physical change. The melting point is a physical property.

Boiling Point The <u>boiling point</u> is the temperature at which a liquid becomes a gas. Each pure substance has a certain boiling point at atmospheric pressure. Atmospheric pressure is the pressure caused by the weight of Earth's atmosphere. The boiling point of water is 100°C at atmospheric pressure. The boiling point of nitrogen is −195.8°C. The boiling point does not depend on the amount of a substance. The boiling point is a physical property. The table shows the melting and boiling points of some substances. ☑

Substance	Melting Point (°C)	Boiling Point (°C)
Hydrogen	−259.31	−252.89
Nitrogen	−209.97	−195.8
Oxygen	−218.79	−182.97
Ethyl alcohol	−114	78
Mercury	−39	357
Water	0	100
Sulfur	119	444.6
Lead	327.5	1750
Silver	960.8	2193
Gold	1063	2660
Copper	1083	2567

✔ **Reading Check**

9. **Determine** What happens to water at 100°C?

_____

_____

Picture This

10. **Use a Table** In what state is gold at a temperature of 800°C? Circle your answer.

   a. solid
   b. liquid
   c. gas
   d. plasma

How can melting and boiling points be used?

The boiling point and melting point can help you identify a substance. If you see a clear liquid boil at 56.1°C, you know it is not water. Water boils at 100°C. You can classify substances based on boiling and melting points.

Metallic Properties

You have learned how you can classify substances as solids, liquids, or gases. You also learned to classify things by color, shape, length, mass, volume, or density. Other physical properties let you classify substances as metals.

What do metals look like?

What is the first thing you notice about a metal? You may notice that it looks shiny. This is because of the way metal reflects light. The shine of a metal is called luster. New handlebars on a bike have a metallic luster. Silver forks, knives, and spoons also have a metallic luster.

How are metals used?

Metals can be used in many ways because of some of their physical properties. Many metals can be hammered, pressed, or rolled into thin sheets. This property of metals is called malleability (mal lee uh BIH luh tee). Artists use malleable metals like copper to make sculptures. The Statue of Liberty is made of copper. Many metals can be drawn into wires. This property is called ductility (duk TIH luh tee). Wires in buildings and most electrical equipment are made from copper. Silver and platinum are also ductile.

Do you have any magnets on your refrigerator at home? Your refrigerator door is made of metal. Magnets are attracted to some metals. This is another physical property of metals. Some metals have groups of atoms that can be affected by the force of a magnet. The metals are attracted to the magnet because of that force. Magnets are often used to find metallic objects.

Using Physical Properties

You have learned that many physical properties can be used to identify substances. Properties like color, shape, length, mass, volume, ability to attract a magnet, density, melting point, boiling point, malleability, and ductility can help you separate and classify substances.

⚡ Think it Over

11. Classify Which of the following is made of metal? Circle your answer.

a. eraser
b. popsicle stick
c. soda bottle
d. tea kettle

FOLDABLES

Ⓑ Classify Make the following Foldable. Find objects and record your observations of physical properties on the Foldable.

Object Observed	Physical Properties

How are physical properties used to identify things?

You can describe salt as a white solid. You can measure the mass, volume, and density of a sample of salt. You could also find out if it is attracted to a magnet. These are examples of how physical properties can be used to identify a substance.

Identifying a Dog Suppose you volunteer to help your friend choose a family pet. You spot a cute dog at the local animal shelter. The sign on its cage says the dog is male and one to two years old. It also says the dog's breed is unknown. What kind of information do you and your friend need to figure out the dog's breed?

First, you need to know all of the physical properties of the dog. What does the dog look like? Second, you need to know the descriptions of different breeds of dogs. Then you can match up the description of the dog with the correct breed. The dog you found is brown, black, and white. He is medium-sized. He also has long ears and short legs. What breed is the dog? ☑

How can you narrow your options?

To find out, you may need to find out more about different breeds of dogs. Sometimes the easiest way to identify something is to find out what it cannot be. This is called the process of elimination. You can eliminate small dog and large dog breeds. You can also eliminate breeds that have short ears. You might want to look at photos of different dog breeds. Then you could see which one looks most like your dog.

Dichotomous Key The figure below shows a dichotomous (di KAH tuh mus) key. The questions in the key help you eliminate dog breeds. Scientists use methods like these to figure out the identities of living and nonliving things.

What Kind of Dog?		
1.	A. Small dog	Jack Russell Terrier
	B. Medium-size dog	go to #2
2.	A. Short ears that stick up	Boxer
	B. Ears hang down	go to #3
3.	A. Long ears, short legs, saggy skin	Bassett Hound
	B. Longer legs, medium-length ears	Beagle

Reading Check

12. **Explain** What are two things you need to know to figure out the dog's breed?

_____

_____

_____

_____

Think it Over

13. **Infer** What breed of dog might the dog at the animal shelter be?

_____

● After You Read

Mini Glossary

boiling point: the temperature at which a liquid becomes a gas

density: the amount of mass a material has in a given volume

matter: anything that has mass and takes up space

melting point: the temperature at which a solid becomes a liquid

physical change: a change where the physical properties of a substance change but the substance does not change

physical property: a characteristic of a material that you can observe or measure without changing the material

states of matter: solid, liquid, gas, and plasma

1. Read the key terms and definitions in the Mini Glossary. Write a sentence using the terms *melting point* and *physical property* on the lines below.

_____

_____

2. In the diagram fill in nine other physical properties of matter that can be used to identify a substance.

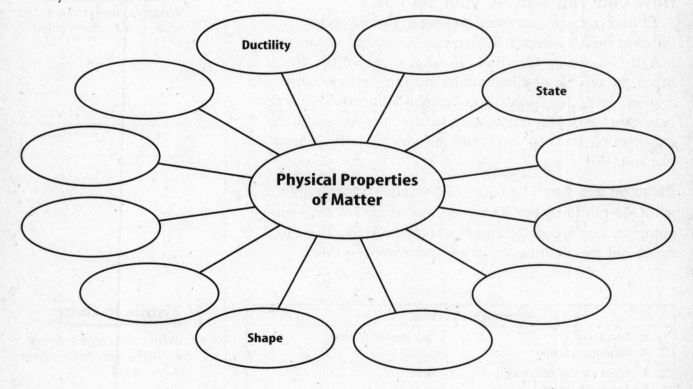

Science Online Visit **in6.msscience.com** to access your textbook, interactive games, and projects to help you learn more about physical properties and changes.

End of Section

 **Matter and Its Changes**

section ❷ Chemical Properties and Changes

 Standard—6.3.18: Investigate and describe that when a new material, such as concrete, is made by combining two or more materials, it has properties ....
Also covers: 6.6.1, 6.6.2, 6.6.3

● Before You Read

How does cake batter change when it is baked in an oven?

_____

_____

● Read to Learn

Ability to Change

Imagine you are at a campfire. What is needed for a campfire? You will need at least several large pieces of firewood and some small pieces of kindling. What happens to these things during the fire? After the campfire, all that is left is a pile of ash. Where did the wood go? What property of the wood is responsible for this change?

All of the properties you learned about in the first section were physical properties. You could see them easily. You also could use them to classify objects. Even when those properties changed, the identity of the object stayed the same. Why is the campfire different? Some properties tell you that the identity of the wood has changed. A **chemical property** is any characteristic that lets a substance change into a new substance.

Common Chemical Properties

Some changes are called chemical changes. A **chemical change** is a change in the identity of a substance because of the chemical properties of that substance. A new substance or substances are formed by a chemical change. You do not have to be in a laboratory to observe chemical changes. The campfire produced chemical changes. The oxygen in the air reacted with the wood. The reaction formed a new substance called ash.

What You'll Learn

- to identify chemical properties and chemical changes
- to classify matter by chemical properties
- the law of conservation of mass

▶ **Mark the Text**

Underline As you read, underline each chemical property you read about.

FOLDABLES

ⓒ Organize Information
Use the following Foldable to list examples of physical changes and chemical changes.

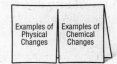

Examples of Physical Changes | Examples of Chemical Changes

Do all things burn?

Wood can burn. This chemical property is called flammability. Some products have warning labels to tell you they are flammable. These products should be kept away from heat or flames. What happens if you throw a stone onto the campfire? It will not burn. It has the property of being incombustible, or unable to burn. ☑

What are some common chemical reactions?

What happens to an unpainted iron gate? Over time it will rust. This is a chemical reaction.

Chemical Reactions with Metals Oxygen in the air reacts with the iron. This causes corrosion. The corrosion makes a new substance called iron oxide. The common name for iron oxide is rust. Other chemical reactions occur when metals react to other elements. Tarnish is a grayish-brown film that appears on silver. Silver reacts with sulfur in the air to form tarnish. The ability to react with oxygen or sulfur is a chemical property.

Chemical Reactions with Food Have you ever peeled a banana and then left part of it on the table? It probably turned brown. The same thing happens to sliced apples or avocadoes. The brown coloring is from a chemical reaction. The fruit reacts with the oxygen in the air. Although nothing is wrong with brown bananas, apples, or avocadoes, they do not look tasty. ☑

Can heat and light cause chemical reactions?

Vitamins often come in dark brown bottles. Do you know why? Many vitamins will change when they are exposed to light. This is a chemical property. The dark bottles protect the vitamins from going through a chemical change with light.

Some substances are sensitive to heat. They will go through a chemical change only when they are heated or cooled. One example is limestone. Some limestone has been around for hundreds of years without changing. But if limestone is heated, it goes through a chemical change. It produces carbon dioxide and lime. Lime is a chemical used in many industrial processes. This chemical property is the ability to change when heated. ☑

Another chemical property is the ability to change because of electrical contact. Electricity can cause a change in some compounds. It can also cause compounds to decompose, or break down. Water can be broken down with electricity.

☑ Reading Check

1. **Identify** Name a chemical property of wood.

_____

_____

☑ Reading Check

2. **Communicate** Why does a banana turn brown without its peel?

_____

_____

Indiana Academic Standard Check

6.3.18: Investigate and describe that when a new material, such as concrete, is made by combining ….

✔ 3. **Determine** What chemical property allows limestone to turn into carbon dioxide and lime?

Something New

The important difference between a physical change and a chemical change is that in a chemical change new substances are made. You enjoy many things because of chemical changes. What about that perfect, browned marshmallow roasted over a campfire? The fire caused a chemical change. The chemical change caused the marshmallow to look and taste different.

Sugar is normally white and made of crystals. When you heat it over a flame, it turns to a dark-brown caramel. A different substance is formed. Eggs, sugar, flour, and other ingredients change chemically when you bake them. If they did not, you could not eat a birthday cake. Cake begins as liquid and ends as solid. The baked cake has different properties than the batter.

What are the signs of a new substance?

Do you know you have a new substance just because it looks different? You could put salad in a blender and make it look different. But this would not be a chemical change. You would still have lettuce, carrots, and the other things that were in the salad.

You can look for signs to tell you if a new substance is made because of a chemical change. When a cake bakes, gas bubbles form. The bubbles grow within the ingredients. Bubbles are often a sign that a chemical change has happened. If you look closely at a piece of cake, you can see the airholes left from the bubbles. Other signs of change are the production of heat, light, smoke, and sound and a change in color.

Can you reverse a chemical change?

Physical changes usually can be reversed easily. Melted butter can become solid again if you put it in the refrigerator. Modeling clay can be smashed to fit back into its container. But chemical changes cannot be reversed by doing something physical. For example, you cannot glue the ashes from a fire together to make wood. You also cannot see the egg or the flour in a baked cake.

How can you classify matter according to chemical properties?

It is sometimes easier to classify by physical properties than it is to classify by chemical properties. You can see the physical properties of a substance easily. You cannot see chemical properties without changing the substance.

Think it Over

4. **Determine** Which of the signs of a chemical change would you see or hear at a campfire?

_____

_____

_____

Think it Over

5. **Conclude** What type of change does modeling clay go through in a person's hand?

_____

_____

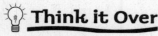 **Think it Over**

6. **Compare and Contrast** How are physical and chemical properties different?

_____

_____

_____

_____

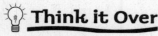 **Think it Over**

7. **Think Critically** Why is it important to keep chemical properties in mind when arranging products in a grocery store?

_____

_____

_____

FOLDABLES™

D Summarize Make the following Foldable. Use it to summarize the law of conservation of mass in your own words. Be sure to include examples.

Law of Conservation of Mass

Comparing Properties Once you know chemical properties, you can classify and identify matter using those properties. Suppose you try to burn what looks like a piece of wood. It does not burn. You can decide that it is not wood. The table below compares the two kinds of properties.

Comparing Properties	
Physical Properties	color, shape, length, mass, volume, density, state, ability to attract a magnet, melting point, boiling point, malleability, ductility
Chemical Properties	flammability; ability to react with: oxygen, electricity, light, water, heat, vinegar, etc.

In a grocery store, the products sometimes are separated because of chemical properties. The produce section is away from big windows where light and heat come in. The fruit and vegetables would ripen too quickly near a window. You also will not find lighter fluid near the bakery where there could be heat and flames.

Architects and product designers also think about chemical properties when they design buildings and merchandise. For example, children's sleepwear and bedding cannot be made of flammable fabric. Architects choose building materials like titanium that do not react with oxygen like other metals.

The Law of Conservation of Mass

Think back to the campfire. After the campfire, all that was left was a small pile of ash. Many kilograms of wood were turned into only a few kilograms of ash. Could this be a solution to the problems with landfills and garbage dumps? Why not burn all the trash? Can the amount of trash be reduced without making unwanted materials?

Can mass be destroyed?

Before you celebrate finding the solution to problems of landfills and garbage dumps, think about it. Did mass really disappear during the fire? It seems that way. There is less ash than there was wood. The **law of conservation of mass** states that the mass of what you end with is always the same as the mass of what you start with.

Has this law been proven to be true?

This law was first studied about 200 years ago. Many experiments have been done since then. They all prove the law to be true. One experiment done by French scientist Antoine Lavoisier was like a small campfire. He determined that a fire does not make mass disappear. But where did the mass go? The ashes are not heavy enough to equal the mass of the pieces of firewood.

Where did the mass go?

The campfire example shows that the law of conservation of mass is true. You just have to look carefully. When flammable materials burn, they combine with oxygen. They produce smoke, gases, and ash. The smoke and gases escape into the air. The mass of the smoke, gases, and ashes is the same as the mass of the original firewood. ☑

How can you show the law of conservation of mass?

Mass is not destroyed or created during a chemical change. The law of conservation of mass is shown in the figure below. In the first picture, there is one substance in the flask. There is another substance in the test tube inside the flask. The total mass is 16.150 g. The substances mix when the flask is turned upside down. (The flask is sealed so nothing escapes.) When the flask is placed on the scale again, the total mass is still 16.150 g. Instead of disappearing or appearing, particles in substances rearrange. They make different combinations of substances which have different properties.

✔ **Reading Check**

8. **Explain** What did the firewood change into?

_____

_____

Picture This

9. **Classify** What kind of change took place in the bottle, a chemical change or a physical change?

_____

Conservation of Mass

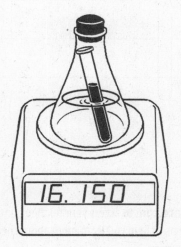

● After You Read

Mini Glossary

chemical change: a change in the identity of a substance because of the chemical properties of that substance

chemical property: any characteristic that lets a substance go through a change that turns it into a new substance

law of conservation of mass: states that the mass of what you end with is always the same as the mass of what you start with

1. Review the terms and their definitions in the Mini Glossary. How is the law of conservation of mass related to chemical changes?

   _____

   _____

2. Fill in the table about chemical properties.

Chemical Property	Example
	wood burning
ability to react with oxygen or sulfur	
	limestone producing carbon dioxide and lime
ability to react with electricity	

3. You were asked to underline different chemical properties. How did this help you understand and learn about chemical properties?

   _____

   _____

   _____

End of Section

ScienceOnline Visit **in6.msscience.com** to access your textbook, interactive games, and projects to help you learn more about chemical properties and changes.

Energy

section ❶ Energy Changes

> **Standard—6.3.17:** Recognize and describe that energy is a property of many objects and is associated with heat, light, electricity . . . .
> **Also covers:** 6.2.7

● Before You Read

On the lines below, write what you think it means when someone says they have a lot of energy.

_____

_____

What You'll Learn
- what energy is
- about different forms of energy
- about kinetic energy and potential energy

● Read to Learn

Energy

Energy is a word you probably use every day. You might say eating a snack gives you energy. You might say a soccer player has a lot of energy. Did you know that a burning fire also has energy? A tank of gas and a bouncing ball have energy too.

What is energy?

The word *energy* comes from the ancient Greek word *energos,* which means "active." You probably have used the word *energy* to mean active. **Energy** is the ability to cause change. Energy can change the temperature of a pot of water. Energy can change the speed and direction of a baseball. Energy in a thunderstorm makes lightning and thunder. You use energy when you change the speed of a bicycle by pedaling harder to go faster and by putting on the brakes. Energy also can change the arrangement of atoms in molecules and cause chemical reactions to happen.

Forms of Energy

Energy comes in different forms and from many different places. Food has chemical energy. Your body changes food into energy it needs to move, think, and grow. Nuclear power plants use energy in the nucleus of the atom to make electricity.

Mark the Text

Underline Underline different kinds of energy as you read about them. Then highlight an example of how that type of energy is used.

FOLDABLES™

Ⓐ Compare and Contrast Use two quarter-sheets of notebook paper to compare and contrast information about kinetic energy and potential energy.

What is an energy transformation?

An energy transformation happens when energy changes from one form to another. Energy transformations, or changes, happen all around you all the time. They even happen inside you. You have chemical energy stored in your muscles. When you push on a bicycle pedal, this chemical energy changes to energy of motion.

What happens to a car sitting in sunlight? The energy in sunlight changes to heat energy. The heat energy warms the inside of the car. Rub your hands together quickly. What happens? Your hands feel warm. The energy you use to move your hands changes to heat energy.

When energy is transformed, the total amount of energy does not change. Energy cannot be lost or gained. Energy only changes form.

How are energy transformations used?

Early humans used the chemical energy in wood when they learned to build fires. They used the energy to cook and stay warm. Today, a gas stove changes the chemical energy in natural gas to heat energy. Heat energy from a gas stove is used to cook food.

You use energy transformations in other ways, too. A hair dryer changes electrical energy into heat energy. A lightbulb changes electrical energy into light and heat energy. The table shows some ways energy transformations are used.

Type of Energy	Device	How Energy Is Transformed
Chemical	Stove	Energy from natural gas is changed to heat and light energy.
Electrical	Lightbulb	Energy from an electric current is changed into heat energy.
Solar	Solar energy collector	Energy from sunlight is changed into heat energy.

Kinetic Energy

Suppose you are bowling. You roll the bowling ball down the lane toward the bowling pins. The moving bowling ball has energy because it can cause change. When the moving bowling ball hits the bowling pins, it causes the bowling pins to fall. The energy an object has because of its motion is **kinetic energy**. A football thrown by a quarterback has kinetic energy. A leaf falling from a tree also has kinetic energy. ✔

💡 **Think it Over**

1. **Explain** How is sunlight an example of energy transformation?

_____

_____

Picture This

2. **Use a Table** What kind of energy does natural gas turn into?

_____

_____

✔ Reading Check

3. **Summarize** What is kinetic energy?

_____

_____

What affects kinetic energy?

All moving objects have kinetic energy. Not all moving objects have the same amount of kinetic energy. The amount of kinetic energy an object has depends on the mass and the speed of the object.

Mass Suppose a small rock and a large boulder are rolling down a hill at the same speed. Which has more kinetic energy? What would happen if they hit something at the bottom of the hill? Would the boulder cause more damage, or the rock? The boulder would cause more damage. The boulder has more kinetic energy because it has more mass.

Speed The kinetic energy of an object also depends on speed. Imagine two bowling balls that are the same size rolling down two bowling lanes. One ball is rolling much faster than the other. The bowling ball that is rolling faster knocks down more pins, even though both bowling balls hit the pins at the same place. When more pins are knocked down, a greater change has happened. The bowling ball that rolls faster has more kinetic energy. Kinetic energy increases as speed increases.

How is kinetic energy transferred?

When objects hit each other, kinetic energy can be moved, or transferred, from one object to the other. Think about the energy in a bowling ball when it hits the pins. The bowling ball does not have to touch all of the pins to knock them all down. The kinetic energy of the bowling ball is transferred to a few pins. Then, these pins fall and bump into other pins. Kinetic energy of the ball transfers from pin to pin until all of the pins fall down.

Look at the figure. A transfer of kinetic energy takes place when dominoes fall. Tapping only the first domino in the row makes it fall against the next domino. The kinetic energy from the first domino is transferred to the second domino. Kinetic energy is transferred from domino to domino until the last one falls. The kinetic energy of the last domino is transferred to the table.

4. Predict Two balls are rolling at the same speed. One ball has a mass of 5 kg. Another ball has a mass of 4 kg. Which ball has the greater kinetic energy?

_____

_____

Picture This

5. Explain What happens to the kinetic energy when you tap the first domino in a row of dominos?

_____

_____

Potential Energy

Look at the figure below. The ski lift takes a skier to the top of a hill. When the skier is standing at the top of the hill, she has no kinetic energy. But as she skis down the hill and moves faster, her kinetic energy increases.

Where does kinetic energy come from?

Gravity pulls the skier down the hill. If she were standing at the bottom of the hill, gravity would not start her moving. When the skier is standing at the top of the hill, she has a form of energy called potential energy. **Potential energy** is energy that is stored in an object because of the object's position. As the ski lift takes the skier up the hill, her potential energy increases. Potential energy is stored inside the skier before gravity pulls her down the hill. Changing her position increased her potential energy. The skier's potential energy gradually changes into kinetic energy as she skis down the hill.

Think it Over

6. **Explain** Why doesn't a skier standing at the top of a hill have any kinetic energy?

_____

_____

_____

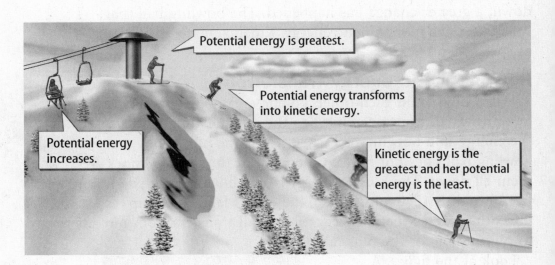

Potential energy is greatest.

Potential energy transforms into kinetic energy.

Potential energy increases.

Kinetic energy is the greatest and her potential energy is the least.

Picture This

7. **Explain** At what point on the hill is the skier's potential energy the least?

_____

_____

How can potential energy be increased?

When you lift an object higher than it was, it has the potential to fall. If it does fall, it has kinetic energy. To lift an object, you have to transfer energy to the object. The ski lift uses energy when it takes a skier up a hill. It transfers some energy to the skier. This energy is stored as potential energy in the skier. The potential energy changes to kinetic energy when the skier goes down the hill. The skier's potential energy would increase if she took a ski lift that went higher. The higher an object is lifted above Earth, the greater its potential energy.

Converting Potential and Kinetic Energy

Potential energy is transformed to kinetic energy when a skier skis down a hill. Kinetic energy can be transformed into potential energy. Suppose you throw a ball straight up into the air. Your muscles cause the ball to leave your hand and move up. The ball has kinetic energy because it is moving. Look at the figure below. As the ball gets higher, its potential energy increases. The ball slows down, and its kinetic energy decreases.

What happens when the ball reaches its highest point? It is hard to see, but the ball stops for an instant. The ball has no more kinetic energy when it stops. The kinetic energy it had when it left your hand has all changed into potential energy. Then, the ball falls back down. As the ball falls, its potential energy changes back into kinetic energy. If you catch the ball at the same height that you threw it from, the ball's kinetic energy is the same as when it left your hand.

Picture This

8. Interpret an Illustration Look at the figure. When does the kinetic energy of the ball increase? Circle your answer.

a. before it is thrown
b. right after it is thrown
c. when it reaches its highest point
d. as it is falling

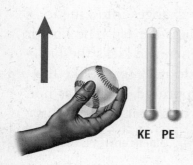

As the ball leaves the person's hand, it is moving the fastest and has greatest kinetic energy.

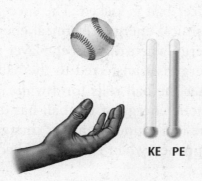

As the ball moves upward, it slows down as its kinetic energy is transformed into potential energy.

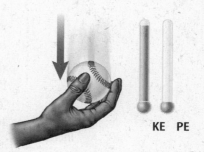

As the ball moves downward, it speeds up as its potential energy is transformed into kinetic energy.

How does energy change in falling water?

Have you ever stood close to a waterfall and listened to the roaring water? The water at the top of a waterfall has potential energy. The potential energy is transformed into kinetic energy as the water falls. ☑

The kinetic energy of falling water can be used to make, or generate, electricity. Dams are built on rivers. Water backs up behind a dam and forms a lake. The water near the top of the dam falls downward. Then, the water's kinetic energy spins generators that produce electricity. The water's potential energy behind the dam is transformed into kinetic energy and then into electrical energy.

Indiana Academic Standard Check

6.3.17: Recognize and describe that energy is a property of many objects ....

✔ **9. Determine** What kind of energy does the water at the top of a waterfall have?

_____

10. Analyze When a ball that is rolling across a field stops, energy is lost. Is this sentence true or false? Explain.

_____

_____

_____

Picture This

11. Draw Conclusions
When is the kinetic energy of the soccer ball greatest—right after the ball is kicked, or as the ball rubs against the grass?

_____

_____

Conservation of Energy

Keeping track of energy as it is transformed can be hard. Sometimes it seems like energy disappears or is lost. But, that does not happen. In 1840, a scientist named James Joule showed that energy cannot be made or lost. The **law of conservation of energy** states that energy cannot be created or destroyed, but can only be transformed from one form to another. The total amount of energy in the universe never changes. Energy only changes form.

Kinetic energy can be changed into heat energy. This happens when two objects rub against each other. Suppose you push a book across a table. It will slow down and stop. But its kinetic energy is not lost. The book's kinetic energy is changed into heat energy as the book rubs against the table.

How can you keep track of energy changes?

Look at the figure. It shows how energy flows when a soccer ball is kicked. The soccer player's leg muscles have chemical energy. Chemical energy changes into kinetic energy when the soccer player swings her leg. The kinetic energy is transferred to the ball when she kicks the ball. After the ball rolls for a while, it stops. It seems like the kinetic energy of the ball has disappeared. But it has not. The ball's kinetic energy changed into heat energy. This happened when the ball rubbed against the grass as it rolled.

A moving soccer player has kinetic energy. Kinetic energy from the player's moving leg is transferred to the ball.

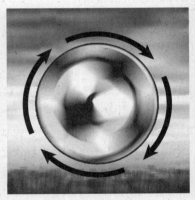

When the ball rolls, its kinetic energy is transformed by friction into heat as the ball rubs against the grass.

After You Read

Mini Glossary

energy: ability to cause change

kinetic energy: energy an object has because of its motion

law of conservation of energy: energy cannot be created or destroyed, it can only be transformed from one form to another

potential energy: energy that is stored in an object because of the object's position

1. Read the vocabulary terms and their definitions in the Mini Glossary. Explain how potential energy can change to kinetic energy.

_____

_____

_____

2. The figure below shows a marble on a ramp. In the boxes, describe the ways the potential energy and kinetic energy of the marble are changing.

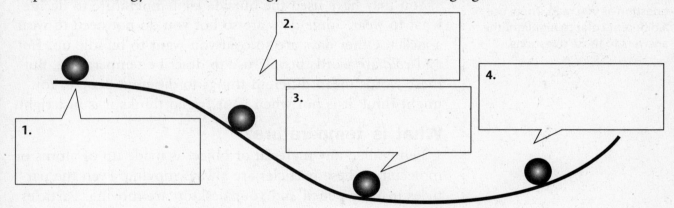

3. You were asked to underline different kinds of energy and then highlight an example of each. Did this strategy help you learn about the different forms of energy? Why or why not?

_____

_____

Science Online Visit **in6.msscience.com** to access your textbook, interactive games, and projects to help you learn more about energy changes.

End of Section

#

section ❷ Temperature

> **Standard—6.3.17:** Recognize and describe that energy is a property of many objects and is associated with heat, light, electricity ....
> **Also covers:** 6.2.7

What You'll Learn
- the difference between temperature and heat
- ways heat is used
- how heat is transferred

Mark the Text

Identify Concepts Look at the section headings. Highlight each heading that asks a question as you read. Then, use a different color to highlight the answers to those questions.

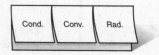

FOLDABLES™

Ⓑ Organize Information Make the three-tab Foldable to write information about conduction, convection, and radiation.

| Cond. | Conv. | Rad. |

● Before You Read

Is it hot or cold today? On the lines below, explain why it feels hot or cold outside.

_____

_____

● Read to Learn

Temperature

You may have used the outside air temperature to decide what to wear. Some days are so hot you do not need to wear a jacket. Other days are so cold you want to bundle up. *Hot* and *cold* are words people use to describe temperature. But these words mean different things to different people. You might think it is hot when your friend thinks it is just right.

What is temperature?

Remember, any material or object is made up of atoms or molecules. These particles are always moving. Even the particles in your pencil and your desktop are moving. Particles move in all directions. In a gas, particles are spread far apart and can move freely. In a liquid, particles are closer together. They cannot move as far. In solids, particles are even closer together than in liquids. They vibrate, or move back and forth.

The particles in solids, liquids, and gases have kinetic energy because they are moving. The faster the particles are moving, the more kinetic energy they have.

Temperature is a measure of the average kinetic energy of the particles in an object. Gas molecules at a low temperature move slowly. Gas molecules at a higher temperature move faster. At the higher temperature, the molecules are moving faster and have more kinetic energy.

Measuring Temperature

You cannot measure temperature by how something feels. What feels warm to some people feels cool to other people. Recall that temperature is a measure of the average kinetic energy of the particles in an object. You cannot measure the kinetic energy of every atom. There are too many of them. Instead, thermometers are used to measure temperature.

What is the Fahrenheit scale?

The Fahrenheit (FAYR un hite) scale is a common temperature scale used in the United States. On this scale, the freezing point of water is 32°F. The boiling point of water is 212°F. There are 180 degrees between the freezing point and boiling point of water. Each degree is an equal amount.

What is the Celsius scale?

The Celsius (SEL see us) scale is used more widely throughout the world. On this scale, the freezing point of water is 0°C. The boiling point of water is 100°C. There are 100 degrees between the boiling and freezing points of water on the Celsius scale. Therefore, a temperature change of one Celsius degree is bigger than a change of one Fahrenheit degree.

Heat

What is heat? **Heat** is the transfer of energy from one object to another due to a difference in temperature. Heat only flows from warmer objects to cooler ones. ☑

Suppose you held a glass of ice water. The water soon warms up. Why? Your hand is warmer than the ice water. Heat flows out of your hand and into the glass. The temperature of the water increases. The temperature of your skin touching the glass decreases. Heat stops flowing from your hand to the glass when both are the same temperature.

Heat and Temperature

How warm will a colder object get when heat is transferred to it? That depends on two things. The first is the amount of material in the object. The second is the kinds of atoms the material is made of. For example, water has to absorb a lot of heat before its temperature rises by one degree. This is why water is used to cool things. Water in a car's radiator carries a large amount of heat away from the engine to keep the engine from overheating.

💡 Think it Over

1. **Compare and Contrast** Describe one way that the Fahrenheit scale is different from the Celsius scale.

_____

_____

_____

✔ Reading Check

2. **Conclude** Does heat flow from warmer objects to cooler objects or from cooler objects to warmer objects?

_____

_____

How do temperatures of water and land differ?

How does the temperature of water in a lake compare to the temperature of the surrounding air on a hot summer day? How do these temperatures compare at night when the air has cooled off? The water in the lake is cooler than the air on a hot day. The water is warmer than the air at night. This is because it takes longer for a large body of water to warm up or to cool down than the air and land around the body of water.

Heat on the Move

Remember that if a warm area touches a cooler area, heat moves from the warmer area to the cooler area. Heat is transferred in three ways—conduction, convection, and radiation. Conduction transfers heat mainly through solids and liquids. Convection transfers heat through liquids and gases. Radiation transfers energy through space. ☑

What is conduction?

<u>Conduction</u> (kun DUK shun) is the transfer of energy through a material by atoms in the material bumping into each other. What happens when you put a metal spoon into a cup of hot cocoa? The spoon gets hot. The part of the spoon in the hot cocoa becomes warmer. The atoms and molecules move faster. These particles hit other slower-moving particles in the spoon. Kinetic energy transfers from the faster-moving particles to the slower-moving particles farther up the spoon's handle.

Conduction transfers kinetic energy from particle to particle in a solid. The figure shows how the particles move back and forth in place, bumping into one another. Energy is transferred from fast-moving (warmer) particles to slower-moving (colder) particles when they bump.

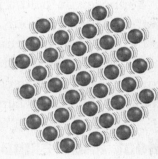

What are thermal conductors?

Thermal conductors are materials that transfer energy easily. Most metals are good conductors of heat. Gold, silver, and copper are the best thermal conductors. Some cooking pans are made of steel but have copper bottoms. A copper bottom conducts heat more evenly. It helps spread the heat across the bottom of the pan so that the food is cooked more evenly.

✔ **Reading Check**

3. **Summarize** What are the three ways heat can be transferred?

_____

_____

_____

Picture This

4. **Describe** how particles in a solid move during conduction.

_____

_____

💡 Think it Over

5. **Apply** Which of these would be the best conductor? Circle your answer.

a. a plastic spoon
b. a wooden chopstick
c. a silver fork
d. a rubber spatula

What are insulators?

You use an oven mitt to take a hot pan out of the oven. The oven mitt keeps the heat from moving from the pan to your hands. The oven mitt is a thermal insulator. Insulators are materials that do not transfer heat easily. When you are cold, you can put a blanket over you. The blanket is an insulator that makes it hard for heat to leave your body. Other good insulators are wood, rubber, plastic, and even air.

What is convection?

<u>Convection</u> (kun VEK shun) transfers heat when particles move between objects or areas that have different temperatures. Convection is most common in liquids and gases. As temperature increases, particles move faster and spread farther apart. So the density of the material decreases. Colder, more dense material forces the warmer, less dense material upward.

The figure shows a thermal. Thermals help some birds stay in the air for a long time without flapping their wings. A thermal is a column of warm air forced up by colder air around it. It is a convection current in the air. The Sun heats the ground. The air near the ground gets warmer and becomes less

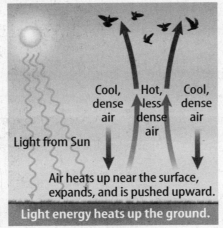

Cool, dense air

Hot, less dense air

Cool, dense air

Light from Sun

Air heats up near the surface, expands, and is pushed upward.

Light energy heats up the ground.

dense. The cooler, denser air pushes the warmer air up. As the air cools, it sinks and pushes more warm air up.

Convection also occurs in liquids. In a pot of boiling water, the warmer, less dense water is forced up as the cooler, denser water sinks. When all the water is warmed to the boiling point, you can see the movement in the boiling water.

What is radiation?

<u>Radiation</u> (ray dee AY shun) is the transfer of energy by waves. When waves hit an object, the object absorbs their energy and its temperature rises. Radiation can travel through air or through a vacuum, like space. Earth gets energy from the Sun through radiation. Your body is warmed by radiation when you stand by a fire or a radiator. You can also use radiation to cook food. A microwave oven uses microwave radiation to transfer energy to the food. ☑

Picture This

6. Label Write "thermal" at its location in the figure.

✔ **Reading Check**

7. Identify In what way is energy transferred in a microwave oven?

_____

_____

● After You Read

Mini Glossary

conduction: transfer of energy by atoms in a material bumping into each other

convection: transfer of heat when particles move between objects or areas that have different temperatures

heat: transfer of energy from one object to another due to a difference in temperature; flows from warmer objects to cooler objects

radiation: transfer of energy by waves

temperature: measure of the average kinetic energy of the particles in an object

1. Review the terms and their definitions in the Mini Glossary. Explain the term *temperature* in your own words.

_____

_____

2. Complete the graphic organizer to give an example of each type of heat transfer.

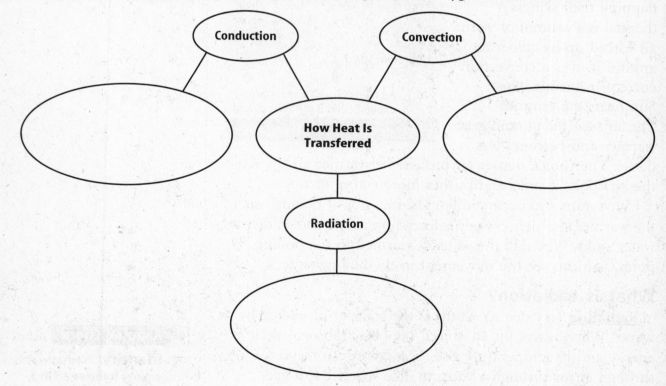

End of Section

Science Online Visit **in6.msscience.com** to access your textbook, interactive games, and projects to help you learn more about temperature and heat.

 Energy

section ⊜ **Chemical Energy**

> **Standard—6.2.7:** Locate information in reference books, back issues of newspapers and magazines, CD-ROMs, and computer databases.
> **Also covers:** 6.2.5, 6.2.6, 6.3.17, 6.3.18

● Before You Read

Have you ever seen fireflies at night in the summer? They make a blinking light. How do you think they make this light?

_____

_____

What You'll Learn
- how chemical energy is changed
- how to make a chemical reaction go faster or slower

● Read to Learn

Chemical Reactions and Energy

Have you ever seen light sticks? They glow for a short time. Energy in the form of light comes from a chemical reaction that happens inside the stick. The same thing happens when you turn on a gas stove. A chemical reaction takes place, and energy in the form of heat and light are given off. You use energy from chemical reactions every day.

What is a chemical reaction?

Some chemical reactions happen when atoms or molecules come together and form new compounds. A chemical reaction also can break the bonds between atoms. These atoms can then join with other atoms. For example, a chemical reaction happens when a fire burns. Bonds between atoms in the compounds of the wood break. Then, the atoms join with other atoms to make new compounds.

What are chemical bonds?

Energy is stored in the chemical bonds between atoms in a compound. The energy is a kind of potential energy called chemical energy. The chemical energy stored in coal, gas, and oil is an important energy source that you use every day. Chemical energy stored in food is a source of energy for your body to move and grow. Muscles change chemical energy into kinetic energy and heat when they move. ☑

Study Coach

State the Main Ideas As you read this section, stop after each paragraph and write down the main idea in your own words.

☑ **Reading Check**

1. **Name** three sources of chemical energy.

_____

_____

_____

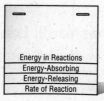
Energy in Reactions

Transformations in energy happen in every chemical reaction. Energy must be added to break chemical bonds. When bonds form, energy is released. Energy often is added to begin a reaction. A lighted match placed in a mixture of hydrogen gas and oxygen gas will cause the mixture to explode and water will form. The heat from the flame of the match is the energy needed to start the chemical reaction. Hydrogen and oxygen atoms will bond together to make water molecules. The energy that is released when the atoms bond results in the explosion.

After atoms bond to form water molecules, it is hard to break the water molecules apart. Energy in the form of electricity, heat, or light, is needed to break chemical bonds.

What is an energy-absorbing reaction?

Some chemical reactions need energy all the time or they will stop. These reactions absorb, or take in, energy. An **endothermic** (en duh THUR mihk) **reaction** is a chemical reaction that absorbs heat energy. Endothermic reactions take place during cooking and baking.

Chemical reactions occur when sunlight hits a plant's leaves. The figure shows how plants use sunlight to make food. This process is called photosynthesis (foh toh SIHN thuh sus). Chemical reactions change the energy in sunlight into chemical energy in sugar that plants produce. Plants use carbon dioxide, water, and sunlight to make oxygen and sugar through photosynthesis.

Picture This
2. **Highlight** Use a highlighter to indicate where sugar is stored after photosynthesis.

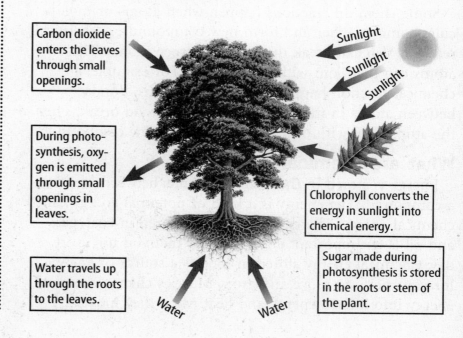

Carbon dioxide enters the leaves through small openings.

Sunlight
Sunlight
Sunlight

During photosynthesis, oxygen is emitted through small openings in leaves.

Chlorophyll converts the energy in sunlight into chemical energy.

Water travels up through the roots to the leaves.

Sugar made during photosynthesis is stored in the roots or stem of the plant.

Water   Water

What is an energy-releasing reaction?

Endothermic chemical reactions, like photosynthesis, are important because they make compounds such as oxygen and food. Other reactions are important because they make energy. **Exothermic** (ek soh THUR mihk) **reactions** are chemical reactions that give off heat energy. When you add a piece of wood to a fire, it burns. Atoms in the wood join with oxygen atoms in the air. An exothermic reaction takes place, and heat energy and light energy are released. This kind of exothermic reaction is called combustion. Burning oil, coal, and gas produces much of the energy needed to heat homes and schools.

How fast do chemical reactions happen?

Chemical reactions can happen at different rates, or speeds. When fireworks explode, chemical reactions happen very fast. When metal is left outside for a long time, it gets rusty. Metals rust when they join with oxygen. Rusting is a kind of chemical reaction that happens much more slowly than a fireworks explosion.

Many chemical reactions happen in your body every second. The reactions happen at different rates. Your body controls the rates of these reactions so that your body will work correctly and stay healthy.

Can the rate of a chemical reaction change?

You can change the rate of a chemical reaction two ways. One way is to change the temperature. For example, if you leave cake batter in a pan on the counter for many hours, nothing happens. If you put the pan in a hot oven, it turns into a cake. Raising the temperature of the cake batter makes the chemical reactions happen more quickly.

Another way to change the rate of a reaction is to add a compound called a catalyst. A **catalyst** (KA tuh list) is something that changes the rate of a chemical reaction without changing itself. Catalysts in your body called enzymes help you grow, breathe, and digest food. The saliva in your mouth has an enzyme in it. When you chew a piece of bread, this enzyme helps break down the starches in bread into smaller molecules. Enzymes help turn the food into the energy your body needs. ☑

Other chemical reactions use catalysts to go faster. These reactions include the production of vegetable shortening, synthetic rubber, and high-octane gasoline.

Think it Over

3. **Infer** Which of the following is an example of an exothermic reaction?

a. candle burning
b. bread baking
c. ice melting
d. photosynthesis

Reading Check

4. **Define** What is a catalyst?

_____

_____

_____

● After You Read

Mini Glossary

catalyst: substance that changes the rate of a chemical reaction without changing itself

endothermic reaction: chemical reaction that absorbs heat energy

exothermic reaction: chemical reaction that gives off heat energy

1. Review the terms and their definitions in the Mini Glossary. In your own words, explain the difference between an endothermic reaction and an exothermic reaction.

_____

_____

_____

2. In the table below, write if each reaction is exothermic or endothermic.

Chemical Reaction	Endothermic or Exothermic?
Exploding fireworks	
Photosynthesis	
Baking cookies	Endothermic
Burning gas	
Hydrogen and oxygen combining to form water	

3. You were asked to write the main idea of each paragraph as you read this section. How did you decide which is the main idea for each paragraph?

_____

_____

_____

End of Section

 Science Online Visit **in6.msscience.com** to access your textbook, interactive games, and projects to help you learn more about chemical energy.

286 Energy

Electricity and Magnetism

section ❶ Electric Charge and Forces

Standard—6.3.19: Investigate that materials may be composed of parts that are too small to be seen without magnification.
Also covers: 6.2.7, 6.3.23

● Before You Read

What are two examples of how you use electricity?

_____

_____

● Read to Learn

Electric Charges

Many things use electrical energy. Electrical energy comes from the forces between the electric charges found in atoms.

Where are the charges found in atoms?

Matter around you is made of atoms. Atoms are particles that are too small to be seen. They are less than a billionth of a meter in size. Every atom has electrons. The electrons move around a nucleus, as shown in the figure. The nucleus contains protons and neutrons. An atom has the same number of protons as electrons.

Protons and electrons have electric charge. Protons have positive charge. Electrons have negative charge. The amount of positive charge on a proton is equal to the amount of negative charge on an electron. Neutrons have no electric charge.

When is an object electrically charged?

An atom has equal amounts of positive and negative charge because it has equal numbers of protons and electrons. The positive and negative charges cancel each other out. An atom can become electrically charged if it gains or loses electrons. An object is electrically charged if the amounts of positive and negative charge are not equal.

What You'll Learn

- how electrical charges apply forces
- what an electrical field is
- how objects become electrically charged
- how lightning happens

▶ **Study Coach**

Create a Quiz After you have read this section, create a quiz based on what you have learned. After you have written the quiz questions, be sure to answer them.

FOLDABLES

Ⓐ Organize Information
Make the following Foldable to organize information about protons, neutrons, electric charges, and electric fields.

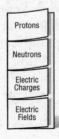

Protons

Neutrons

Electric Charges

Electric Fields

The Forces Between Charges

Two objects that are electrically charged exert forces on each other. These electric forces can bring objects together, or attract them. They also can push objects apart, or repel them. Look at the figure. If two objects are positively charged, they repel each other. If two objects are negatively charged, they also repel each other. But if one object is positively charged and the other is negatively charged, they attract each other. Like charges repel and unlike charges attract.

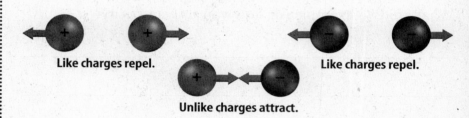

Like charges repel.

Unlike charges attract.

Like charges repel.

Picture This

1. **Highlight** Highlight the direction of the forces in each example in the figure.

How does distance affect electric force?

The distance between two charged objects affects the electric force between them. As the distance between charged objects increases, the electric force between them decreases. Suppose two electrons are moving apart. As they move farther apart, the force that repels them decreases.

How does charge affect electric force?

The amount of charge on two objects affects the electric force between them. If the amount of charge on either object decreases, so does the electric force. If the amount of charge increases, the electric force increases.

Think it Over

2. **Apply** When two electrons move closer together, how does the force between them change?

_____

_____

Electric Field and Electric Forces

Electric charges can exert forces on each other even when they are not touching. What happens when you rub a balloon on your hair and then hold the balloon a little away from your hair? Your hair moves toward the balloon. The balloon and your hair are not touching, but they are exerting forces on each other.

How do electric charges exert forces if they are not touching?

An electric charge is surrounded by an area called an electric field. The electric field exerts a force on other electric charges. Every proton and electron is surrounded by an electric field that exerts a force on all other protons and electrons. ✓

✔ Reading Check

3. **Identify** What parts of an atom are surrounded by electric fields?

_____

_____

How can you describe an electric field?

The electric field surrounding an electric charge is invisible. The figures show a way to describe an electric field for a positive charge and a negative charge. The arrows show the direction of the force the electric field exerts. The figures show the electric field at only a few points in space surrounding a charge, but the electric field is at every point in space surrounding a charge.

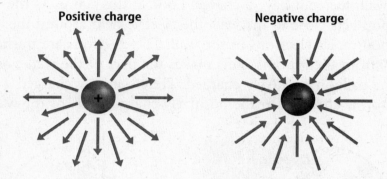

Positive charge   Negative charge

Picture This

4. **Compare** How are the electric fields of positive and negative charges different?

_____

_____

_____

_____

Making Objects Electrically Charged

A balloon becomes electrically charged when you rub it on your hair. The balloon no longer has an equal number of protons and electrons. Electric charges move from your hair to the balloon. This is how the balloon becomes electrically charged.

How does touch make an object electrically charged?

When you rub the balloon on your hair, the atoms in your hair and in the balloon are close together. Electrons move from atoms in your hair to atoms in the balloon. This is an example of charging by contact. **Charging by contact** is the movement of electric charges between objects that are touching, or in contact. ☑

The balloon gains electrons from your hair making it have more electrons than protons. Remember electrons have a negative charge, so the balloon is negatively charged. Your hair loses electrons to the balloon making it have more protons than electrons. Since protons are positively charged, your hair is positively charged. The amount of negative charge gained by the balloon equals the amount of positive charge left on your hair.

✓ **Reading Check**

5. **Summarize** For charging by contact, what must two objects do?

_____

Static Cling Another example of charging by contact is the static cling your clothes can get when they are in a dryer. Your clothes rub against each other when they tumble in a dryer. Electrons move from one piece of clothing to another. This can cause pieces of clothing to stick to each other.

Are there other ways to charge objects?

What happens when you rub a balloon on your hair and then try to stick it to a wall? It sticks. Why? You make the balloon negatively charged by rubbing it on your hair. But the wall does not have a charge. Look at the figure. As the balloon gets close to the wall, the electric field around the balloon repels electrons in the wall. The electrons are pushed away from their atoms. This makes the part of the wall close to the balloon positively charged. The negatively charged balloon is attracted to the positively charged part of the wall.

Picture This

6. Circle the negatively charged part of the figure.

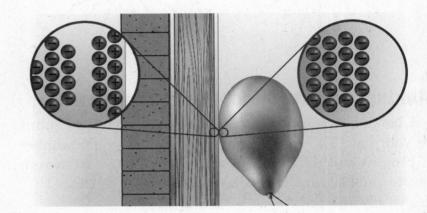

<u>**Charging by induction**</u> is the rearrangement of electric charge because of the presence of an electric field. One part of the object becomes positively charged and another part becomes negatively charged. However, the whole object stays electrically neutral.

Insulators and Conductors

<u>**Insulators**</u> are materials in which electric charges cannot move easily. Electrons in insulators are held tightly by the atoms and cannot move easily. Plastics, glass, rubber, and wood are examples of materials that are insulators. <u>**Conductors**</u> are materials in which electric charges can move easily. Electrons in conductors are not held tightly and can move rather easily. The best conductors are metals such as copper and gold.

FOLDABLES

B Compare and Contrast
Make the following Foldable to compare and contrast conductors and insulators.

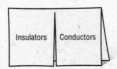

Static Charge

When charging by contact happens, the object that loses electrons has more positive charge than negative charge. The object that gains electrons has more negative charge than positive charge. The imbalance of electric charge on an object is <u>static charge</u>.

What is electric discharge?

Have you ever walked across a carpet and then touched a metal doorknob? Did you feel an electric shock or see a spark? The spark is an example of an electric discharge. An <u>electric discharge</u> is the movement of static charge from one place to another. The spark you saw was the result of a static charge.

How did this happen? Electrons move from the carpet to your body. Your hand then has an electric field that repels electrons in the doorknob. The electrons in the doorknob move away. This leaves a positively charged place on the doorknob. If the attractive electric force on the extra electrons is strong enough, these electrons can be pulled from your hand to the doorknob. The spark you see and the shock you feel are caused by this quick movement of electrons. ☑

What is lightning?

Lightning is an example of an electric discharge. Air currents in storm clouds sometimes cause electrons to move from the top of the cloud to the bottom. The electric field surrounding the bottom of the cloud repels electrons in the ground. This makes the ground positively charged. Lightning is the quick movement of the charges between the ground and the cloud.

What is grounding?

A lightning flash has a lot of electrical energy. If lightning hits a tree, it can start a fire. If it hits a building, the building can be damaged or burn. Buildings are protected from lightning by metal lightning rods on their roofs. A thick wire is connected to each lightning rod. The other end of the wire is connected to the ground. If lightning hits the lightning rod, the electrical charges go through the wire into the ground. Earth can be a conductor. Earth is so big that it can absorb a lot of extra electrical charge. The charge from the lightning goes into the ground and not the building. Making a path for electrical charge to go into the ground is called grounding. ☑

✓ Reading Check

7. Identify What moves from your hand to a doorknob when you get a shock?

_____

✓ Reading Check

8. Identify What acts as a conductor for a lightning rod?

_____

● After You Read

Mini Glossary

charging by contact: the movement of electric charges between objects that are touching, or in contact

charging by induction: the rearrangement of electric charge because of the presence of an electric field

conductors: materials in which electric charges can move easily

electric discharge: the movement of static charge from one place to another

insulators: materials in which electric charges cannot move easily

static charge: the imbalance of electric charge on an object

1. Read the key terms and definitions in the Mini Glossary above. On the lines below, explain how the terms *charging by induction* and *static charge* are related.

_____

_____

2. Write the letter of each statement in the correct location in the Venn diagram to compare and contrast charging by induction to charging by contact.

   a. **Objects must be touching**
   b. **Makes part of an object positively charged and part negatively charged**
   c. **Move electric charge**
   d. **Objects are not touching**
   e. **Makes the charge of an object positive or negative**

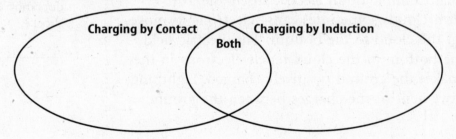

Charging by Contact   **Charging by Induction**

Both

3. You were asked to create a quiz and answer the quiz questions after you read this section. How did this help you learn the material in this section?

_____

_____

End of Section

Science ● nline Visit **in6.msscience.com** to access your textbook, interactive games, and projects to help you learn more about electric charge and forces.

chapter 19

Electricity and Magnetism

section 2 Electrical Current

Standard—6.3.23: Explain that electrical circuits provide a means of transferring electrical energy from sources such as generators to devices ....
Also covers: 6.2.7

● Before You Read

When you turn on a lamp, where does the light come from?

_____

_____

What You'll Learn
- about electric current
- how electrical energy is moved to a circuit
- current, voltage, and resistance

● Read to Learn

Electric Current

A TV produces light waves and sound waves. Where does this energy come from? An electrical outlet provides electrical energy. Electrical energy is available only when an electric currant flows in the TV. The TV changes the electrical energy into sound and light.

What is an electric current?

An **electric current** is the flow of electric charges. An electric current flows in a wire when electrons move along the wire.

A wire is electrically neutral. It has the same number of protons and electrons. The electrons move along the wire when electric current flows in the wire. At the same time, electrons flow into one end of the wire and flow out of the other end of the wire. The number of electrons that flow into one end is the same as the number of electrons that flow out of the other end. This keeps the wire electrically neutral. ☑

What is the unit for current?

The amount of electric current in a wire is the amount of electric charge that flows into and out of the wire every second. The SI unit for electric current is the ampere (A). One ampere of electric current means a huge number of electrons (about six billion billion) are flowing into and out of the wire every second.

◀ Mark the Text

Locate Information
Underline every heading in the reading that asks a question. Then, use a different color to highlight the answers to those questions.

✔ Reading Check

1. **Determine** What keeps a wire electrically neutral?

_____

_____

_____

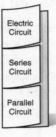

Organize Information
Make the following Foldable to help you understand the different kinds of circuits.

Electric
Circuit

Series
Circuit

Parallel
Circuit

A Simple Electric Circuit

When lightning flashes, electric energy turns into heat energy, sound energy, and light energy. This happens in an instant. When you watch TV, electricity must be turned into light energy and sound energy for as long as you have the TV on. An electric current must keep flowing in the TV.

Electric current will flow only if the charges can flow in a closed, or non-stopping, path. A closed path in which electric charges can flow is an **electric circuit**. The figure at the bottom of the page shows a simple electric circuit. Current flows in this circuit as long as the conducting path between the battery, wires, and lightbulb is not broken. If the switch is open, the path is broken and the current will not flow. Also, if a wire or the filament in the lightbulb is broken, the path is broken and current will not flow.

Making Electric Charges Flow

A force must be exerted on electric charges to make them flow. Remember that a force is exerted on an electric charge by an electric field. To make electric charges flow in a circuit, there must be an electric field in the circuit that moves electrons in one direction.

What can make charges flow?

The battery in the figure produces the electric field that can make electrons flow. Chemical reactions happen in the battery when it is connected in a circuit. These chemical reactions cause one post, or the negative terminal, of the battery to become negatively charged and the positive terminal to become positively charged. The negative and positive charges on the battery terminals make the electric field in the circuit. The electric field causes electrons to flow from the negative terminal toward the positive terminal. ☑

Reading Check

2. **Summarize** What kind of reactions make an electric field in a battery?

_____

Picture This

3. **Draw** In the figure, draw arrows along the wire that show the flow of the electric current when the circuit is closed.

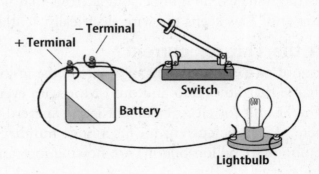

What is electric resistance?

Electrons are always hitting atoms and other electric charges as they flow. This causes electrons to change direction. But the electric field in the circuit keeps the electrons moving in the direction the current is flowing.

A measure of how hard it is for electrons to flow in an object is **electric resistance**. The resistance of insulators is usually much higher than the resistance of conductors. The unit for electric resistance is the ohm (Ω).

How can you model electron flow?

Look at the figure of a ball bouncing down a flight of stairs. The ball hits the steps and changes its direction many times. Its overall motion is in one direction—downward. The ball is like an electron moving through an electric circuit. Electrons in a circuit change direction after they hit atoms and other electric charges. But their overall motion is in one direction—the direction of the current flow.

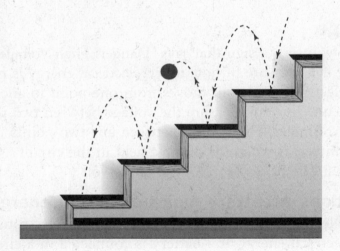

Picture This

4. Analyze Draw an arrow to show the overall direction of the ball in the figure.

Why do electrons flow slowly in a wire?

If the ball had fallen without bouncing, it would have gotten to the bottom of the stairs much faster. Changing directions from bouncing on the steps slowed the ball down. In the same way, electrical resistance in a wire causes electrons to flow slowly. An electron in a circuit may take several minutes to move only a centimeter. If that is true, why does a lighbulb light up as soon as you flip a switch? When you flip a switch, you close a circuit. An electric field moves through the circuit at the speed of light. The electric field causes electrons in the lightbulb to start flowing almost immediately after the switch is flipped.

Think it Over

5. Apply How would turning on a light be different if the electric field were much slower?

_____

_____

Transferring Electrical Energy

When a current flows in a material, kinetic energy moves to the material. This is because the electrons and atoms bump into each other. The energy that flowing electrons move to the circuit also is called electrical energy. Electrical energy is changed into other forms of energy. When current flows to a lightbulb, it is changed to heat and light.

Electrical Energy and the Electric Field

The electrical energy that electrons move to a circuit depends on the strength of the electric field. If the electric field becomes stronger, the electric force exerted on electrons increases as they move from one point to another in the circuit. This causes electrons to move faster between hitting other atoms and electric charges. Since the speed of the flowing electrons increases as the electric field gets stronger, their kinetic energy also increases. A stronger electric field causes more electrical energy to move to the circuit.

Voltage

Have you seen a sign that says "Danger! High Voltage?" **Voltage** is a measure of how much electrical energy is moved by an electric charge as it moves from one point to another in a circuit. You can measure the voltage between two points with a voltmeter. The voltage between any two points in the circuit increases when the electric field in the circuit increases. The SI unit for voltage is the volt (V).

How does a battery make electrical energy?

The electric field in a circuit causes flowing electrons to have electrical energy. If a battery is connected in a circuit, chemical reactions in the battery make the electric field. In a battery, chemical energy is changed into electrical energy. This electrical energy can be changed into other forms of energy in the circuit. The battery is the source of energy.

What is battery voltage?

Battery voltage is the voltage between the positive and negative terminals of a battery. The battery voltage is related to how much electrical energy an electron would move to a circuit from the negative terminal to the positive terminal. When the voltage of a battery increases, more electrical energy is moved to a circuit. The voltage a battery makes depends on the chemical reactions in the battery. ☑

Think it Over

6. Apply What happens to voltage in a circuit when the electric field decreases?

_____

_____

Reading Check

7. Summarize What happens when the voltage of a battery increases?

_____

_____

What happens if the voltage in a circuit is increased?

The voltage, current, and resistance in a circuit are all related. If the voltage in a circuit increases, the electric field in the circuit increases. Electrons speed up between bumping into atoms and other electric charges. This makes the current in a circuit increase. If the resistance in a circuit increases, it increases the number of times that electrons bump into atoms and other electric charges every second. This makes it harder for electrons to flow in the circuit. Because of this, increasing the resistance reduces the current.

What is Ohm's law?

The relationship between the voltage, current, and resistance of a circuit is known as Ohm's law. Ohm's law can be written as the following equation.

$$\begin{array}{ccc} \textbf{voltage} & = & \textbf{current} \times \textbf{resistance} \\ \text{(in volts)} & & \text{(in amperes)} \quad \text{(in ohms)} \end{array}$$
$$V = IR$$

Series and Parallel Circuits

There are probably a lot of devices connected to circuits in your home. There are two ways that devices can be connected in a circuit. One way is a series circuit, shown in the top figure. The other way is a parallel circuit, shown in the lower figure.

Series Circuit

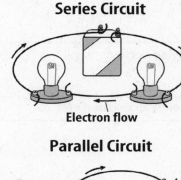

Electron flow

Parallel Circuit

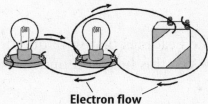

Electron flow

In a **series circuit**, there is only one closed path for the current to follow. If any part of the path is broken, the current will not flow in the circuit. In a **parallel circuit**, there is more than one closed path for current to follow. If the current flow is broken in one path, current will still flow in other paths in the circuit. The electric circuits in your house are parallel circuits. This means you can switch off the light in one room without turning off the lights in the whole house.

Applying Math

8. Apply The current in a circuit is 0.10A. The resistance of the circuit is 30.0 Ω. What is the voltage in the circuit? Show your work.

_____

_____

_____

Picture This

9. Observe Look at the lightbulb in the middle in the parallel circuit. How many closed paths is it a part of?

_____

● After You Read

Mini Glossary

electric circuit: a closed path in which electric charges can flow

electric current: the flow of electric charges; measured in amperes (A)

electric resistance: a measure of how hard it is for electrons to flow in an object; unit is the ohm (Ω)

parallel circuit: a circuit where there is more than one closed path for current to follow

series circuit: a circuit where there is only one closed path for the current to follow

voltage: a measure of how much electrical energy is moved by an electric charge as it moves from one point to another in a circuit

1. Review the terms and their definitions in the Mini Glossary. Write a sentence comparing and contrasting a parallel circuit and a series circuit.

   _____

   _____

2. Complete the flow chart about how electrons flow to make a lightbulb glow.

   Electrical Energy in a Circuit

   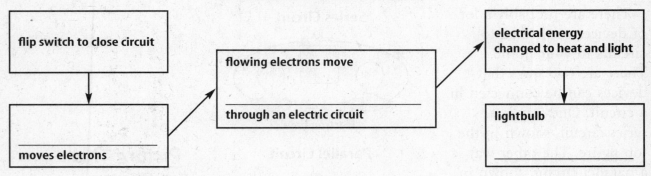

   | flip switch to close circuit |
   | flowing electrons move _____ through an electric circuit |
   | electrical energy changed to heat and light |
   | _____ moves electrons |
   | lightbulb _____ |

3. You were asked to underline the headings that were questions and then highlight the answers to each question. How did this help you understand more about electric current?

   _____

   _____

End of Section

 **Science Online** Visit **in6.msscience.com** to access your textbook, interactive games, and projects to help you learn more about electric current.

Electricity and Magnetism

section ❸ Magnetism

> **Standard—6.3.23:** Explain that electrical circuits provide a means of transferring electrical energy from sources such as generators to devices ....
> **Also covers: 6.2.5, 6.2.6**

● Before You Read

What happens when you put a paper clip close to a magnet?

_____

_____

● Read to Learn

Magnets

Did you use a magnet today? If you have watched TV or used a computer, you used a magnet. Magnets are a part of TVs, computers, and other devices. Magnets can exert forces on objects that are made from, or contain, magnetic materials. Magnets also can exert forces on other magnets. The forces of magnets make them very useful.

What are magnetic poles?

Every magnet has two ends or sides. Each of these ends or sides is called a magnetic pole. There are two kinds of magnetic poles. One is a north pole. The other is a south pole. Every magnet has a north pole and a south pole.

How do magnets exert forces on each other?

Magnetic Poles Magnetic poles of a magnet exert forces on magnetic poles of other magnets. Look at the figure at the top of the next page. If two north poles or two south poles are near each other, they repel or push away. If the north pole of one magnet is near the south pole of another magnet, they attract. Like poles repel and unlike poles attract.

What You'll Learn

■ how magnets exert forces on each other
■ why some materials are magnetic
■ how an electric generator works

> **Mark the Text**

Identify Specific Ideas
As you read through this section, highlight information about how magnets exert forces.

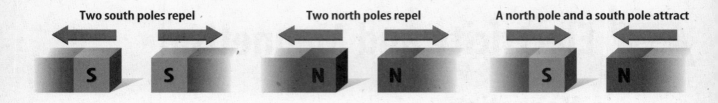

Two south poles repel **Two north poles repel** **A north pole and a south pole attract**

S   S   N   N   S   N

Picture This

1. **Compare** In the figure, how are the magnets whose unlike poles are near each other different from the magnets whose like poles are near each other?

_____

_____

Think it Over

2. **Determine** Which of these will stick to a magnet?

   a. drinking glass
   b. pencil
   c. sewing needle
   d. plastic cup

Distance The magnetic forces between two magnets get stronger as the magnets get closer. The magnetic forces between two magnets get weaker as the magnets get farther apart.

What is a magnetic field?

Have you ever held like poles of two magnets near each other? They push each other apart. You can feel this even when they are not touching. Recall that electric charges exert forces on each other even when they are not touching. This is because an electric charge is surrounded by an electric field. In the same way, a magnet is surrounded by a magnetic field. It exerts a force on other magnets.

If iron filings are sprinkled around a bar magnet, they will line up in a pattern of curved lines. These lines are called magnetic field lines. They help show the direction of the magnetic field around a magnet. The magnetic field lines are closest together at the magnet's poles. This is where the magnetic field is strongest.

Magnetic Materials

A paper clip will stick to a magnet if you hold a magnet near it. But a piece of aluminum foil will not stick to a magnet. Both are made of metal. Why is one attracted to the magnet and not the other?

Not all metals are attracted to magnets. Only metals that contain the elements iron, nickel, cobalt, and a few other rare-earth elements are attracted to magnets. Materials that contain these elements are magnetic materials. Magnets contain one or more of these metals. The steel paper clip contains iron, so it is a magnetic material.

Why are some materials magnetic?

Atoms of magnetic elements, like iron, nickel, and cobalt, also are tiny magnets. Each atom has a north pole and a south pole. If an element is not magnetic, its atoms are not magnets. Objects that are made of elements that are not magnetic will not be affected by a magnetic field.

What are magnetic domains?

In a magnetic material, forces that atoms exert on each other cause the magnetic fields around atoms to line up. So the atoms have their magnetic poles pointing in the same direction. A group of atoms that have their magnetic poles pointing in the same direction is called a **magnetic domain**. ☑

The magnetic fields of all the atoms in a magnetic domain add together. This means each magnetic domain has a south pole and a north pole. Each magnetic domain also is surrounded by a magnetic field. One magnetic domain may have trillions of atoms. But it is still too small to see. There may be billions of magnetic domains in a small piece of iron.

Do domains line up in permanent magnets?

What happens if you hold two paper clips together? They both are made of magnetic material. But they do not attract or repel each other. Why do they stick to a magnet and not each other? The magnetic domains in a paper clip point in all different directions. As a result, the magnetic fields around each magnetic domain cancel each other out and the paper clip does not have a magnetic field. ☑

In a permanent magnet, like a bar magnet, most of the magnetic domains point in the same direction. The magnetic fields around each magnetic domain do not cancel each other out. They add together to make a stronger magnetic field. The magnetic field that surrounds the magnet is a combination of the magnetic fields around the magnetic domains.

Why are magnetic materials attracted to a magnet?

A paper clip is not a magnet. But it has magnetic domains that are small magnets. Usually the domains point in all directions. But when a permanent magnet gets close to a paper clip, the magnetic field of the magnet exerts forces on the magnetic domain of the paper clip. These forces make the magnetic poles of the domains in the paper clip line up. The magnetic poles point in a single direction when a permanent magnet is nearby. The nearby pole of the permanent magnet is always next to the opposite poles of the magnetic domains. This causes the paper clip to be attracted to the magnet.

Because the magnetic fields of the domains are lined up, they do not cancel each other out. When the paper clip is attached to the magnet, it is a temporary magnet. It has a north pole and a south pole.

✓ Reading Check

3. **Explain** Why do atoms in a magnetic material have their magnetic fields pointing in the same direction?

_____

_____

_____

✓ Reading Check

4. **Summarize** Why won't two paper clips attract or repel each other?

_____

_____

_____

FOLDABLES

ⓓ **Compare** Make the following Foldable to help you compare different kinds of magnets.

Permanent Magnet

Temporary Magnet

Electro-magnet

Electromagnetism

Electricity and magnetism are related. A wire carrying an electric current is surrounded by a magnetic field. Any moving electric charge also is surrounded by a magnetic field. The connection between electricity and magnetism is called electromagnetism.

What are electromagnets?

You can make the magnetic field of a wire that is carrying a current stronger by wrapping it around an iron core. A wire, carrying a current, wrapped around an iron core is an **electromagnet**. The figure shows an electromagnet. An electromagnet has a north pole and a south pole. If the direction of current flow in the wire coil of an electromagnet is changed, the north pole and the south pole switch places.

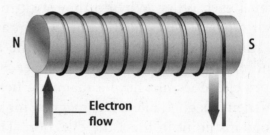

N   S

Electron
flow

The strength of a magnetic field made by an electromagnet depends on the amount of current in the wire coil. Increasing the amount of current increases the magnetic field strength. If there is no current, there will be no magnetic field. So, an electromagnet is a temporary magnet. The properties of an electromagnet can be controlled. Electromagnets are used in doorbells and telephones.

Generating Electric Current

An electric current makes a magnetic field. Can a magnetic field make an electric current? The answer is yes. If a magnet is moved through a wire loop that is part of a circuit, it will make an electric current flow through the circuit. The current flows only as long as the magnet is moving. It also would work if the magnet was still, but the wire loop was moving. The making of an electric current by moving a magnet through a wire loop or moving a wire loop around the magnet is **electromagnetic induction**. Electromagnetic induction makes an electric field in a circuit that causes electrons to flow. This is just like a battery.

Picture This

5. Observe From which pole does the electric current flow in the electromagnet?

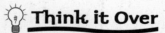

Think it Over

6. Apply If the amount of current in an electromagnet decreases, what will the electric field do?

What is an electric generator?

What makes the electrical energy in an electrical outlet? It is made by an electric generator. The figure shows a simple electric generator.

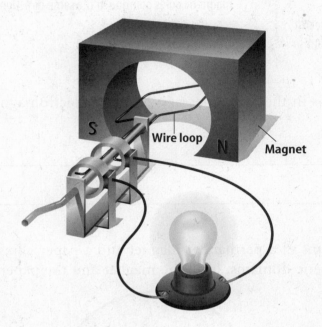

S   **Wire loop**   N   **Magnet**

In an electric generator, a wire loop is rotated within a magnetic field. The movement of the wire loop in the magnetic field makes an electrical field in the wire. This electrical field causes a current to flow. The current flows as long as the wire loop is rotating. How can you keep the wire loop rotating? Mechanical energy is used to keep the wire loop rotating. The generator turns mechanical energy into electrical energy. ☑

Where does electricity you use come from?

The electrical energy in an electrical outlet comes from generators in electric power plants. Electromagnets are rotated past wire coils in these generators. Power plants use mechanical energy to rotate the electromagnets. The mechanical energy is usually in the form of kinetic energy. Moving water or moving steam provide the kinetic energy to make electrical energy.

Some power plants burn fossil fuels like gas and coal. The fossil fuels heat water and make steam that spins generators. In hydroelectric power plants, water flowing from behind a dam provides mechanical energy. This mechanical energy is turned into electrical energy.

Picture This

7. Locate Where is the magnetic field strongest in the simple generator?

_____

_____

Indiana Academic Standard Check

6.3.23: Explain that electrical circuits provide a means of transferring electrical energy from sources such as generators ....

✔ **8. Identify** On the lines below, write the words that make this sentence true: An electric generator changes ____a____ energy, in the form of kinetic energy, into ____b____ energy.

a._____

b._____

● After You Read

Mini Glossary

electromagnet: a wire, carrying current, wrapped around an iron core

electromagnetic induction: the making of an electric current by moving a magnet through a wire loop, or moving a wire loop around the magnet

magnetic domain: a group of atoms that have their magnetic poles pointing in the same direction

1. Review the terms and their definitions in the Mini Glossary. Describe electromagnetic induction in your own words.

_____

_____

2. The figures show the magnetic domains of a permanent magnet and a paper clip. Using information you learned about magnetic domains, label the magnet and the paper clip.

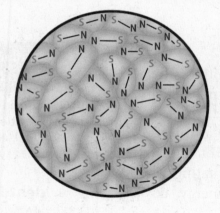 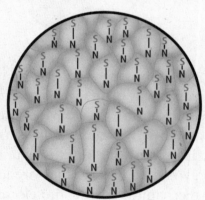

_____   _____

3. You were asked to highlight information you read about how magnets exert forces. How did this help you to understand more about magnets?

_____

_____

_____

End of Section

Science ●nline Visit **in6.msscience.com** to access your textbook, interactive games, and projects to help you learn more about magnetism.

Waves

section ❶ What are waves?

> **Standard—6.3.22:** Demonstrate that vibrations in materials set up wavelike disturbances, such as sound and earthquake waves, that spread away ....

● Before You Read

Describe what comes to mind when you think of waves.

_____

_____

What You'll Learn

■ how waves, energy, and matter are related
■ the difference between transverse waves and compressional waves

● Read to Learn

What is a wave?

Imagine that you are floating on an air mattress in a swimming pool and someone jumps into the pool near you. You and your air mattress bob up and down after the splash. What happened? Energy from the person jumping in made your air mattress move. But the person did not touch your air mattress. The energy from the person jumping in moved through the water in waves. **Waves** are regular disturbances that carry energy without carrying matter. The waves disturbed, or changed the motion of, your air mattress.

What do waves do?

Water waves carry energy. Sound waves also carry energy. Have you ever felt a clap of thunder? If so, you felt the energy in a sound wave. You also move energy when you throw a ball. But, there is a difference between a moving ball and a wave. A ball is made of matter. When you throw a ball, you move matter as well as energy. A wave moves only energy.

A Model for Waves

How can a wave move energy without moving matter? Imagine several people standing in a line. Each person passes a ball to the next person. The ball moved, but the people did not. Think of the ball as the energy in a wave and the people as the molecules that move the energy.

Study Coach

Create a Quiz As you read this section, write quiz questions based on what you have learned. After you write the quiz questions, answer them.

FOLDABLES

Ⓐ Identify Make the following Foldable from a sheet of notebook paper to help you organize information about waves.

What are waves?

Mechanical Waves

In the model of the wave, the ball (energy) could not be moved if the people (molecules) were not there. The same thing happens when a rock is thrown into a pond. Waves form where the rock hits the water. The molecules in the water bump into each other and pass the energy in the waves. The energy of a water wave cannot be moved or transferred if there are no water molecules.

Waves that use matter to move or transfer energy are **mechanical waves.** Water waves are mechanical waves. The matter that a mechanical wave travels through is called a medium. In a water wave, the medium is water. Solids, liquids, and gases are also mediums. For example, sound waves can travel through air, water, solids, and other gases. Without one of these mediums, there would be no sound waves. There is no air in outer space, so sound waves cannot travel in space.

What are transverse waves?

One kind of mechanical wave is a transverse wave. Transverse means to pass through, across, or over. In a **transverse wave,** the energy of the wave makes the medium move up and down or back and forth at right angles to the direction the wave moves. Think of a long rope stretched out on the ground. If you shake one end of the rope up and down, you make a wave that seems to slide along the rope, like the wave shown in the figure.

Picture This

2. **Draw and Label** In the figure, draw a circle around each crest in the wave. Then, use a different color of pen or pencil to draw a square around each trough.

Transverse Wave

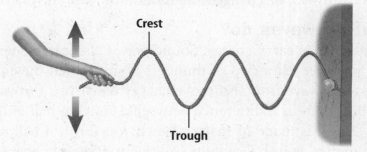

Crest

Trough

It might seem that the rope is moving away from you, but only the wave is moving away from your hand. The energy of the wave travels through the rope. But the matter in the rope does not move. Look at the figure. You can see that the wave has peaks and valleys that are spaced apart at even and regular distances. The high points of transverse waves are called crests. The low points are called troughs.

What are compressional waves?

Mechanical waves can be either transverse or compressional. Compress means to press or squeeze together. In a **compressional wave,** matter in the medium moves forward and backward along the same direction that the wave travels.

An example of a compressional wave made with a coiled spring is shown in the figure. A string is tied to the spring to show how the wave moves. Some coils on one end are compressed and then let go. As the wave begins, the coils near the end are close together. The other coils are far apart. The wave travels along the spring.

Compressional Wave

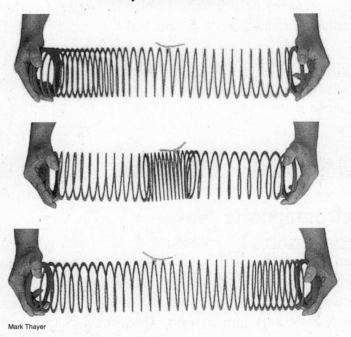

Mark Thayer

The coils and string move only as the wave passes them. Then, they go back to where they were. Compressional waves carry only energy forward along the spring. The spring is the medium the wave moves through, but the spring does not move along with the wave.

Sound Waves Sound waves are compressional waves. How do you make sound waves when you talk or sing? Hold your fingers against your throat while you hum. You can feel your vocal cords vibrating, or moving back and forth very quickly. You can also feel vibrations when you touch a stereo speaker while it is playing. All waves are made by something that is vibrating. ✔

Picture This

3. **Describe** Look at the figures. Describe the coils of the spring when the wave passes through them. Are they close together or far apart?

_____

Indiana Academic Standard Check

6.3.22: Demonstrate that vibrations in materials set up wavelike disturbances, such as sound and earthquake waves, that spread away from the source.

✔ **4. Identify** What kind of waves are sound waves?

_____

Picture This

5. Identify Look at the figure. What do the dots above the drum represent?

_____

_____

Making Sound Waves

A vibrating object causes the air molecules around it to vibrate. Look at the figure. When the drum is hit, the drumhead vibrates up and down. When the drumhead moves up, the air molecules next to it are pushed closer, or compressed, together. The group of compressed molecules is called a compression. The compression moves away from the drumhead.

When the drumhead moves down, the air molecules near it have more room and can spread apart. This group of molecules is a rarefaction. Rarefaction means something that has become less dense. The rarefaction also moves away from the drumhead. As the drumhead vibrates up and down, it makes a series of compressions and rarefactions in the air molecules that make up a sound wave.

 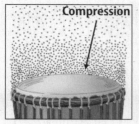 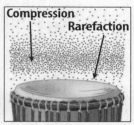

Electromagnetic Waves

Electromagnetic (ih lek troh mag NEH tik) **waves** are waves that can travel through space where there is no matter. There are different kinds of electromagnetic waves, such as radio waves, infrared waves, visible light waves, ultraviolet waves, X rays, and gamma rays. These waves can travel in matter or in space. For example, radio waves from TV and radio stations travel through air. They can be reflected from a satellite in space. Then, they travel through air and the walls of your house to your TV or radio.

How does the Sun emit light and heat?

The Sun emits electromagnetic waves that travel through space and reach Earth. The energy carried by electromagnetic waves is called radiant energy. Almost 92 percent of the radiant energy that reaches Earth from the Sun is carried by infrared and visible light waves. Infrared waves make you feel warm. Visible light waves make it possible for you to see. Some of the Sun's radiant energy is carried by ultraviolet waves. These are the waves that can cause sunburn. ☑

● After You Read

Mini Glossary

compressional wave: a type of mechanical wave in which matter in the medium moves forward and backward along the same direction that the wave travels

electromagnetic waves: waves that can travel through space where there is no matter

mechanical waves: waves that use matter to move energy

transverse wave: a type of mechanical wave in which the energy of the wave makes the medium move up and down or back and forth at right angles to the direction the wave travels

waves: regular disturbances that carry energy without carrying matter

1. Read the key terms and definitions in the Mini Glossary above. Write a sentence using the term *mechanical wave* on the lines below.

_____

_____

2. Use the Venn diagram to compare and contrast transverse and compressional waves. Arrange the characteristics of the waves according to whether they are true for transverse waves, compressional waves, or both.

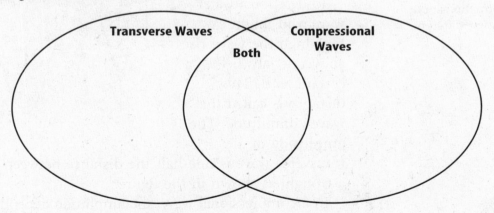

Transverse Waves   Both   Compressional Waves

3. How did the examples of the rope and the spring toy help you understand the difference between transverse and compressional waves?

_____

_____

_____

 Science Online Visit **in6.msscience.com** to access your textbook, interactive games, and projects to help you learn more about waves.

End of Section

Waves

section ❷ Wave Properties

 Standard—6.3.22: Demonstrate that vibrations in materials set up wavelike disturbances, such as sound and earthquake waves, that spread away ....
Also covers: 6.2.5, 6.2.7

What You'll Learn

■ about the frequency and the wavelength of a wave

■ why waves travel at different speeds

Mark the Text

Underline Terms As you read this section, underline each property of a wave. Then, highlight information about each property in a different color.

FOLDABLES

Ⓒ Organize Information
Make the following Foldable to help you organize information about the different properties of waves.

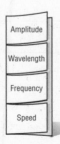

⬤ Before You Read

Think about waves in an ocean and waves in a pond. How would you describe each kind of wave?

_____

_____

⬤ Read to Learn

Amplitude

To describe a water wave, you might say how high the wave rises above, or falls below, a certain level. This distance is called the wave's amplitude. The **amplitude** of a transverse wave is one-half the distance between a crest and a trough, as shown in the figure.

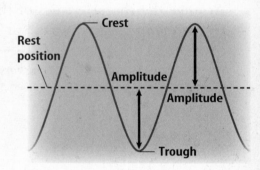

In a compressional wave, the amplitude depends on how close together the particles of the medium are. The amplitude is greater when the particles of the medium are squeezed closer together in each compression and spread farther apart in each rarefaction.

How are amplitude and energy related?

A wave's amplitude is related to the energy that the wave carries. For example, electromagnetic waves of bright light carry more energy and have greater amplitudes than electromagnetic waves of dim light. Loud sound waves carry more energy and have greater amplitudes than soft sound waves. A very loud sound can carry enough energy to damage your hearing.

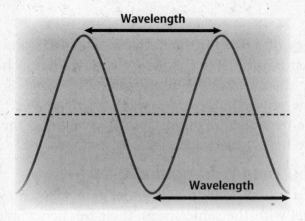

Transverse Wave

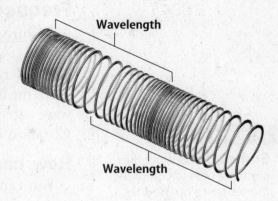

Compressional Wave

Wavelength

You also can describe a wave by its wavelength. Look at the figure above. For a transverse wave, **wavelength** is the distance from the top of one crest to the top of the next crest, or from the bottom of one trough to the bottom of the next trough. For a compressional wave, the wavelength is the distance between the center of one compression and the center of the next compression, or from the center of one rarefaction to the center of the next rarefaction.

The wavelengths of electromagnetic waves can vary from extremely short to longer than a kilometer. X rays and gamma rays have wavelengths that are smaller than the diameter of an atom.

This range of wavelengths is called the electromagnetic spectrum. The figure at the right shows the names given to different parts of the electromagnetic spectrum. Visible light, or light you can see, is only a small part of the electromagnetic spectrum. The wavelength of visible light gives light its color. For example, red light waves have longer wavelengths than green light waves.

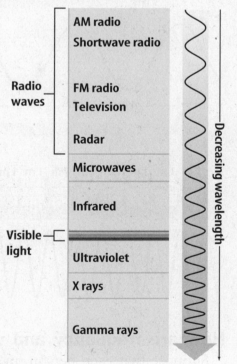

Picture This

1. **Describe** Look at the figure of the transverse wave. Compare the wavelengths between two crests to the wavelength between two troughs. Describe what you find.

_____

_____

Picture This

2. **Use Graphs** Which of the following has the greatest wavelength?
   a. microwaves
   b. X rays
   c. AM radio waves
   d. FM radio waves

Frequency

The **frequency** of a wave is the number of wavelengths that pass a given point in 1 s. Frequency is measured in hertz (Hz). Hertz are the number of wavelengths per second. So, 1 Hz means one wavelength per second. Remember that waves are made by something that vibrates. The faster the vibration is, the higher the frequency is of the wave. ☑

How can you model frequency?

You can use a model to help you understand frequency. If two waves travel with the same speed, their frequency and wavelength are related. Look at the figure below. Imagine people on two moving sidewalks next to each other. One sidewalk has four people on it. They are spaced 4 m apart. The other sidewalk has 16 people on it. They are spaced 1 m apart.

Imagine both sidewalks are moving at the same speed. The sidewalks move toward a pillar. On which sidewalk will more people go past the pillar? The sidewalk with 16 people on it has a shorter distance between people. Four people on this sidewalk will pass the pillar for every one person on the other sidewalk.

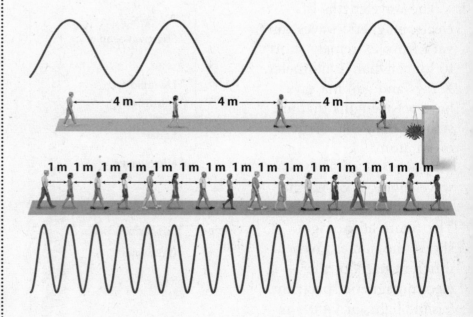

How are frequency and wavelength related?

Suppose that each person on the sidewalks represents the crest of a transverse wave. The movement of the people on the first sidewalk is like a wave with a 4 m wavelength. For the second sidewalk, the wavelength would be 1 m.

☑ Reading Check

3. Summarize Write the correct words to complete the sentence on the lines below.

Waves that vibrate fast have _____a._____ frequencies. Waves that vibrate slowly have _____b._____ frequencies.

a._____

b._____

Picture This

4. Use Models On the bottom sidewalk, circle groups of four people each. Then draw a line from each group of four people to one person on the top sidewalk.

Applying Math

5. Calculate If three people on the top sidewalk pass the pillar, how many people on the bottom sidewalk will have passed the pillar?

_____

The sidewalk with the longer, 4 m, wavelength carries a person past the pillar less frequently. Longer wavelengths have lower frequencies. On the second sidewalk, people pass the pillar more frequently. There, the wavelength is shorter—only 1 m. Shorter wavelengths have higher frequencies. This is true for all waves that travel at the same speed. As the frequency of a wave increases, its wavelength decreases.

What makes different colors and pitches?

The color of a light wave depends on the wavelength or the frequency of the light wave. For example, blue light has a higher frequency and shorter wavelength than red light.

Pitch is how high or how low a sound seems to be. Either the wavelength or the frequency determines the pitch of a sound wave. The pitch and frequency increase from note to note when you sing a musical scale. High-sounding pitches have higher frequencies. As the frequency of sound waves increases, their wavelengths decrease. Lower pitches have lower frequencies. As the frequency of a sound wave decreases, their wavelengths increase. ☑

Wave Speed

You have probably watched a thunderstorm on a hot summer day. You see lightning flash between a dark cloud and the ground. If the thunderstorm is far away, it takes many seconds before you will hear the sound of the thunder that goes with the lightning. This happens because light travels much faster in air than sound does. Light travels through air at about 300 million m/s. Sound travels through air at about 340 m/s. You can calculate the speed of any wave using this equation. The Greek letter lambda, λ, represents wavelength.

Wave Speed Equation

wave speed (m/s) = **frequency** (Hz) × **wavelength** (m)
$$v = f\lambda$$

Mechanical waves, such as sound, and electromagnetic waves, such as light, change speed when they travel in different mediums. Mechanical waves usually travel fastest in solids and slowest in gases. Electromagnetic waves travel fastest in gases and slowest in solids. For example, the speed of light is about 30 percent faster in air than in water.

✔ **Reading Check**

6. **Summarize** What determines color and pitch? Circle your answer.
   a. wavelength
   b. frequency
   c. wavelength and frequency
   d. wavelength or frequency

Applying Math

7. **Use an Equation** What is the speed in m/s of a wave with a frequency of 50 Hz and wavelength of 2 m? Show your work.

_____

_____

_____

● After You Read

Mini Glossary

amplitude: transverse wave—one-half the distance between a crest and a trough; compressional wave—how close together the particles of the medium are

frequency: the number of wavelengths that pass a given point in 1 s

wavelength: transverse wave—the distance from the top of one crest to the top of the next crest, or from the bottom of one trough to the bottom of the next trough; compressional wave—the distance between the center of one compression and the center of the next compression, or from the center of one rarefaction to the center of the next rarefaction

1. Review the terms and their definitions in the Mini Glossary. Explain in your own words how wavelength and frequency are related.

_____

_____

2. Label the parts of the transverse wave in the diagram below.

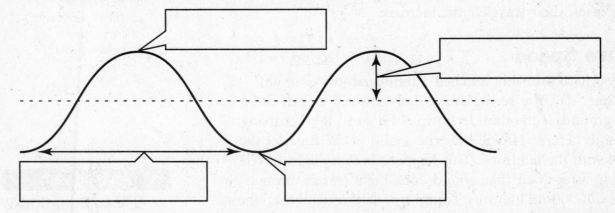

3. You were asked to underline properties of waves and highlight information about them. How did this help you understand and learn about properties of waves?

_____

_____

_____

 Visit **in6.msscience.com** to access your textbook, interactive games, and projects to help you learn more about properties of waves.

Waves

section ⊜ Wave Behavior

 Standard—6.3.21: Investigate, using a prism for example, that light is made up of a mixture of many different colors of light, even though . . . .
Also covers: 6.2.5, 6.2.7

● Before You Read

Have you ever shouted and heard an echo? On the lines below, write about what you think causes an echo.

_____

_____

What You'll Learn
- how waves can reflect
- how waves change direction
- how waves can bend around barriers

● Read to Learn

Reflection

You can see yourself in a mirror because waves of light are reflected. Reflect means to throw back. **Reflection** happens when a wave hits an object or surface and bounces off. Light waves from the Sun or a lightbulb bounce off of your face. The light waves hit the mirror and reflect back to your eyes. So you see your reflection in the mirror.

You can see your reflection in the smooth surface of a pond, too. But, if the water has ripples or waves, it is harder to see your reflection. You cannot see a sharp image when light reflects from an uneven surface like ripples on the water. This is because the reflected light goes in many different directions.

Refraction

A wave changes direction when it reflects from a surface. Waves can also change direction in another way. Have you ever tried to grab a sinking object in a swimming pool, but missed it? You were probably sure you grabbed right where it was. But, the light waves from the object changed direction when they moved from the water to the air. The bending of a wave as it moves from one medium to another is **refraction**.

Mark the Text

Identify Details Highlight each question head. Then use another color to highlight the answer to each question.

FOLDABLES

Ⓓ Organize Information Use four quarter-sheets of paper to take notes about reflection, refraction, diffraction, and interference as you read.

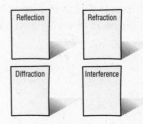

How are refraction and wave speed related?

Remember that the speed of a wave can be different in different materials. For example, light waves travel faster in air than in water. Refraction happens when the speed of a wave changes as it moves from one medium to another.

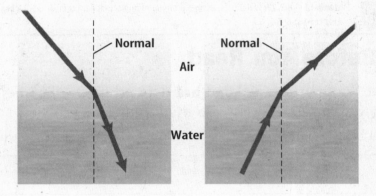

Wave Speed The figures above show how a light wave bends when it passes from air to water and water to air. A line that is perpendicular to the water's surface is called the normal. A light ray slows down and bends toward the normal when it passes from air into water. A light ray speeds up and bends away from the normal when it passes from water into air. If the speed of the wave changes a lot between mediums, the direction of the wave will change a lot too.

Refraction The figure below shows refraction of a fish in a fishbowl. Refraction makes the fish appear to be closer to the surface. It also appears farther away from you than it really is. Light rays reflected from the fish are bent away from the normal as they pass from water to air. Your brain assumes that light rays always travel in straight lines. So, the light rays seem to be coming from a fish that is closer to the surface.

Refraction

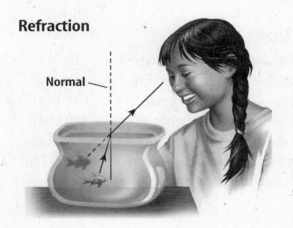

How does refraction make color?

Recall that different wavelengths make different colors. You can separate the colors in sunlight using a prism. A prism is an object or medium used to break light into its different wavelengths. Light is refracted twice when it passes through a prism—once it when it enters and once when it leaves. Since each color has a different wavelength, each color is refracted by a different amount. The colors of light are separated when they leave the prism. Violet light has the shortest wavelength. It is refracted, or bent, the most. Red light has the longest wavelength. It is refracted the least.

How are the colors of a rainbow made?

Each raindrop is a tiny prism. Light rays refract when they enter and again when they leave a raindrop. The colors refract at different angles because they have different wavelengths. The wavelengths separate into all the colors you can see. The colors you see in a rainbow are in order of decreasing wavelength: red, orange, yellow, green, blue, indigo, and violet.

Diffraction

Why can you hear music from the band room when you are down the hall? Sound waves bend as they pass through an open doorway. This is why you can hear the music. This bending is caused by diffraction. **Diffraction** is the bending of waves around a barrier. ☑

Light waves can diffract, too. But, they cannot diffract as much as sound waves. You can hear the band playing music when you are down the hall, but you cannot see the musicians until you actually look inside the band room door.

How are diffraction and wavelength related?

The wavelengths of light are much shorter than the opening of the band room door. This is why the light waves do not diffract as much as the sound waves do when they pass through the door. Light waves have wavelengths that are very short—between about 400 and 700 billionths of a meter. The doorway is about 1 m wide. The wavelengths of sound waves you can hear can be as long as 10 m. Sound waves are much closer in measurement to the opening of the door. A wave diffracts more when its wavelength is similar to the size of the barrier or opening.

💡 **Think it Over**

3. **Explain** why the color violet is refracted the most.

_____

_____

✔ **Reading Check**

4. **Define** What is diffraction?

_____

_____

_____

💡 **Think it Over**

5. **Communicate** A garage door is 3 m wide. Which sound waves will diffract most easily when they pass through the door—ones with a wavelength of 2 m or ones with a wavelength of 0.2 m?

_____

Can water waves diffract?

Imagine water waves in the ocean. What happens when the waves hit a barrier like an island? They go around the island. If the wavelength of the water waves is close to the size and spacing between the islands, the water waves diffract around the islands and keep moving. If the islands are bigger than the wavelength of the water waves, the water waves diffract less.

What happens when waves meet?

Suppose you throw two pebbles into a still pond. Waves spread out from where each pebble hits the water. When two waves meet, will they hit each other and change direction? No, they pass right through each other and keep moving. ☑

How do waves interfere with each other?

What happens when two waves overlap? The two waves add together, or combine, and make a new wave. The ability of two waves to combine and make a new wave when they overlap is **interference**. There are two kinds of interference—constructive and destructive as shown in the figure.

Constructive Interference In constructive interference, the crest of one wave overlaps the crest of another wave. They form a larger wave with greater amplitude. Then the original waves pass through each other and keep traveling as they were before.

Constructive Interference

Destructive Interference In destructive interference, the crest of one wave overlaps the trough of another. The amplitudes of the waves combine to make a wave with a smaller amplitude. If the waves have equal amplitudes, they will cancel each other out while the waves overlap. Then the original waves pass through each other and keep traveling as they were before.

Destructive Interference

✔ **Reading Check**

6. Infer What happens when two waves meet?

_____

_____

Picture This

7. Conclude Look at the figure of destructive interference. When can two waves cancel each other out?

How are particles and waves different?

Diffraction When light travels through a small opening, it spreads out in all directions on the other side of the opening. What would happen if particles were sent through the small opening? They would not spread out. They would keep going in a straight line. Diffraction, or spreading, happens only with waves.

Interference Interference does not happen with particles, either. When waves meet, they interfere and then keep going. If particles meet, either they hit each other and scatter, or miss each other. Interference and diffraction both are properties of waves but not particles. ☑

How can noise be reduced?

A lawn mower and a chain saw make loud noises. These loud noises can damage hearing.

Ear Protectors That Absorb Noise Loud sounds have waves with larger amplitudes than softer sounds. Loud sound waves carry more energy than softer sound waves. You have cells in your ears that vibrate and send signals to your brain. Energy from loud sound waves can damage these cells and can cause you to lose your hearing. Ear protectors can help prevent loss of hearing. The protectors absorb, or take in, some of the energy from sound waves. The ear is protected because less sound energy reaches it.

Ear Protectors That Interfere With Noise Pilots of small planes have a similar problem. The airplane's engine makes a lot of noise. But, pilots cannot wear ear protectors to shut out all of the engine's noise. If they did, they would not be able to hear instructions from air-traffic controllers.

Instead, pilots wear special ear protectors. These ear protectors have electronic circuits. The circuits detect noise from the airplane. Then they make sound frequencies that destructively interfere with the noise. Remember that destructive interference makes a smaller wave. The frequencies interfere only with the engine's noise. Pilots can still hear the air-traffic controllers. So, destructive interference can be helpful.

✔ Reading Check

8. **Determine** What two properties do waves have that particles do not have?

_____

_____

💡 Think it Over

9. **Explain** How do the ear protectors some pilots wear work?

_____

_____

_____

● After You Read

Mini Glossary

diffraction: the bending of waves around a barrier

interference: the ability of two waves to combine and make a new wave when they overlap

reflection: occurs when a wave hits an object or surface and bounces off

refraction: the bending of a wave as it moves from one medium to another

1. Review the terms and their definitions in the Mini Glossary. Write one or two sentences describing how refraction can make a rainbow.

   _____

   _____

   _____

2. In the graphic organizer below, name the four different wave properties. Give an example of each.

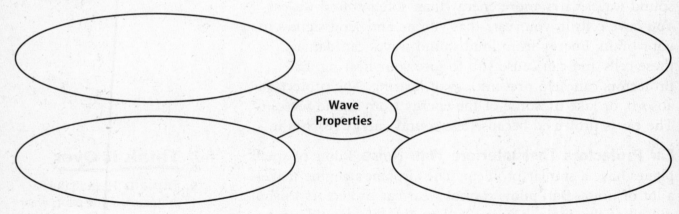

3. You were asked to highlight each question head and the answer to each question as you read this section. Name another strategy that would help you learn the properties of wave.

   _____

   _____

   _____

End of Section

 **Science Online** Visit **in6.msscience.com** to access your textbook, interactive games, and projects to help you learn more about wave behavior.

PERIODIC TABLE OF THE ELEMENTS

Gas
Liquid
Solid
Synthetic

Columns of elements are called groups. Elements in the same group have similar chemical properties.

Element — Hydrogen
Atomic number — 1
Symbol — H
Atomic mass — 1.008

State of matter

The first three symbols tell you the state of matter of the element at room temperature. The fourth symbol identifies elements that are not present in significant amounts on Earth. Useful amounts are made synthetically.

1

	1	2		3	4	5	6	7	8	9
1	Hydrogen 1 H 1.008									
2	Lithium 3 Li 6.941	Beryllium 4 Be 9.012								
3	Sodium 11 Na 22.990	Magnesium 12 Mg 24.305								
4	Potassium 19 K 39.098	Calcium 20 Ca 40.078	Scandium 21 Sc 44.956	Titanium 22 Ti 47.867	Vanadium 23 V 50.942	Chromium 24 Cr 51.996	Manganese 25 Mn 54.938	Iron 26 Fe 55.845	Cobalt 27 Co 58.933
5	Rubidium 37 Rb 85.468	Strontium 38 Sr 87.62	Yttrium 39 Y 88.906	Zirconium 40 Zr 91.224	Niobium 41 Nb 92.906	Molybdenum 42 Mo 95.94	Technetium 43 Tc (98)	Ruthenium 44 Ru 101.07	Rhodium 45 Rh 102.906
6	Cesium 55 Cs 132.905	Barium 56 Ba 137.327	Lanthanum 57 La 138.906	Hafnium 72 Hf 178.49	Tantalum 73 Ta 180.948	Tungsten 74 W 183.84	Rhenium 75 Re 186.207	Osmium 76 Os 190.23	Iridium 77 Ir 192.217
7	Francium 87 Fr (223)	Radium 88 Ra (226)	Actinium 89 Ac (227)	Rutherfordium 104 Rf (261)	Dubnium 105 Db (262)	Seaborgium 106 Sg (266)	Bohrium 107 Bh (264)	Hassium 108 Hs (277)	Meitnerium 109 Mt (268)

The number in parentheses is the mass number of the longest-lived isotope for that element.

Rows of elements are called periods. Atomic number increases across a period.

The arrow shows where these elements would fit into the periodic table. They are moved to the bottom of the table to save space.

Lanthanide series	Cerium 58 Ce 140.116	Praseodymium 59 Pr 140.908	Neodymium 60 Nd 144.24	Promethium 61 Pm (145)	Samarium 62 Sm 150.36
Actinide series	Thorium 90 Th 232.038	Protactinium 91 Pa 231.036	Uranium 92 U 238.029	Neptunium 93 Np (237)	Plutonium 94 Pu (244)